A Mother's
Place

A MOTHER'S PLACE

*Taking the Debate about Working
Mothers beyond Guilt and Blame*

SUSAN CHIRA

HarperCollins*Publishers*

HarperCollins books may be purchased for educational, business, or sales promotional use. For information please write: Special Markets Department, HarperCollins Publishers, Inc., 10 East 53rd Street, New York, NY 10022.

FIRST EDITION

Designed by Ruth Lee

Library of Congress Cataloging-in-Publication Data

Chira, Susan
    A mother's place: taking the debate about working mothers beyond guilt and
blame / Susan Chira.—1st ed.
      p. cm.
    Includes index.
    ISBN 0-06-017327-0
    1. Working mothers—United States.   2. Motherhood—United States.
  I. Title.
  HQ759.48.C48   1998   97-44916
  306.874'3—dc21

---

98 99 00 01 02 ❖/RRD 10 9 8 7 6 5 4 3 2 1

For Michael, Eliza, and Jake

CONTENTS

PROLOGUE

For years, I believed I had to choose between work and children, and I allowed my fears to still my desire to become a mother. Everywhere I looked, everything I read, and nearly everyone I talked to told me that what I wanted was impossible—to be serious about both my work and motherhood. I have been trying to tune out those voices for most of my life.

I grew up in the 1960s and early 1970s in an affluent, complacent suburb of New York, on the cusp of two worlds. The first was the tidy conformity of the 1950s, with its rigid rules about women's place. The fathers I knew rode the train to an office in the city, and the mothers, like mine, stayed at home. I was always a little out of step with that neat suburban existence. Other kids played outside, making use of the yards their parents had so thoughtfully procured for them. I closeted myself in my room, reading. In school, I raised my hand too much in class. I even had the temerity to speak up for the women's movement in our junior high school debate, "Women's rights: pro or con?" Con won, hands down; the girls in my class insisted that they wanted boys to open doors for them.

Increasingly, though, the world that had dominated my childhood came under assault. I watched, enthralled, as barriers fell and the world seemed heady with possibilities. I searched for a school where I would not feel so out of place, and I arrived at Andover in 1973, just as the boarding school was admitting its first class of girls. I had new freedom, but I also noticed that this freedom was awakening old resentments. The women's movement was being caricatured as a group of man-hating harridans, and the moral seemed to be that a woman who did not know her place would end up without a man.

For solace, I turned to the mysteries of Dorothy Sayers, particularly *Gaudy Night,* written in 1936, in which the intellectual, prickly, and independent Harriet Vane agonizes over her love for the aristocratic detective Lord Peter Wimsey. The novel is an extended meditation about whether a woman can love a man without losing herself. The mystery, set in a women's college at Oxford, ultimately concludes that she can, but only if the man is as sensitive, as intelligent, and as much of a paragon as Wimsey. Sayers's vision of an emotional and intellectual partnership became a model for the life I hoped to lead.

In the real world, though, Wimseys were hard to find. By the time I got to college, I discovered that it was futile to mask myself. At Harvard, there were even some men who found the real me appealing. My college experience, though, did not offer much reassurance about combining love and work. For four years, I tried, with mixed success and much heartache, to juggle a serious commitment to my studies, working on and then running the college newspaper, and tending a roller-coaster romance.

A disturbing pattern emerged: My accomplishments helped drive a wedge between me and the man I'd fallen in love with. It was as if we were living out the conflicts of an already-married, two-career couple—and as if I was trapped in the plot of all the movies that warned of the sad and lonely fate that awaited women like me. I was elected to head the newspaper; as my responsibilities consumed my days and nights, my boyfriend began sleeping with someone else. I got a fellowship to go to Japan after college; he told me I shouldn't pass up the chance, but that my moving would end our relationship.

I struggled without much guidance, personal or theoretical.

There wasn't much talk, in my circles anyway, about how other women had managed such conflicts. Since I had not read the feminist classics of previous generations, I remained ignorant of the passion and thoughtfulness that other women had brought to bear.

The conclusions I drew then from my experience were bleak. I did not think that my boyfriend might have been an example of the kind of man to avoid; I thought he was just reflecting the way most men felt and would always feel. I thought of myself as unmaternal, impatient with the sacrifices that children would require. I had no emotional or practical model of a different way to be a mother; my own mother had set a high standard of devotion, and I did not see how I could meet it if I left home to work. I did not foresee a husband being a real partner, and I believed children would be my responsibility alone. When I looked ahead, I thought that trying to combine a job and a husband would be hard enough; to fit babies in, too, seemed not only impossible but an act of hubris for which I certainly would suffer.

Everything around me seemed to drive home this message. In the early 1980s, when I was beginning a career in journalism, I picked up a copy of *New York* magazine in a dentist's office and felt a familiar stab of anxiety. The headline was "You Can't Have It All." Inside were the stories of formerly fast-track women who had become mothers. Their lives, as the magazine recounted them, were unadulterated hell. Defeated by the demands of their careers, children, and unhelpful husbands, these once-confident superstars were bailing out. It was a theme that would be reprised in countless articles, news accounts, and movies of the decade. The optimism of the 1970s was giving way to stern warnings that women had dared to want too much, and their children were paying the price.

In my first few years at the *New York Times,* I moved three times in a little more than three years: first to Albany to cover politics in the New York State legislature, then to Stamford to report on Connecticut, and then to Tokyo. Most of the men I knew joined the chorus of naysayers, telling me I couldn't hope that any self-respecting man would put up with my constant relocations and unpredictable hours.

One day in a restaurant in 1983, a male friend told me that *I* was the one who shouldn't put up with *them*. I was stunned; I fell back in my chair and felt one myth blown apart. I had the sense to marry that man and the great good fortune to learn that it is possible to make a marriage in a different mold.

When my husband and I arrived in Tokyo in 1984, I observed the families of foreign correspondents there carefully. At first, most of what I saw was traditional: man tends career; woman tends kids. Some of the women were able professionals, but their careers were usually secondary to their husbands' and they had taken virtually sole responsibility for the logistics of child rearing overseas. While I was in Tokyo, Deborah Fallows published *A Mother's Work,* one of the earliest and most influential of the growing "backlash" genre: a professional woman leaves the work force to honor her greater obligation to her children. I read about the book and wondered whether she was just telling a painful truth, hard as it was to hear.

Then some of my friends began having babies, and their lives challenged that assumption. Many of them were managing to work and raise children. My trepidation gave way to an overwhelming longing for a child.

When my daughter was born in 1990, I felt a surprising triumph and lightheartedness, an odd sense of freedom even though I was tied to a demanding new creature. I now realize that this was the headiness that came from defying the Furies. Frightened as I was, I had taken my stand and become a mother without losing my commitment to the world of work.

My elation was soon vanquished by an onslaught of doubts. My new daughter filled my heart and engaged my mind, and I knew that tending her would mean hard work, sustained attention, and rigorous thought. How could I possibly meet this standard while pushing myself in my job?

The cultural jeremiads against working motherhood resonated with my own fears. Children are this young only once, I kept hearing. These years come and are gone forever. When you work, you arrive home so tired you have nothing left to give the children. When you travel, your children are inconsolable, torn between desperation and rage. Hiring a baby-sitter is merely paying someone else to love your child for you; if you're lucky, the baby will love her so much she'll call her mommy; if you're not, the baby will wither under her arid indifference or cringe from her abusive blows.

To my astonishment and growing delight, I found that the defeatists were wrong. When I returned to work, I left behind a gnawing sense of oppression, boredom, and guilt that had cast a pall over my maternity leave. My husband, a writer and journalism professor, brought to fatherhood great zest and assurance, as well as a commitment equal to my own. He also enjoyed flexible hours that helped us through many a crisis. Nanny horror stories notwithstanding, I found a responsive and loving baby-sitter, one who is still with us after seven years.

My daughter did not fall apart the first time I worked past 8 P.M. I arrived home, stomach in knots, only to find her playing happily with her father. I traveled as little as I could manage, but when I did, she was fine—happy to see me and the small presents (a T-shirt, a seashell) I brought back with me. When my son was born in 1994, I worried all over again. I'd been told that one child might just be manageable for a working mother, but two would defeat me. I would feel torn in half, unable to give either child enough attention and tend to my job as well. Two is unquestionably harder, and there have been moments when I walk in the door and am dizzy with the effort of swiveling my head and heart around to accommodate both my children. Yet those moments pale before the many times I come home and marvel at the two distinct individuals who greet me. When my job seems a round of petty battles, returning to my family banishes my frustration and restores my perspective; there is life beyond work, and my fatigue lifts when I see my children's faces.

Yet my experience was almost never reflected in what I read or heard about working mothers. These women were always teetering on the verge of collapse, haunted by the damage they were causing their children, dragging themselves heavyhearted to work.

Some of my friends, indeed, felt that way. Many mothers have been left reeling by a genuine revolution over the past twenty-five years. In 1970, less than half of all mothers held jobs; in 1997 nearly three-quarters were employed—a dramatic leap at a dizzying pace.

To be a working mother is often to struggle with a profound sense of dislocation and loss. My friends were devastated when their children called the baby-sitters mommy. They loved their work, but they ached for more time at home, and whenever a problem surfaced with their children, they feared that their jobs were the culprits.

I often felt alone in my relative contentment and worried that I was deceiving myself. Every new study that appeared about the impact of work, every news story about nannies or neglectful mothers, and every new feature about women leaving their jobs seemed addressed to me.

When I talked to other women, I felt as if a bomb could explode every time the subject of children came up. A mother at home said she was "too much of a perfectionist" to entrust her children to another woman. A working mother talked of how much she missed her children and how she would quit in a heartbeat if she could afford it. I felt an unspoken reproach, my devotion to my children questioned. Should I engage or draw back? Should I mouth a half-truth or forge on to confrontation?

I wanted to say that for me, it was possible, even exhilarating, to have a job and raise children. At times, out of defensiveness, I think I must have sounded smug. Yet I, too, am prey to guilt and anxiety.

When I returned to my job at the newspaper after an eighteen-month leave of absence largely spent working on this book, I decided to try assignments I had rejected in the past as too demanding and too intrusive on my family life. I negotiated what I thought would work: an editing job based not directly on the news, with its unpredictability, but on feature articles, which I had reasoned I could take home with me if the hours stretched too long. Yet for the first time in my working life, I felt my job cut me off from my family.

My days were longer, and the work felt relentless. As a reporter, I had frantic days and slow ones, times when I waited for appointments to be set up or calls to be returned and had lulls in the interim when I could call home. As an editor, the pace never slackened; it only ricocheted from busy to crazy and back to busy again.

In the first weeks of my new job, as I struggled to learn unfamiliar skills and absorb a different way of working, I was exhausted, distracted, and, much of the time, sad. It was far harder than usual to shed work like a skin and embrace the joyful chaos of home. I arrived home and my children rushed to greet me, but I felt desolate at how much time I had missed with them. My husband took on several tasks I had once assumed: calling the pediatrician, investigating and setting up after-school classes for the children, talking to our baby-sitter. Rather than feeling relief that he was lessening my burdens, I was oddly bereft, as if performing those jobs had helped me feel close to the children.

Worst of all, I was hit by waves of unusual jealousy and self-doubt. Every time my son stretched out his arms to his father, I worried he had learned to turn to him instead of me. Eager for intimacy with my daughter, I found myself pressing her too intently for news about her day. I noticed how I clung more tightly to my son when I put him to bed, how I stayed with him longer than necessary because I needed to smell his skin and nuzzle his hair. One weekend morning, when I was too exhausted even to play with the children, I struggled to hold back tears, lashing myself with the same accusations that enraged me when others leveled them at working mothers.

Eventually, I realized that I was suffering from the uncertainty and insecurity that accompany most transitions. I began taking time at work to call the baby-sitter when I needed to touch base. I put through calls to the pediatrician. I continued visiting my daughter's class one morning a week before work, which gave me a glimpse into her world at school. And I discovered that although I still chafed at my work hours, I could detect no impact on my children. There were no nightmares, no sleep interruptions, no wistfulness that I could observe. My children continued to confide in me. What was most important, I found that I was still able to read the children's moods—to figure out when something was amiss, soothe them when they were sad, and exult with them over their triumphs.

Yet outside the reassuring confines of my home, I encountered a growing conventional wisdom that labeled mothers like me neglectful, children like mine damaged, and a life like mine impossible and bad for society. Mothers today were smarter than their feminist forebears, that wisdom ran. They were waking up to the harsh but timeless truth that work and motherhood did not mix, and they were fleeing the workplace for home. They had underestimated the visceral pull of children and had failed to understand that becoming mothers would upend their world and extinguish their desire to work. A new cult of domesticity extolled the joys of tending children at home and trumpeted the dangers of abandoning them to work.

In the vitriol that infused the attacks on working motherhood, I sensed a broader assault on the very idea of women's fulfillment. Women have grown too bold, too selfish. In pursuing their dreams, they have blighted their children's lives. No one questions the costs, both to women and their children, of denying mothers the freedom to make choices. The debate about work and children implies that given such freedom, mothers will not take the moral path, will not honor their obligations to their children if they work outside the home.

My resentment at the cultural and political forces pounding away at mothers prompted me to write this book. I fear that the societal message convinces many women, both mothers and those who want to be, to lose hope that anyone can combine work and motherhood. Women are encouraged to give up instead of fighting to change the conditions that make working and child rearing so wrenching. The voices of despair, disguised as postfeminist realism, shout down any murmur of hope.

The commentators tell us that much of society's ills can be cured by large doses of mothers staying home. They proclaim that working mothers do not raise their children, that they are not really mothers at all. Our society remains in thrall to a long-standing idea that there is only one way to be a good mother. The powerful, enduring image of the good mother as sacrificial, perfect, and at home still tugs at most mothers' hearts. Many mothers, I among them, are suspended uneasily between an ideal of motherhood we know we cannot meet and a reality that defies our entrenched ideas of what good mothers feel and do.

Yet working motherhood is not second-class motherhood; it is an honorable and devoted one, worthy of respect. Our culture does not offer a stringent, responsible alternative vision of motherhood. Mothers are not given a psychological explanation of why such a different model could also satisfy children and meet their needs.

I believe that the way we talk about working mothers and the fate of their children is fraudulent, distorted by half truths and shot through with sanctimony. I want to recast that debate so that we can look clearly at the problems that do threaten children and their parents and work to solve them.

I recognize that I write as an upper-middle-class professional woman, one who finds her work demanding and satisfying and whose husband takes on far more at home than most fathers do. That is why I include the voices of other women and men, with different backgrounds and different opinions from my own. I interviewed more than forty mothers for this book: employed or at home; married, single, and divorced; well off, working class and on welfare; white, African American, Latina, and Chinese. I also talked to a dozen fathers. They are not a scientifically representative sample; I found them the way most reporters do. Some I had interviewed before on other assignments. Some were friends of friends or friends of other women and men I interviewed. Some I found through unions, and some through organizations that help mothers who are or were on welfare. I deliberately chose people who I thought might hold different opinions from my own.

Just as I cannot speak for all mothers, neither can the pundits who insist that one solution fits all. Sometimes I, and all mothers I know, long for some clarity, a tidy list of answers, a how-to manual. In writing this book, I sometimes felt as if I was laying out my motherhood, my uncertainties and my missteps, to be judged by a stern public. My children are still young. There are times when I worry about having them shake this book in my face when they are older. Sometimes the voices on the outside join the ones inside my head in a malevolent chorus of condemnation.

In the end, I have to rely on the power of my experience. The psychologists who preach about the security of children's bonds to their mothers would say that my son should be even less secure than my daughter because I "left" him when he was less than three months old to begin working on this book. Instead, I am a far more relaxed and confident mother now than I was during those six months I dutifully stayed home with my daughter because the experts told me that was a bare minimum. Experience and perspective helped, but I noticed a striking difference in my time with my son when I began, even gradually, to turn to my own work. A new verve, energy, and delight infused my hours with him.

During that first maternity leave, I proposed an article for the *Times,* to dip back into my other world. Cradling my nursing baby in one arm and the phone in my ear, conducting an interview with some serious personage, I could hardly contain my happiness. I don't really advocate trying to interview with a baby on one arm. But that one moment, ridiculous as it sounds, stands out because it was the first time I felt both my selves fit together with an audible click. Our culture does not acknowledge such moments of joy and power—and I am writing this book to celebrate them.

PART ONE

THE ICON OF
THE GOOD MOTHER

The Drumbeat

Small wonder that I felt besieged before and after I became a working mother. The headlines blared the bad news: "The Myth of Quality Time: How We're Cheating Our Kids," "Working Parents' Torment: Teens After School," "Can Your Career Hurt Your Kids?" "Working Women: Goin' Home."[1]

I watched as the trial of a nineteen-year-old English au pair charged with killing the eight-month-old boy in her care turned into an extraordinary public indictment of the baby's mother, Deborah Eappen, and all working mothers. The verdict: Guilty—of careerism, of callousness, of hiring someone to do a job only a mother should do.

I listened to Dr. Laura Schlessinger, a talk radio psychologist with a following second only to Rush Limbaugh's, and heard her rail against mothers who allowed their children to be "raised" by child care centers. By contrast, Dr. Laura declared in her signature slogan, "I am my kid's mom."

I saw audiences cheer movies like *Mrs. Doubtfire,* in which the working mother is heartless and shrill and the real mother is the nonworking, irresponsible father.

Wherever I turned, I could find articles and experts bemoaning the state of children and laying the blame at the door of two-career families—the 1990s' code word for working mothers. Journalists and judges, politicians and psychologists, moviemakers and myth-makers chanted in a grim chorus that the mother who works is the mother who fails.

They outlined the themes of a new conventional wisdom, which sounded much like the old one: When mothers forsake their rightful place at home, children are the victims. A working mother either allows her children to stay home unsupervised, where they drift into drug-taking, sex, and a life of crime, or she herds them into after-school programs, where they are deprived of precious time to hang out. Children are at the mercy of neglectful day care workers who may also be sexual perverts or a trusted nanny who beams on them when their mother is at home and beats them when she is away. Reluctant working mothers slave away at demeaning jobs, pining for the days when they could be at home waxing the kitchen floor and buffing their children's consciences.

Some of today's truisms are, in fact, true. There are legitimate reasons to worry about the plight of children, and plenty of evidence that much child care in the United States is abysmal. It would be wrong to dismiss these concerns merely because working mothers may feel uncomfortable or slighted. One can find examples of every statement just mentioned. Yet there is no evidence that working mothers are the cause of these problems. The endless parade of examples amounts to a concerted attack on working motherhood that substitutes an ugly caricature for the light and shadow of a faithful and complicated portrait.

The good mother who sacrifices, the selfish mother who works, the evils of day care, the obsessions with men's and women's differ-ent natures, the public laments by mothers torn from the arms of their children by jobs, the breast-beating over the state of chil-dren—these are the themes of the chorus bewailing a lost paradise, the days when mothers stayed at home. Too often, the first impulse is to blame mothers for cultural corrosion, because they are still expected to be the ones shoring up civilization, inculcating the virtues that children and society need.

Although many of those who attack working mothers are political conservatives, they are not alone in seeing this society spinning out of control and children vulnerable to a culture saturated with gratuitous sex and violence. I share the yearning for vanishing hallmarks of a civilized society—respect, diligence, self-restraint, public safety, family ties. I agree that too many adults dodge their responsibilities to children and rationalize away their children's pain.

And yet, too many pundits reflexively seize on the quick fix: keep mothers at home. "The Motherhood Revolution has been a disaster for our children," declared the computer scientist David Gelertner in an article entitled "Why Mothers Should Stay Home." From the religious right to such mainstream publications as the *Wall Street Journal* and *U.S. News & World Report* come lectures to mothers that they do not really need to work, that they are abandoning their children not to help pay a mortgage but to buy fancy sneakers, VCRs, or trips to Disneyland.[2]

In the superheated world of talk radio, Dr. Laura Schlessinger has won legions of fans with a snappy sound-bite morality, preaching that selfish adults have abandoned children. During one tirade at a 1995 book reading in New York City to promote her best-seller *How Could You Do That?!* she elaborated: "I remember one painful call I got from a woman who went so far as to adopt a kid and got this kid a full-time baby-sitter nanny and hardly ever saw this kid, because she came home later from work and left early, and on the weekends the kid wanted to go with the lady. That was Mommy. Who do you think Mommy is?"

By contrast, Dr. Laura is the good mother, the one mothers today should emulate. She described how when her son was little, he was playing with a ball and it rolled under a chair. Instead of picking it up for him, she encouraged him to get it himself. "The easier thing would be now if I were a day care person, I'd get the ball. So he finally got the ball and he turned and he looked at me with the greatest sense of achievement and pride. That's what we call a quality moment."

Working mothers also have their champions. Positive portrayals compete with the negative ones. Women's magazines and advertisements that virtually spoke with one voice championing the mother at home in the 1950s now speak with many, trying, with exquisite tactfulness, to offend no one and appeal to everyone. The April 1995 issue of *McCall's* featured a mother of a disabled child who left her job explaining "What I Sacrificed for My Son," whereas the November 1994 issue offered busy working mothers tips when they're "Too Tired." Advertisements increasingly show a woman at work whose heart is at home. One advertisement for Quaker oatmeal read: "Catering is an all day job, but my job as a Mom always comes first. For Moms who have a lot of love, but not a lot of time."

Indeed, many conservatives argue that a cultural elite, the reigning experts, and popular culture in general preach a completely opposite message than the one ringing in my ears: anything goes, as long as adults are happy. In "Putting Children Last," an article in the May 1995 issue of *Commentary,* Mary Eberstadt read many of the same books and articles that I did (even some that I wrote as a reporter for the *New York Times*) and came away enraged because she found them extolling the mother at work above the mother at home. The message today, she wrote, "is that parents need feel no guilt—in fact they should feel good—about putting their own wants and needs ahead of their children's." She rightly skewered the vacuity of articles that suggest, straight-faced, that busy parents pencil in their children for occasional fifteen-minute doses of "quality time."

There is enormous cultural confusion all around us, but what I think critics like Eberstadt miss is the undercurrent of second-bestness that accompanies most of the advice she lampoons. It is all about making do with, making up for, such mothers' inevitable, damaging deficiencies.

Moreover, the messages that strike a public nerve and dominate the public debate are the negative ones. In the mid to late 1990s, several books were published offering reassuring or sympathetic assessments of working mothers. The book that caught on, though, was one that portrayed working mothers as joining fathers in neglecting their children and condemning them to speeded-up, emotionally deprived lives: Arlie Russell Hochschild's *The Time Bind: How Work Becomes Home and Home Becomes Work*. An excerpt from the book appeared on the cover of the *New York Times Magazine,* and its themes were the subject of cover stories that same week in *Newsweek* and *U.S. News & World Report.*[3]

Then, in the fall of 1997, came the trial of the English au pair that transfixed the country. It was covered gavel to gavel by Court TV and prompted impassioned exchanges about working mothers and child care on radio call-in shows, opinion columns, Internet chat rooms, and living rooms in the United States, Britain, and beyond.

The "nanny" trial showed just how divided opinions are about working mothers: For all the vitriol flung at Deborah Eappen, there were many who rallied with equal passion to her side. Yet the ferocity of the attacks on her—the cruelty, self-righteousness, and smugness—was what stayed with me and many other working mothers I know. There is no single drumbeat anymore, but it is easy to hear the attacks, particularly if they resonate with our own fears.

BAD MOTHER, SAD CHILDREN: TWO EMBLEMATIC TALES

As the nanny trial unfolded in Cambridge, Massachusetts, Deborah Eappen became a public whipping girl for the anger and unease that working mothers continue to evoke. Deborah and Sunil Eappen, doctors living in the Boston suburb of Newton, hired Louise Woodward, an eighteen-year-old English au pair, in November 1996 to care for their two young sons. They grew uneasy, because Woodward was staying out late, had trouble waking up in the morning to care for the children, and had left them unattended when she went to the basement to do laundry. In early February 1997, just a few days after her employers had imposed new restrictions, Woodward paged Deborah Eappen at work, telling her that eight-month-old Matthew was not breathing normally. Doctors at the hospital found a two-and-a-half-inch skull fracture. Matthew died five days later. Woodward was charged with murder.

Eappen tried to maintain her composure during the trial; she was castigated in cyberspace for being "cold and creepy" and "emotionless"—not the way a mother should act. She and her husband were denounced for hiring a young and less expensive au pair rather than an older, more experienced, and more expensive nanny. The caustic comments about her profession exposed the widespread belief that the only acceptable reason for a mother to work is because she must. The many defenders of Louise Woodward even suggested that Eappen had abused her son herself and was accusing the au pair to cover her crime.

Many of the accusations hurled at her were vicious and exaggerated, but they also echoed many of the themes of a broader cultural and political attack on working mothers. "The kid comes first, bottom line, end of story," one radio show caller pronounced. That is the central theme in the attack on working mothers: the charge, as powerful as it is wrong, that mothers with a job do not put their children first.

"Are you willing to make the sacrifice in lifestyle?" scolded another caller. Sacrifice is supposed to be the cornerstone of motherhood. It seemed that Deborah Eappen's decision to pass up a prestigious offer to be a chief resident and her choice to work three days a week were not sufficient sacrifices; only total self-annihilation would do.

"Apparently the parents didn't want a kid and now they don't have one," another caller declared.[4] That is the clincher, the implicit threat of retribution that hovers over most discussions of working motherhood. At best, buying child care is like hiring a prostitute, paying for services a good mother would perform herself; at worst, it's like arranging for a hired killer. Either way, there will be a cost. If the children live, they will be emotionally scarred or intellectually damaged.

The au pair trial became such a national obsession in part because it struck at the fear every working parent has of entrusting a child to someone else. It is a fear that has been exploited in a renewed assault on day care and the very premise of mothers working outside the home. Predictably, a rash of nanny horror stories were rehearsed in the press in the wake of the trial. Even before that trial, however, such accounts were legion. One of the most chilling appeared in a fall 1995 report on *Prime Time Live* by ABC's Diane Sawyer. She had families place hidden cameras in their homes to spy on their nannies. The resulting footage was riveting, the stuff of every mother's nightmares. A nanny who smiles and coos at an eleven-month-old and takes her to the window to wave good-bye abruptly dumps her in her playpen the moment the mother is out of sight. She leaves the baby there most of the day, crying, while she talks on the telephone. In a horrifying episode that Sawyer showed to the child's weeping parents, the nanny, incensed at the baby's screams, hits her over the head several times with the portable phone.

It is not until the middle of the program, though, in a quick aside, that the audience learns that most of the caregivers *Prime Time Live* taped were, in fact, warm and loving. The wrenching scenes of abuse and neglect the program focused on were the tragic exception, not the rule. News is made from such exceptions, of course, but as in the nanny trial, mothers were led to believe that every time they leave their children in the care of another, they court their death.

A few months before the nanny trial consumed the country in the fall of 1997, Arlie Hochschild's book appeared, garnering wide and mainly uncritical publicity. With chilling anecdotes, Hochschild painted a bleak picture of working mothers that confirmed society's worst fears. She opened the book with a scene of a guilty mother bribing her daughter with a candy bar so she would go quietly to day care. Another mother, instead of taking her son to the hospital immediately to see if he was having an epilectic seizure, dropped him off at the baby-sitter because both she and her husband had important presentations at work. A third mother and her husband took on so much overtime between them that the children were shuttled between two baby-sitters, both parents' mothers, and a cousin.

Like many other commentators, Hochschild attributed all children's problems to their sadness and resentment about their mothers' work schedules. She described a four-year-old child whose executive mother had spent less time with her than usual the preceding week. The girl first said she wanted to dance for her parents, and then stopped in the middle, refusing her parents' gentle entreaties to continue. Offering no evidence other than her own speculation, Hochschild decided the dance was akin to a sit-down strike, with the child declaring, "If you won't give me time, then I won't give you time, and I won't finish the dance."[5]

Hochschild offered stern moral judgments, using the language of loss and longing typical of the debate about working mothers. Working parents "stole time from their children," she declared. Working parents long for "time to throw a ball with their children, or to read to them, or simply to witness the small dramas of their development," as if work put these activities out of reach. She contemptuously described an executive as an "outsourcing mom," paying for services that good mothers still performed by themselves: cooking Thanksgiving turkeys, making Halloween costumes, planning their children's birthday parties.[6]

Her provocative thesis captured the public imagination: Women have joined the ranks of men, running away from the endless messy emotional demands of home and escaping to the ordered, companionable, and newly supportive world of work. That is why, she reasoned, even women who could afford to do so were not cutting back their work hours. She ignored another plausible explanation: Many women, particularly but not exclusively professional women, like work because it offers them intellectual challenge, adult company, money, independence, and an identity outside the home. They have the temerity to want both absorbing work and a full family life.

Hochschild also suggested that if women's work at home were valued more, women would spend more time at home. Yet the vivid accounts she offered of women confessing that home life is often frantic and exhausting suggest that factory workers as well as professionals find being at home all day with children taxing. The dirty little secret is that some women have always felt that way, but were not allowed to say so.

Few questioned these and other obvious holes in Hochschild's arguments. She studied one company with family-friendly policies. Can one really generalize her findings about one company to the entire country or to people who work in less hospitable companies? Even while the book distorted the reasons women may want to work, it also overstated the appeal of work for many parents, both men and women. Countless parents find their jobs regimented and oppressive; many have told pollsters they would rather be at home.

Hochschild's book prompted an outbreak of head-shaking and finger-pointing about the price children pay for working mothers. A typical account appeared in *Newsweek,* with the subtitle slamming home the moral: "How We're Cheating Our Kids." Both Hochschild's book and the *Newsweek* article tried to avoid targeting only the mother, and both aimed their critique of loss of family time at busy fathers, too. Yet many of the most pointed examples involved mothers.

The *Newsweek* article began with an account of a lawyer whose children began to act up in the grocery store. After the cashier said snidely, "Oh, you're the mother," the mother had an epiphany: "Sitters don't raise kids. Parents do." She made the choice the article implied all devoted mothers should make: work part-time, or at the very least, cut back on their hours.

This anecdote was supposed to be telling, but it didn't tell me much. Why should we assume that the children were misbehaving in the grocery store because they have a baby-sitter? Maybe they felt safer to act up with the mother, the way kids often do because they sense the mother will not withdraw her love. Maybe they were just doing what lots of kids do, getting wired in a store with lots of things they want and are forbidden to have.

The article invoked the authority of experts declaring that children are being shortchanged: "I see apathy, depression—a lack of the spunkiness I associate with being a kid," says a Harvard psychologist. Many of the scenarios these experts describe as typical of children of two-career families could apply broadly to any mother or father, at home or at work, who is failing to give children a sense of order, ritual, and limits.

GIVE UP, GO HOME, OR ELSE

The prescription for this widespread social malaise is clear: The wise mother curbs her ambition and refuses to pay the price for having it all. Follow Brenda Barnes, the head of PepsiCo, and leave work to spend more time with family. For those unlike Barnes who feel they cannot afford to do so, "voluntary simplicity" is the answer: pare down financial expectations, sell off unnecessary belongings, rent instead of own, and escape the tyranny of work. Indeed, the authors of a *U.S. News & World Report* cover story in the spring of 1997 were just two of many voices lecturing women that they were telling "lies" about their need to work. Most middle-class families, the magazine insisted, could send their children to public universities and afford a decent home without two incomes.

Cover stories in magazines like *Fortune* and *Barron's* offer profiles of working mothers who are giving up and going home. Articles abound with tales of younger women who have seen the folly of an older generation. Having it all, they say smugly, is just too exhausting and stressful, a delusion that older women ruined their lives pursuing.

An article in the December 1995 *Wall Street Journal* and a March 1996 National Public Radio broadcast featured a new generation of daughters spurning the example of their own working mothers; neither included even one daughter who was inspired to emulate her working mother. One daughter in the *Wall Street Journal* article remembered throwing up in the taxi her mother had sent to the high school to pick her up when she was sick because she was too busy to take time off. The NPR broadcast featured a daughter whose mother routinely put her to sleep under her conference-room table as she worked late into the night. She chose not to have children at all.

The NPR report also discussed two mothers who had managed remarkably well to meet their children's needs while rising in the business world. These mothers worked; baked cookies; coached softball; and, their daughters said, were there when they needed them. Yet their daughters thought their mothers had too little time for themselves; they chose to stay at home with their children.

Women who have managed to forge careers and raise children

report that young women do not believe they can do the same. Sandra Scarr, a prominent child care researcher and mother of four, said, "I'm really amazed at the number of young women today who are graduating from a very good university and who feel very strongly that they want to stay home with their own children because they are irreplaceable. That tells you the culture's still out there telling them it's really better if you could stay home, and they feel guilty if they don't want to. You need to say, why, why would children be better off if you stayed home and were miserable?"[7]

Shirley M. Tilghman, a Princeton scientist who raised two children on her own while climbing to the top of her field, spoke of facing a group of Yale students who insisted, despite her own experience and her protestations, that they would have to choose between children and science.[8]

The outrage turned on Deborah Eappen showed how jaundiced a view society takes of mothers who defy this conventional wisdom and insist they need or want to work. From child-rearing authorities like Penelope Leach to the influential radio psychologist and religious-right leader James C. Dobson Jr., experts proclaim that working mothers do not raise their own children and paint them as less caring and less dedicated—in a word, unmotherly.

The idea that working mothers are acting contrary to their own natures flows from long-held beliefs about differences between men and women that are now making a cultural comeback. Pop sociologists, conservatives, academics, and feminists alike are trumpeting the idea that women are more relationship oriented, more empathic. Witness the popularity of John Gray's *Men Are from Mars, Women Are from Venus* and Deborah Tannen's books. Carol Gilligan and a host of "difference feminists" have pointed to distinctive ways that women solve moral dilemmas or that women learn. While one camp of feminists celebrates women for their "maternal thinking" and suggests that they will change the world for the better, religious fundamentalists like Dobson and even some mainstream scholars like the Rutgers sociologist David Popenoe argue that women's nature uniquely suits them for child rearing.

BIG SCREEN, LITTLE SCREEN

Mothers in popular culture today appear in a dizzying variety of guises, good and bad. Roseanne has supplanted June Cleaver on television, and working mothers looking for encouragement can find it. All too often, though, the mirrors of culture continue to distort the reality of mothers' lives. When I went to the movies or turned on the television, it was all too easy to feel branded.

Working mothers seldom surface in the movies, and it is difficult to find a movie in the past few years that presented working mothers as attractive. Hollywood did offer Demi Moore in *Striptease*, leading the film critic Molly Haskell to snipe in an interview with me, "That's Hollywood's idea of the sexy working mother."

In *Mrs. Doubtfire*, one of the smash hits of 1993, the working mother, played by Sally Field, was the villain. She juggled birthday parties and office business on her cell phone, screamed at her ex-husband (Robin Williams), yelled at her children, plunged into a postseparation affair at the office, and insisted on separating the children from their doting father.

Nora Ephron, whose witty novels and romantic film comedies often capture the zeitgeist of the upper middle class, hammered home the new conventional wisdom in her 1992 film, *This Is My Life*. Ephron adapted the movie from a novel by Meg Wollitzer called *This Is Your Life*. Although the novel's themes encompass fame, coming-of-age, female self-hatred, and the destructive and redeeming faces of motherhood, Ephron turned the movie into a straightforward morality play about working and its inevitable damage to children. The movie tells the story of the daughters of Dottie Engels, a divorced mother who at last fulfills her dream of becoming a famous comic. But in her quest for the big time, she neglects her daughters, Erica and Opal. In the movie's pivotal scene, which does not appear in the book, her daughters confront her. The dialogue is entirely Ephron's.

DOTTIE: Don't I ever get a turn? Isn't it ever O.K. for me to have a life? I really don't understand this. When I was unhappy my daughters were happy. Now that I'm happy, you're miserable. Is that fair? Is it?

Erica and Opal walk out, and later run away to their estranged
father, who has never communicated with them or sent money.
Dottie turns to her boyfriend.

DOTTIE: I'm a terrible person. I mean, I did think about them. Erica was
right. I really didn't think about them. . . . In the beginning I thought of
them all the time. I spent sixteen years doing nothing but thinking about
them and now I spent three months thinking about myself and I feel like
I murdered them.

HE: You had to travel. It's part of your work. Look, kids are happy when
their mother is happy.

DOTTIE: No, they're not. Everybody says that but it's not true. Kids are
happy if you're there. You give kids a choice, your mother in the next
room on the verge of suicide versus your mother in Hawaii in ecstasy and
they choose suicide in the next room, believe me. . . .

On television, where women are among the most faithful view-
ers and the ones sponsors are loath to offend, good working mothers are far easier to find. Where once the only mothers on television
were the sentimentalized ones like Donna Reed, television mothers
today include the blue-collar working mothers on *Roseanne* and
Grace Under Fire; the caricatures of *The Simpsons* or *Married . . .
with Children,* which talk back to the old picture-perfect images;
and the much-reviled, much-defended upper-middle-class single
unmarried mother on *Murphy Brown.*
    Roseanne was a television phenomenon whose decade-long suc-
cess proved how starved mothers were to see someone on television
who yelled at her kids and worked outside the home in unglam-
orous, unrewarding jobs, but whose bond with her children was
true and deep. *Grace Under Fire,* an unabashed *Roseanne* clone, was
also an instant hit.
    Yet many of the most popular shows on television today con-
tinue to gloss over the realities of working mothers' lives. Bill
Cosby's wife was a lawyer, but she appeared at home only as the
perfect mom (still the sideshow to the perfect dad); after all the fuss,

Murphy Brown's child disappeared from the story line for several seasons, though he returned in 1997.

Home Improvement, the number one show on television until *E.R.* displaced it, builds all its gags on the *Men Are from Mars* gambit. Every joke on *Home Improvement* stems from the men not understanding how the women feel, making them mad, and having to make it up to them. I watched it dutifully for months, but I could never figure out whether Jill, the wife, worked or not. Once, I caught a reference to Jill's plans to go to graduate school. The mystery was finally solved when I read a profile of the actress who plays Jill; she has a part-time job. Though Tim's job hosting *Tool Time* is central to the show's gags, Jill never appears at work; she is always seen in her domestic role.

Despite Roseanne, the stereotypes of the selfish careerist continue to air. On a spring 1996 episode of *Law and Order,* a baby dies mysteriously, possibly at the hands of a depressed, resentful au pair. Although both parents work, the father is shown sympathetically, as someone who drops by to check on the baby. The mother is a monster; the day the baby died, she was away on a business trip. The detectives learn that she did not want a baby; while they investigate the baby's death, the mother is obsessively working on a $300 million deal. She is a pointed contrast to the nanny's former employer, a mother who quit her job because, she tells the detectives, "It became obvious no one could take care of the baby as well as I could." The good mother installed a hidden television camera to spy on the nanny and didn't like what she saw; the bad mother relied on an agency recommended by her secretary's sister.

The climactic scene comes when the mother is grilled by the nanny's attorney, herself a working mother. The young businesswoman cannot tell her how many times her baby napped or her baby's favorite toy. When Claire, the prosecutor, confronts the defense attorney about her hypocrisy, she says, "Believe it or not, I do worry about what Andrew's missing and what I'm missing. Who knows? Maybe my priorities are a little screwed up."

On a January 1997 episode of the hit show *NYPD Blue,* Sylvia Costas, the prosecutor married to Andy Sipowicz, the costar of the series, tells him she wants to leave her job to stay at home with their young son. She can't concentrate on her work, she tells him, and the cases don't seem to matter "when I could be thinking about his dopey mug without feeling guilty, or be at home holding him." When he assures her he'll work another job if necessary to afford it, she says, "Does anyone have the right to be that happy?"

THE CULT OF DOMESTICITY REDUX

Today's drumbeat of concern and condemnation echoes with the themes of the past. What we see and hear today under the guise of putting children first is a new cult of domesticity and a new campaign to sway women to embrace it. Virtually no one, not even the religious right, suggests a simple return to the 1950s; feminism has made too many inroads for that. But there are uncanny, unsettling similarities.

For decades, women have been told that there is something unwomanly about ambition; mothers are not supposed to have lives that extend beyond their children. Today we are told that working mothers are one of the root causes of juvenile delinquency, alienation, and psychological upheaval. After World War II, as the era of domesticity dawned, fingers pointed to the mother at home. She was overprotective and overpermissive. Edward Strecker, a consultant to the army and navy, wrote in 1946 that the "self-sacrificing mom" was to blame for the large numbers of boys found psychologically unsuitable for the military: "From dawn until late at night she finds her happiness in doing for her children. . . . Failing to find a comparable peaceful haven in the outside world, it is quite likely that one or more of the brood will remain in or return to the happy home, forever enwombed."[9]

Mothers in the 1950s were told, just as they are today, that if they must work, they should work part time. In 1958, the *Ladies' Home Journal* told mothers they could work part time when their children were in school, then move up to full-time work when their children left home for college. Today, "sequencing"—pulling back when children are young and picking up the pace of work as they grow—is hailed as the answer to women's problems.[10]

The authors of a *Parents* magazine article in 1988 wrote approvingly of a type of mother they called "the Adapter," who "works paid employment around the needs and schedules of her family . . . her goal is to successfully integrate paid employment with her top priority, a family-oriented life." [11]

In contrast to the harried working mother who barely has a chance to see her children, writers extol the mother at home, who spends leisurely days with her children "watching the clouds drift by in a brilliant summer sky" and "baking cookies together for a superstar day in kindergarten."[12]

Unlike the 1950s, the new cult of domesticity is not about staying home to be a helpmeet for your husband or devoting yourself to making your floors spick and span; it is about making sure your babies are the best they can be. By the 1990s, the term *housewife* had virtually vanished, to be replaced by *full-time mother*.

WHIPSAWED: JAN FLINT AND BRENDA COFFEY

The criticism and the call to come back home keep working mothers alternating between fury and shame. So it was for Jan Flint and Brenda Coffey, mothers and factory workers at a Welch's plant in central Michigan, whose debate on working and child rearing has stretched over the long years of their friendship.

I first met them in 1992, when I was researching an article on working mothers for the *New York Times*. We talked at a coffee shop in Kalamazoo early in the morning after they came off their night shifts. Brenda, a divorced mother of two, was the laconic foil to Jan's intensity. Jan smoked cigarette after cigarette as she vented her rage at an economy that forced her to work even though she believed God meant her to stay at home; at welfare mothers whose checks came out of Jan's much-grudged, much-needed salary; at herself for failing to be the kind of mother she thought she should be. Brenda's composure only cracked twice: when she spoke of her ex-husband with a contempt more striking because it was so contained and when she broke down in tears describing her older daughter's struggle with cancer.

In winter 1996, I drove to Jan's home in central Michigan to talk again. Brenda's older daughter was well, but her younger daughter had given birth to a son, whom Brenda looked after during the day while her daughter worked.

Jan, who had chosen the overnight shift while her husband worked days so he could care for their three children at night and she could be home for them during the day, had changed schedules. She changed to the second shift, working from about 3 P.M. to 11 P.M. while her husband worked nights. She did so to fulfill a long-held dream: starting a business at home that could free her from factory work. But until she saved up enough money to quit, Jan was juggling two jobs and feeling more stress than ever before.

We sat in the office of Jan's fledgling photography business, Lasting Memories, surrounded by pictures of earnest young brides and grooms, as Jan and Brenda talked.

"I feel that God put me here to rear my children, and I've screwed with that," Jan said. "I think that's what's broken down the family, women going to work."

"I don't think you've done anything to your kids," Brenda countered. "You see teenagers in trouble who had mothers home all their lives. You see these kids, from well-to-do families. They had anything they ever wanted. I think you're putting too much blame on yourself."

"But does society think they're better moms than us? I think so," Jan said. "They're better because they're at home."

"I don't totally agree with that," Brenda said quietly. "I wouldn't look at so-and-so down the road and say she's a better mom."

"But they look down on me," Jan said.

Jan seemed to voice every contradiction that bedevils the debate about working mothers and women today. Sometimes she seemed to be talking in the voices of the very critics she resented, accusing herself of neglect. Then she would rally to her own defense, comforting herself with the knowledge that two of her three children consistently made honor roll and that, inexplicably, the one who was the weakest in school was the child she had reared at home. Sometimes she sounded like Phyllis Schlafly, denouncing women for taking good jobs from men and asking herself whether she was doing the right thing by teaching her daughter to use her brain rather than to learn sewing and cooking to be a good wife. At other points, she sounded like Gloria Steinem, carping at men who plopped down on couches while their working wives worked a second shift at home.

Brenda was torn between her pride at supporting her two daughters by herself and her guilt about her daughter's teenage pregnancy. In the fifteen years since her divorce, Brenda's ex-husband had given her a onetime payment of fifty dollars in child support. For the first few years after her divorce, she worked swing shifts, alternating between days and nights, a time she remembers as a nightmare because she could never keep baby-sitters or settle on a fixed schedule. She asked to work from 9 P.M. to 7 A.M. because she could spend the most time with her daughters during the day—pick them up at school, supervise their homework, feed them dinner, and then have a baby-sitter come in when they were asleep.

Brenda spoke proudly of her ability to manage without a husband who belittled her and without resorting to welfare. "It took me a good five, six years to get on my feet," she said, remembering times when she and her daughters ate only eggs (and jelly from Welch's, of course) because that was all she could afford to buy. "My ex had the talent of making me feel I was worthless. I was going to prove I could make it on my own, and I have."

Brenda was a conscientious mother. Her daughters never stayed alone until they were in their teens, and even then, Brenda called regularly from work. But she worries that her daughter got pregnant because she was not at home late at night.

"I have these twinges of guilt," Brenda said. "I should have been there. But I wasn't out running around. I was out working to provide. I don't look at myself as a bad mom because of what happened. I think it contributed to the problem, though she probably would have gotten pregnant no matter what shift I worked. When she got pregnant, I was really upset. I've asked my kids, do you feel you suffered? Kelly tells me no. Tina says, 'Mom, you did what you had to do, and we're fine.'"

As much as Jan and Brenda blame themselves, they also resent others blaming them. "I run to the grocery store and buy cookies because I don't have time to make them," Brenda said. "Why is it that stuff makes us feel bad? We're out making money for our kids. Does it ever stop?"

"I do get tired of feeling guilty," Jan said.

"I feel I'm a good mother," Brenda said.

"Me, too," Jan said. "I'm a mother to half of the kids around. I can't be too bad."

The Good Mother

When I was a child, it was clear who the good mother was. She lived in my first reader: the bland suburban homemaker mother of Sally, Dick, and Jane. She lived in my television set: Mrs. Cleaver, the ever-aproned, ever-available mother of Wally and the Beav. She even lived in my house.

When I thought about becoming a mother, images of my own mother came to me: the touch of her cool, soft hand on my forehead when I had a fever or the talks we'd had sitting on stools at the ice cream place downtown. They were memories of comfort, warmth, and safety, the essence of motherhood for me. Yet I did not see how I could offer these gifts to my children while leading a life very different from my mother's suburban stay-at-home one or the model of motherhood enshrined in the culture around me.

That model was an extension and yet a distortion of my own memories. That good mother was a blissful creature, a stranger to rage or boredom. She was the only one who could properly care for a child, the one magically and entirely responsible for a child's fate. Above all, she proved her love by her willingness to sacrifice.

As a mother, I have often felt like an outlaw, my love for my children suspect, because I did not fit that ideal of the good mother.

I want to work, but society tells mothers that the only acceptable reason for working is dire financial necessity. I often found staying at home with an infant frustrating and lonely; mothers I talked to and read about treasured the precious hours with their new babies. They were blissful; I was crying in the shower after the baby had thrown up again. I was not tempted to work part time, but many women who could afford it were finding that an ideal solution. I still battle a sense of shame, a belief in a secret corner of my heart that my emotions brand me as a bad mother, alone amid a tide of rapture.

That is why the drumbeat of criticism still rings so loudly in my ears and those of so many mothers I know—it echoes the reproaches we level at ourselves. The mother at home remains the gold standard, and, by that definition, the majority of mothers today are tin.

Yet the icon of the good mother is equally destructive for mothers at home, who can no more meet such relentless standards of perfection than can mothers who work outside the home. A motherhood cloaked in gauze, with its bouts of despair and rage obscured in favor of greeting-card treacle, serves no one. What is the most crippling, though, is the way we have confused the idea of devotion with sacrifice.

Devotion is an offering of motherhood we should honor and preserve, but sacrifice has no place in the motherhood pantheon. A mother who has lost all sense of herself, whose sacrifices make her feel unhappy and ineffectual, is someone whose self-denial has become poisonous to herself and may well poison others around her. Yet the sacrificial mother has remained one of the most appealing and most resonant ideals throughout history, across class, race, and culture.

THE SACRIFICIAL MOTHER: MYTH AND REALITY

The image of the good mother has always had a tenuous link with reality; instead, over time these ideals usually served as moral parables, representative less of how most mothers lived than how they were supposed to live. The very childhood memories that many of us cherish make motherhood a powerful, and freighted, symbol. Just as we idealize our own mothers, we tend to idealize mothers in general, creating cultural icons that are unyielding and unrealistic because they are a product of fantasies we cling to even as adults.

Mothers have been worshipped for millennia, though in many different forms. No one knows, but many speculate, about the role of the earliest mothers. The oldest religious icons so far unearthed are figures of naked pregnant women, and some archeological excavations show the most prominent burial places given to mothers, prompting some historians to conjure up a society in which mothers evoked power and sensuality, as well as devotion and the rhythms of the earth. One early artifact, uncovered in a Neolithic excavation site in Turkey, shows two female bodies back to back, one nursing an infant and the other embracing a lover (who is smaller than she is).[1]

In contrast to these early images, the portraits of mothers that have shaped the Western tradition are largely those of self-denial and loss. The story of Moses that Jewish families recite every year at Passover is also the story of his mother, Jochebed, who gave up her son to save him from the pharaoh's death sentence and watched an Egyptian woman raise him as her own.[2] Greek myths show powerful, vengeful mothers, but one of the enduring portraits of mother love is the myth of Demeter, who braves the underworld to try to rescue her daughter Persephone and whose mourning turns the earth barren for part of every year.

Romans venerated Cornelia, the mother of the Gracchi, who forswore remarriage and devoted herself instead to her sons, Tiberius and Gaius.[3] And there is no symbol of maternal devotion more powerful in the West than Mary. The Renaissance paintings of the Madonna and child, by their very familiarity, have etched upon our consciousness the ideal mother: tender, comforting, self-sacrificing.

Yet as Shari Thurer documents in *The Myths of Motherhood,* what good mothers actually did in many societies would label them bad mothers today. In classical Greece, some historians estimate that as many as 20 percent of female babies were killed at birth. In medieval and Renaissance Europe, parents sent their children away from home as young as seven or eight years old to become apprentices or servants. For centuries, until the mid- to late 1700s, infants in well-off families were routinely handed over to wet nurses, who, in many cases, did not even live in the same household.[4]

Many of the ideals of good motherhood today are at odds with how mothers have lived for centuries. In most agricultural societies, mothers worked alongside fathers and children in large, extended households. Work did not separate them from their families, but neither did parents have the time to pay undivided attention to their children.

With the rise of towns, mothers also worked in shops and in trades. These family enterprises were small communities in themselves. A seventeenth-century London baker's household would typically consist of the baker, his wife, four paid employees, two journeymen, two apprentices, two maidservants, and three or four children.[5] Benjamin Franklin's wife, Deborah, helped both to run their family print shop and to rear their children.[6]

Unlike the ethos today that mothers bear ultimate responsibility for children, fathers were charged with this obligation well until the eighteenth century. Women, as descendants of Eve, were thought too innately sinful and irrational to be allowed to do much more than provide for children's physical needs. Fathers, not mothers, had the intellectual and moral capacity to educate children and instill moral values.

SEPARATE SPHERES

The nature of mothers' work began to change in the eighteenth and nineteenth centuries. The Industrial Revolution, the rise of manufacturing, and the gradual migration from the countryside to cities helped move the workplace out of the home, sending fathers into the world of work and leaving mothers at home with children. As more and more fathers left the home to work in factories or offices, mothers were told it was now their sacred duty to preside over a new, separate domestic sphere. Mothers were no longer too sinful to rear children; they were the embodiment of purity, and the future of civilized society depended on their ability to mold their children into moral citizens. The reform causes of the nineteenth century— crusades for temperance or against slavery and child labor—were ardently championed by many middle- and upper-class women, who were thought to bring their higher moral sensibility to issues of public life.[7]

In paintings, poems, ladies' magazines, novels of domestic life, and child-rearing manuals, the sentimentalization of motherhood reached new heights. "The roots of all pure love, of piety and honor must spring from this home," Mrs. Beecher wrote in the early 1800s. "To preside there with such skill that husband and children will rise up and call her blessed is nobler than to rule an empire."[8]

Here in the beginning of the Victorian age are the roots of the later cult of domesticity in the 1950s, as well as the still-thriving notion that men are driven to compete in the public sphere while women are called to adorn the private sphere of home.

Mothers' Work

Angel of the hearth notwithstanding, many working-class, poor, and immigrant mothers had to earn money, and often their children did, too. Just how many mothers worked is impossible to say precisely because few surveys listed a separate category for mothers. As the economic historian Claudia Goldin points out, statistics in the late nineteenth and early twentieth centuries vastly under-counted mothers' labor. Mothers worked at home, sewing piece-work, taking in laundry, and running boardinghouses, as well as continuing to labor on family farms.[9]

There was a vast gulf between the races: The 1890 U.S. census listed 4.6 percent of white married women as working, compared to 22.5 percent of nonwhite married women. Goldin estimates, how-ever, that if unpaid work or work done at home were counted, the percentage of white married women working would have risen to about 12.5 percent.[10]

Mothers at home remained the cultural ideal, and as the twentieth century dawned, they were charged with a mission only slightly updated from Mrs. Beecher's: apply the new insights of science in rearing children who would lead society ever onward to progress. Gradually, technical skills and educational achievement supplanted inherited social position as the key to upward mobility, making mothers' ability to devote themselves to their children's education even more important.[11]

Theodore Roosevelt urged American women to serve society by bearing children and raising them responsibly. "The good mother," he said, "is more important to the community than even the ablest man."[12]

In the 1920s, as clerical work offered new opportunities for educated women, the percentage of working women began to climb, although the majority of mothers remained at home. The new medium of moving pictures reflected this reality in the 1930s, featuring a number of self-confident working women—though few mothers—in such films as *Female* (1933) and *A Woman Rebels* (1936).[13]

As the Great Depression struck and economic opportunity withered, women began to be depicted as stealing jobs from men in literature, business magazines, and even Department of Labor publications.[14] The Women's Bureau of the Labor Department was established, in part, to convince a hostile public that women had a right to work and were usually doing so because they had dependents to support.[15]

Many movies of that era updated the lingering historical and religious ideals of the good mother and beamed them to millions. Barbara Stanwyck played the lead role in *Stella Dallas* (1937) in what remains a classic portrayal of a sacrificial mother. In a heroic act of selflessness, Stella pretended to reject her child for a man, pushing her away because she had been too loyal to leave on her own. Stella was afraid her lower social standing would hobble her daughter. In one of the lasting images of the film, she peers through the windows of the mansion on her daughter's wedding day, tears streaming down her face.

From the Andy Hardy series to *Little Lord Fauntleroy* to *How Green Was My Valley,* the good mother in the movies remained in the background where she belonged, a quiet inspiration and reassuring presence. She was always there to cook and sew and comfort and clean up; she offered no hint of conflict under her serene surface.

The outbreak of World War II changed that picture, if only for a brief interval. Until the 1940s, most women stopped working when they got married; most women in the workforce were single or had lost their husbands. With the advent of war, work became mothers' patriotic place, and even if most Rosie the Riveters were teenage girls, many mothers also flocked to the factories.[16]

Propaganda films and posters cheered these women on, showing scenes of an admiring family gathered around a mother in work clothes, listening as she recounted her day. During the war, Congress allotted modest funds to pay for child care centers for children of some mothers working for the war effort; many factories even provided hot dinners that the mothers could take home. The employment of women leaped from 25 percent in 1940 to 36 percent in 1945.[17]

Even the patriotic fervor that gave mothers permission to work did not spare them the public hand-wringing over the fate of their children. Congress held hearings, and psychologists and other experts began warning of the damage that working was inflicting on an innocent generation now transformed into "victory vandals."[18] With the end of the war, women were chased out of factories and into the home to make room for returning soldiers, as a cult of domesticity even more widespread than the Victorian one took hold.

JUNE CLEAVER AND BEYOND

The movies offered cautionary tales of what would happen to those mothers who did not heed the call home. *Mildred Pierce* (1945) featured Joan Crawford in a mesmerizing film portrayal of a working mother. Mildred Pierce works her way up from waitress to wealthy owner of a chain of restaurants. Along the way, she alternately spoils and neglects her daughter. The daughter grows up to be a murderer who seduces her own mother's husband. When Crawford finds the two in bed, she tries to strangle her own child.

Mildred Pierce was one of the early blows for domesticity in what would become a chorus, sounded in novels, popular and business magazines, government newsreels, and particularly the new medium of television. The chorus celebrated the mother who found ultimate fulfillment in tending her children and branded anyone who broke the mold as unnatural or neurotic.

Pop-Freudian experts decreed that a healthy woman gloried in motherhood; a discontented mother was a case for the couch. Children could be reared properly only by such a healthy mother, the psychologists Marynia Farnham and Ferdinand Lundberg pronounced in their 1947 best-seller *Modern Woman: The Lost Sex:* "If a girl has the good fortune to have a mother who finds complete satisfaction, without conflict or anxiety, in living out her role as wife and mother, it is unlikely that she will experience serious difficulties."[19]

Television sitcoms drove home this message, with shows that created a portrait of the good mother that many mothers today remember from their childhoods. Popular shows, such as *The Adventures of Ozzie and Harriet, Father Knows Best,* and *Leave It to Beaver,* all featured mothers like June Cleaver, mother of Wally and Beaver. Few crises more serious than a child's temporary misbehavior ever flared up, and a solution was never more than a phone call away to Dad at the office.

Even if the good mother was briefly tempted to stray outside her proper role, she soon found her way back home. In one episode of *Father Knows Best,* for example, Margaret, the mother, frets because she has never won a trophy, and everyone else in her family has outside interests. She enters a ladies fishing contest, but soon succumbs to the perils of ambition. Rushing upstairs to boast about her skills, she falls and sprains her wrist and cannot enter the contest after all. But her family gives her a trophy anyway: a frying pan labeled "Most Valuable Mother."[20]

On *The Donna Reed Show,* Donna decides to run for city council. Her husband and children do not really want her to run, but they pretend to be doing fine without her. Donna goes to meetings; they burn the toast. Finally, her husband has a nightmare about how he has become the president's husband; just as the psychological writings of the era linked feminism with castration, he feels unmanned. He breaks down and confesses that he can't bear it any longer; the family cannot survive without her at home. She is so happy to be needed that she pulls out of the race. When she calls to withdraw, the woman who answers the telephone tells her that she would give anything to have a family of her own to tend.[21]

The very years when television shows were championing domesticity saw the beginning of an explosive rise in the number of working married women, mothers among them. Women had more education and fewer children, and they found more opportunities to work as the number of clerical jobs increased and as part-time work became widely available. Goldin has also shown that many married women did not work before the 1950s because they could not; many companies and many school boards would not hire married women. When these barriers fell, the floodgates opened for working women.[22] From 1950 on, the percentage of married women in the workplace increased by 10 percentage points a year.[23] The number of employed women with children under age six rose from 12 percent in 1950 to 16 percent in 1960.[24]

Even as many films and television shows extolled the traditional mother in the 1950s, movies like *Rebel Without a Cause* had begun to hint at the strains beneath the surface calm. Then feminism arrived, and motherhood would never be completely the same. From political movements to popular culture, the old images came under assault.

Portraits of noble working mothers began to compete with images of neglect; television aired series like *One Day at a Time,* starring Bonnie Franklin as a divorced mother raising two daughters, and *Julia,* starring Diahann Carroll as a widow working to support her son, and Hollywood made movies like *Norma Rae.*

Mothers were thrown into a time of transition that continues thirty years after the second wave of the women's movement began. Feminists broke old taboos by talking about the boredom and desperation of a life confined to the home, and a few even urged women to abandon motherhood entirely. Many women who wanted to be at home were left furious and insulted. Neither the old mother nor the new one felt entirely comfortable, and mothers working inside and outside the home believed that society condemned their choices.

OTHER GOOD MOTHERS

The traditional good mother icon was largely a white, middle-class one, but there were distinct cultural variants. For many black mothers, in particular, work held little of the stigma attached to white working mothers. From 1900 through 1950, the proportion of nonwhite married women who were working was around 30 percent, and that proportion soared to over 60 percent by the late 1980s.[25] Generations of black women had to work, and their children saw their work as evidence of devotion, not neglect.

"For me, for black women, this is nothing new," said Chandra Irwin, a mother of three who runs a consulting business from home in Winston-Salem, North Carolina, and who has worked since her children were infants. "We never had June Cleaver or Ozzie and Harriet. My mother always worked. My grandmother always worked." Chandra pointed to a small painting in her kitchen of a simple log house with an old-fashioned washing machine sitting on the front porch.

"This picture reminded me so much of what my grandmother had," Chandra said. "This washing machine she only got much later in life, and it was in the back. She had to wash clothes. She would do laundry for white women, but they wouldn't let her come inside and warm her hands. She had seven kids. My mother's mother worked at night, the midnight shift at a hospital as a nurse's aide. When I feel discouraged, I think of my grandmothers with all those children. They had to work away from home. That's where some of my strength comes from."

In contrast to the televised image of the white middle-class mother tending her children at home by herself, it was far more common for black, Hispanic, poor, working-class, or immigrant mothers to live in larger extended families, with older relatives who provided advice, companionship, and often child care. Many black mothers I interviewed talked about growing up understanding that the entire community was responsible for them—and would report any transgression. This experience led them to discount one of the most powerful elements of the good mother ideal: the belief that only a mother could raise a child properly.

Yet the most important element of the good mother icon—the sacrifice she makes for her children—transcended race and class. Many mothers might not have been able to afford to stay at home, but they all could emulate the ideal of sacrifice. Elesha Lindsay, a hospital administrative assistant who is raising her own daughter while working and attending night school, remembers her own working mother's sacrifices vividly. "I could tell when she went without for us to have something," she said. "She wouldn't go somewhere; she made it sound like she wasn't interested in it."

Indeed, many children understood that working was a sacrifice that their mothers made for them. The image of the black mother, trudging off to work as a domestic in a white woman's house, bearing insults with dignity so her children would never have to do the same, is an icon in itself.

Hispanic women speak of the ideal of *marianisimo,* patterning their lives after the Virgin Mary's example of sacrifice and duty. Women are supposed to live for their husbands and children, deriving joy from making others happy.[26]

Other children knew their families were different from the ones they watched on television. "I grew up in the Donna Reed syndrome," said Delynn Andrews, a mother of five now studying at Kalamazoo Valley Community College in Michigan, who was raised by her mother in a single-parent household. "For me, Donna Reed was just a fantasy. I looked at it and I thought, That's not real. I was taught how to take care of the home and the finances. I can remember being five years old, climbing up to the stove and fixing breakfast."

Even if they lived with two parents in a suburban split-level house, many women grew up knowing that the mothers on television were too good to be true. That understanding has fueled the widespread ridicule of the old shows and the images they presented and has created some of today's biggest television hits, shows like *Roseanne, The Simpsons,* and *Married . . . with Children.*

"I always thought June and Ward Cleaver were kind of boring," said Kay Greene, a thirty-eight-year-old divorced mother of three who is studying to become a physician's assistant at the same college in Kalamazoo. "Our household is a lot more like Roseanne's."

That was a sentiment I heard echoed again and again in my interviews. Representative or not, though, the image of the mother at home was the cultural ideal held before generations of American women, and many of those whose lives did not conform to it dreamed that one day it would be within their reach. Maybe they could not live that way, but their daughters could.

"Everyone would look at TV and think, Oh yeah, that's wonderful," Chandra Irwin said. "That's the way it's supposed to be."

THE NEW GOOD MOTHER AND THE OLD

There is enormous confusion today about motherhood and enormous anxiety. One Mother's Day, I wandered into a greeting card shop, scanning the cards for messages. It was a study in cultural schizophrenia. Some cards were old sentimental favorites, adorned with hearts, pink script, and tributes in verse, whereas others aimed sly digs at June Cleaver.

Yet the old image of the good mother is still burnished in many quarters. Leaders of the religious right venerate the ideal of the sacrificial mother, quoting the biblical precept that "the last shall be first" as proof of her moral superiority and of homemaking as a separate but worthy vocation in God's eyes. Pat Robertson shows reruns of *Father Knows Best* on the Family Channel he used to run; Gary Bauer, the newly powerful Washington voice of the most conservative fundamentalists, says he and most real Americans love the old sitcoms and the country they portray despite sneers from an effete elite. Classic psychological theory still celebrates the good mother as someone who exists only for her child and denies the mother a separate sense of self. The sacrificial mother is the good mother, too, to many judges who decide custody battles.

Many mothers today are struggling to understand how they can reconcile the old ideals of good motherhood with the different lives they lead. One study of mothers found that women's internalized ideas of the good mother guided their decisions about whether to work and how they felt about their choices. Those mothers who felt the good mother was always at home, who agreed with sentiments like "only a mother just naturally knows how to comfort her distressed child" and "my child prefers to be with me more than anyone else," stayed home if they could.

The working mothers who were satisfied with their lives were able to achieve peace of mind because they had redefined some of the traditional images of motherhood. They were most likely to agree with the statements, "Exposure to many different people is good for my child" and "My child needs to spend time away from me in order to develop a sense of being an individual."[27]

THREE GOOD MOTHERS

The working mother as harried, neglectful, and tortured has become a stock character in a cultural morality play. In interviewing dozens of mothers, I found plenty of guilt and plenty of stress. I also found that these caricatures do not begin to do service to the complexity, confusion, and richness of real mothers' lives today. Toni Rumsey may not love her work inspecting Gerber baby food, but she is grateful for the financial security it offers and has learned that she can still honor her commitment to her children. Sue Henderson thrives as a bank executive, but her responsibilities did not prevent her from monitoring her children and taking action when something went awry. Ahling Deng works long hours in a Chinatown sweatshop in New York City and has little time with her children, but her force of character and her determination to instill Chinese family values shape her children's lives.

Toni Rumsey

When I first met Toni Rumsey, in fall 1992, her guilt about working was all but consuming her. Toni punched in at the Gerber factory when she was eighteen, straight out of high school. She has worked there ever since, with the brief exception of ten-week unpaid leaves when each of her children was born. Growing up in Hesperia, Michigan, in a largely blue-collar world where layoffs were a fact of life, Toni found that the comfortable certainties of June Cleaver's America were already out of reach.

After she had her first child, Toni knew her choice was to work or raise her children in a trailer. Yet she measured herself against the mothers she had grown up watching on television. "I never feel like I'm a full mom," she told me then. "I make the clothes, the homemade costumes for Halloween. I volunteer for everything to make up to them for not being there. I try to do it all. When I do all that, I make myself so tired. Then they lose a happy cheerful mom. Then I'm cheating them again. It's a constant guilt, no matter what I do. It's hard when you were raised with Donna Reed and the Beav's mom."

In those early years, Toni said, there were many mornings she drove to work teary-eyed after waking her children at dawn, bundling them into the car with their pajamas on, and dropping them off at the baby-sitter's so she could reach work by the time her shift started at 7 A.M.

"I've stood in the kitchen and I start crying," she said. "The house is filthy. I've got eighteen things to do. I don't know what's going to happen."

Now, after years of reproaching herself, Toni is finally beginning to accept that she is a good mother. I visited her again in winter 1996. As she sat in her cheerful living room, curled up on an outsized Delft blue sofa, I had the sense that she was trying to reassure me, that she wanted to pass on her newfound confidence to a mother whose children were still young.

"You just grow out of the guilt of not being that perfect scenario mom, maybe not the one you had at home, but the one you saw on TV," she said. "When teachers tell you, oh, your child is doing very well, has nice leadership abilities, you're doing OK. I think after you hear that enough you can kind of relax a little. You can just trust what you're doing. I'm a little bit on the compulsive side, so I'm used to worrying."

Toni learned to let up on herself, to let the house get dirtier. She hired an aunt to help her clean and now assigns chores to her children. "I don't know where I got this drive that everything had to be spick-and-span," she said. "It's OK to be guilty and normal to feel guilty. It's OK if the kids don't always like it."

Yet Toni has always driven herself hard to make sure her children did not suffer from her work. She baked cookies and sewed Halloween costumes late into the night, even though she had to be out of the house by 5:45 A.M. each day for her job inspecting baby food. She and her husband have immersed themselves in the life of their children's school, joining the children at games and coaching sports teams.

After her shift ends at 2:18 P.M., Toni drives to school to pick up her fourteen-year-old daughter, Lisa, and eleven-year-old son, Michael. Then they scatter to their full schedule of sports—Lisa to cheerleading, volleyball, or softball, Michael to football or baseball, Toni to the coaching of cheerleaders she has taken on as a way to keep tabs on her children's world. Her husband, Bill, coaches the football team and runs the local Little League, where both children play in games four or five times a week.

When practice ends, the family eats dinner together. On game nights, they usually attend as a family, and then Bill leaves about 10 P.M. to report to his job on the overnight shift at SPX, a branch of the Seal Power Corporation. On Saturdays, Michael plays basketball. On Sundays, they hang around the house or go to the movies.

Toni is used to running hard; she was brought up to work. Her father held down a second-shift factory job, and her mother had to take a job when Toni was eight. Nobody was happy about her mother working. "I had a cranky mom," Toni said, adding that she believed it was worse for her than for her own children because she was not used to her mother working. "I would have liked my mom to be home, and that's what I wanted."

Toni understood that was an unattainable luxury. "In the mid-seventies, when I graduated from high school, the idea of getting a husband to take care of you was already gone," she said. "I wasn't raised with that attitude. I knew I would find a job."

Toni, like many other mothers today, would have welcomed some way to stay out of work longer when her children were young, but feared the price of leaving would be too high. "Maybe the best thing is to stay home when they are small. When they're little, because it's such a big change in your life, the helpless part of you says I wish so bad he [the husband] could take care of you. But I always felt that would be a terrible burden. I would feel really bad if I'd given up my pay. A lot of things in our community here do close up. We don't have big cities to draw on. I would have tried to go back to the plant, and I would have lost eight years of seniority. I remember thinking, who would have me? I've baby-sat and worked in a factory and I'm a mom. Most jobs in the classifieds need a college education, and the job titles sounded scary."

Toni was grateful she had made the decision to keep working when her first husband was killed in a car accident, leaving her with an infant daughter. After she remarried and had another child, she continued to work, dropping the children at the house of a baby-sitter, a local woman whom Toni knew and who cared for a small group of children. Even on a budget, paying comparatively little for child care, Toni was able to find warm, reliable sitters for her children and has used only two baby-sitters in all her years of working. During summer vacations, Toni's cousin or daughters of Toni's friends stayed with them to look after the children.

"I was so lucky—they were wonderful, loving, caring when they were sick," Toni said. "That's what's nice about living in a small town. There is wonderful word of mouth."

For Toni, as for so many other working mothers, a child's illness would upset her carefully constructed balance between home and work. "When one's sick and three days later the other gets it—those are the terrible times. There should be a period when being a mom comes first, but in the real world they don't care if your child is sick. That was when I would sit down and say, 'I just want to quit. Is this worth it?' Then all things pass, and you realize that would not be a good decision."

Now that Toni and her husband are older, they earn a comfortable income, but Toni says it would still be hard to stay home. She is proud that her money has helped them afford a nice house, an extra car, and the ability to go on weekend family trips. Most important, her salary enables them to save to help pay for their children to go to college and get the degrees she realizes will be essential for them to land and keep good jobs.

Financial security is one of the gifts her work has conferred on her children. "I think they have a better sense of security if parents both work and if parents aren't quietly talking about how are we going to pay for this and how are we going to pay for that," she said.

As her children have grown, Toni has found that they seem to need her presence less. They want to be with their friends, and, increasingly, she seems in the way. She has not eased up on her commitment to them. "As busy and hectic as our life is—sometimes I can hardly write on our calendar what goes on—even so, it's really rare to go a day when I don't see my kids or connect. They see a mom that still puts her time in with them. That's why I had kids. I'm not going to shirk that responsibility."

Sue Henderson

Few of Sue Henderson's neighbors in her North Carolina city are working mothers; few of her friends or relatives kept their jobs after they had children. Sue does not have to work; her husband is a textile executive. Yet she has realized, as she puts it, that her work as a bank executive keeps her alive. Her television heroine was not June Cleaver, but the witch-turned-housewife on *Bewitched*, whose sense of adventure Sue admired.

That zest was evident when we met in March 1996, in a conference room at her bank, hidden away from telephones so we could talk uninterrupted. A warm, buoyant person, Sue practically radiates energy and drive. "I do well with a lot on my plate," she said. "I like lots of stimulation."

Sue manages twenty-five bank branches in five counties while raising her two daughters. Often, she does so alone during the week because her husband's job requires frequent travel. She leaves the house in the morning when her children do and returns home at 6 P.M., bringing with her about two hours of work she completes after her daughters are asleep.

Sue relies on the same baby-sitter she hired when her first child was born, an older woman who picks her children up from school, cooks dinner a few nights a week, and can spend the night when Sue has an occasional business trip.

Each time Sue took on more responsibility at work, she worried how she could continue to manage. And each time, the doubts eventually dissipated. "That last time I was offered a promotion, I thought, This is going to destroy my work-family balance," Sue said. "But I found I grew more taking on this challenge. I felt better about me. I felt so alive, upbeat, and great about things."

Yet Sue has had times when she reexamined her life and questioned her choices. When we first talked, she told me she was at one of her lowest points in years. Her older daughter was having trouble keeping up with the two hours of homework assigned nightly in fourth grade. She was balking at Sue's authority as she approached adolescence. And Sue was weathering a tough period at work.

"I'm at a crossroads," she told me then. "I love what I do, but something has to happen. The mornings are crazy. This morning, I wanted to pick up the phone and say to my children, 'Mommy really does love you.' I don't like the pattern. I'm overextended."

Sue struggled to understand whether the issue was working or the onset of adolescence. Her daughter swung between pride and resentment about Sue's work. "I know what she says to other people; they think I own the bank," Sue said. "But she knows I'm vulnerable right now, and she's playing it to the hilt: 'Mom, we need you here. I don't want you to work.' I have been very honest in talking to her about why I work. It's mentally stimulating. I enjoy helping and working with people. It's security for our family. Hopefully, I'm modeling working in a way for her. But right now she needs a lot of personal attention. And she's not getting it."

Sue thought about job sharing or asking for less responsibility.

She seriously considered an offer of part-time work in another business. Some days, she leaned toward leaving; on others, she could not imagine how to go on without work. Her husband would be gone all week; would she simply sit around the house, smoldering?

The very qualities she has sharpened at work as a manager, Sue found, eventually helped her navigate her problems at home. "I'm very proactive," she said. "I will call if I have a concern and ask for help."

Sue knew her baby-sitter was not confident about helping her daughter with her homework, and she knew that she herself could not be home by 3 P.M. So she brought up her concerns at a teacher's conference, and the teacher recommended a student at a nearby college who would serve as a "study buddy," showing her daughter how to plan her time. She also consulted a child psychiatrist to see if her daughter had a learning disability or if the answer was emotional.

Shaken, Sue asked the psychiatrist if she was part of the problem. "I was thinking, Why am I doing all of this? My family is my priority. You feel such guilt when they're not doing well. I said, 'Do I need to find something else to do?' And he was the one who said, 'Don't overreact. Let's try to work on some strategies for her to see what impact that has on you.' He helped me realize that probably work was one of the things that kept me whole."

When Sue and I spoke again several months later, her voice was calmer. Life was better, at home and at work. Her husband had received a promotion that enabled him to move his office closer to home. The college student was helping her daughter learn to manage the homework assignments. The child psychiatrist had recommended some strategies to help her daughter focus and reassured Sue about her own course. When Sue and I last spoke in winter 1998, her daughter was excelling, academically and socially. Their relationship was thriving, and Sue looked back on her earlier fears with a new perspective.

"Life is full of imbalance," she said. "If you react in a state of emotion, you can make the wrong decision. Letting myself come to the decision that it was okay to quit has also given me a sense of freedom. If I ever hit a time when it's not working out, I can make that choice."

Sue recalled a similar struggle after her daughter was born. Her husband said he would support any decision she made, although he wanted her to stay home. Her relatives could not believe she was thinking of any other course.

Torn, she turned to her mother, who had worked as a nurse beginning when Sue was in elementary school. "My mother said, 'Sue, don't throw it all away without giving it a fair shake.' I said, 'How long is a fair shake?' She said, 'You'll know when you've given it a fair shake.' Those were the best words. I still feel like I'm giving it a fair shake ten years later."

Ahling Deng

Ahling Deng sat in her Chinatown tenement, dismissing thoughts of guilt about her long hours away from her children. "We have two purposes in life," she announced. "One is to make money so we can live. The other is to make sure our children grow up to be educated and stay upright."

Ahling works long and hard—more than ten hours a day, at least six and sometimes seven days a week—at a succession of Chinatown sweatshops in New York City so her family can live. She usually arrives home at 9 P.M., just in time to check her daughters' homework before they go to bed.

Ahling has worked these grueling hours bent over her sewing machine since she arrived in the United States in 1982 from China. Not for a moment does she believe she has fallen short of the other life purpose: bringing up smart and moral children.

Indeed, for her, the two goals are intimately connected. "If we are walking on the street, and my children see other children with something better than they have, before they can even say anything, I say, 'Whatever Mommy does, she does to buy you clothes so you can go to school. Mommy has to buy food so we can eat. And that way your children can have these things.'"

She uses her work to impart moral lessons of perseverance, diligence, and self-denial. When her two daughters were small, she took them with her to the factory after school, both to keep an eye on them and to impress on their minds the image of her hard at work.

"You don't go home from the factory until you're done," she said. "By my example, they know you don't finish something half-way. The only way to achieve something is by doing it to the end."

It is an ethic she absorbed as a child in a Chinese village in Guangdong province. Both her parents worked in a factory. From the age of four, Ahling's job was to go to the seashore and lug back buckets of water for the family. She had to leave school in the fifth grade to help take care of her younger brother after he had an accident. "He broke his head, and I left the Ping-Pong paddle there on the table and went home," she said.

When she was twenty-seven, she borrowed money from her father's sister to emigrate to America. No sooner had she gotten off the plane than her aunt asked her to repay the loan in two months. Ahling worked seven days a week—six days at the union factories, which do not allow employees to work seven days straight, and the seventh day at the small nonunion shops that sprout and wither all over Chinatown.

Within a year, she had saved enough to bring over her boyfriend. They married, and a year later, her first daughter, Shujing, was born. After a month, Ahling returned to the factory, leaving Shujing with her brother's wife, who lived nearby and had a child about the same age. For the first six years of Shujing's life, Ahling continued to work seven days a week; her husband worked equally hard at his job. She had another daughter, Shuyen, and a son, Zhao Liong.

After each child was born, she took off about a month, without pay, and then returned to work. I asked her if that was hard for her, and she smiled at the very question. "Americans think so much of sentiment, and they worry so much," she said. "Of course I worried about my children, but what else could I do? There is a Chinese principle: Do the best you can under the circumstances. Either I stay home with them and we have no money to live or I go to work."

In fact, she said, the hardest times for her were just after her children were born, when she could not contribute her share to the family. Like so many other women I interviewed, Ahling would never label herself a feminist, yet she is proud of the independence that money brings her.

"The hardest thing for me is not to be able to count on making money. When I first gave birth, I had no income, except for my husband's, and that was a strange feeling. The thought never entered my mind to be financially dependent on my husband. I am an equal partner. I make the money and so when I spend it, I feel good about it."

Even with both the Dengs' salaries, they can afford only a tiny, three-room railroad flat up six flights of stairs. They share the three rooms with her sister and nephew. Often, there is no heat. A few weeks before we met, Ahling had been forced to cancel a planned interview because her young son was in the hospital with pneumonia, contracted after living weeks without heat in New York's snowiest winter in more than 100 years.

Ahling returned to work about a month after each of her children was born. She said that she has been lucky to rely on a mix of relatives and subsidized day care. When they turned three, her middle daughter and her son attended a local day care center from 8 A.M. to 6 P.M. She paid only $5 a week, a sum based on her income, which is now about $140 a week.

Her sister walks the children to school in the morning (her son is in a prekindergarten program at the local elementary school) and picks them up at school, brings them home, feeds them a hot lunch, and then drops them off at an after-school Chinese program. Her sister, too, is studying, but her school lets out at 1:30 P.M. When the children are sick, Ahling stays home with them, and her sister takes her place at the factory.

If Ahling had all the money she wanted, she would rather have stayed home with the children when they were younger. "The most ideal situation would be when the children are young to stay at home so you could be with them," she said. "But once they are in school, you should start working whether you need the money or not. It keeps you from boredom and vice, like mahjong. It's also good for a parent to work, so when her children go to college she wouldn't be all by herself and wouldn't need to learn new things. When you're older, it's harder to learn, and no one would want to have you."

For Ahling, the challenge is far more how to keep her children Chinese amid a sea of American self-indulgence than how to work and mother at the same time. She is ever alert for opportunities to instruct them.

"We are trying to preserve Chinese family values," she said. "I let them watch some American TV. They get the feeling of how American parents don't care about their children, how they will leave them and go out to eat and to a party. I tell them, 'Everywhere Mommy goes, Mommy goes with you. You are loved by Mommy. Mommy doesn't have as much money as they do, but you are loved. Mommy thinks about you.' So they know how Mommy is good compared to the mothers on TV."

American parents, Ahling said, are too afraid to enforce authority. She teaches her children to respect their parents and to understand their obligation to them. If she works hard for them, they owe her and themselves diligence at school. She is comfortable that her older daughter, who is eleven, is already well on the way. She earns good grades and learned responsibility early on. Ahling taught her at age seven how to wash dishes, wash vegetables, and make rice.

She is more worried about her younger daughter, Shuyen, who, she said, lied to her a few times and pretended she had no homework. Ahling told Shuyen that if she caught her again, she would smack her (although she hastens to add that was a threat she did not have to carry out). She polices Shuyen's homework vigilantly with Shujing's help.

"I make a point, every day, to look over her homework and ask her, 'Have you completed it?' I tell her, 'If you don't finish, I will sit here until you finish.' I don't understand English, but my daughter does. And she will make sure she finishes before she goes to bed. She's like me. She sets a good example."

3

The Baby Care Bibles

When I was pregnant with my first child, I desperately sought reassurance about the prospect of impending motherhood. I started loading up on manuals even before my daughter arrived. I had never changed a diaper and seldom even handled a baby before I had one of my own. I was dutifully appreciative of others' babies, but the truth was, I wasn't all that interested. When I got pregnant, I figured I'd better start learning fast. I quizzed all my friends about what they liked, and I got back the standard answers: Penelope Leach; T. Berry Brazelton; Burton White for advice on stimulating them; and, almost as an afterthought, Dr. Spock.

I found little comfort in the pages of most of these books. The books offered vague and pat blessings about working motherhood, but I got the distinct feeling that their authors were cool toward the idea. They offered rigid formulas about how long I should stay home, without citing or describing any research to substantiate their opinions. Flying blind, I decided that the six months my employer allowed me would put me in a safe zone.

Then, sleepless, tentative, and overwhelmed, I awoke to the reality of infancy. My daughter was energetic, outgoing, and utterly engaging, but she was not a sleeper. She had colic for an excruciating two months. I began to think I was the only mother whose baby did not lie, cooing gently, on her lambskin rug watching the shafts of sunlight move slowly across the room. I could never put her down without her crying. I could never get her to nap. I could never even get her to sleep more than two hours without waking up, night or day.

Why wasn't I loving every minute, the way I was supposed to? Why was I sitting in my bathrobe at two in the afternoon crying because the baby spat up again and I had never even gotten close to the shower? Why couldn't I measure up to the selfless, beatific mother of television and movie fame, the mother pictured in the baby care books? There were moments of ecstasy: staring at her hands sketching balletic movements in the air; the weight of her soft, warm body when she drifted to sleep on my chest; her first laugh. But I was drowning. For the most part, my new bibles were not life rafts; they were millstones pulling me deeper under the water.

The authors of these books are our newest gurus, the latest in a succession of experts preaching to mothers how to bring up their children. Reading many of these books, the mother enters a world in which her needs do not count; indeed, they exist only to be subordinated to the cult of babyhood.

These are views that should alarm any mother, whether at home or at an office, but they are particularly corrosive to a working mother. In ways overt and subtle, large and small, most classic baby care books convey a vision that the mother at home is the norm, and the desired one; that children just may survive a working mother, but it would be far better if she stayed at home; that combining working with mothering is an endless succession of crises, featuring coldhearted baby-sitters, heartless bosses, and heartbroken children.

Mothers who want to do their best by their babies eagerly devour the advice, but they seldom realize that the precepts they absorb are little more than opinions based on child-rearing fashions that have changed as swiftly and arbitrarily as long and short hemlines. These beliefs, often based on little more than the experts' per-

sonal experiences and philosophies, have acquired the force of com-
mandments.

Their first commandment is, Mother, sacrifice thyself.

PENELOPE LEACH

Penelope Leach is the high priestess of the baby cult, the most
relentlessly focused on the child at the expense of the mother. In
Leach's eyes, at least at the beginning of infancy, a good mother has
no separate self and does not want one: "The mother will scarcely
be able to distinguish the infant's needs from her own because her
prime need will be to meet his and she will suffer when he suffers
and find her own pleasure channeled through his."[1]

Of course, a new mother wants desperately to satisfy her new
baby, and a new joy graces her life when she learns how to do so.
Many new mothers are consumed by their infants, so engrossed that
the larger world narrows to a circle of two. This is a state the great
British psychoanalyst Donald W. Winnicott called "primary maternal preoccupation"; Leach is describing what has become a psychoanalytic truism about a mother's early experience.

A mother may be obsessed, but her interests are not identical to
her baby's. Sometimes they are in direct conflict. Her battered body
craves sleep, and her howling infant demands food. Flashes of
resentment and bewilderment punctuate her happiness.

Good mothers do not give in to these bad feelings, in Leach's
eyes. If they do, it is merely a sign of their own neurosis, a residue of
bad mothering from their own childhoods, according to Leach.
Describing a mother who finds a baby's possessiveness overwhelming, Leach writes: "Taught, all her life, to keep her own feelings
under control, neither displaying nor giving way to them, she is
faced with a baby who is simply demanding to be cuddled and
kissed, patted and stroked. . . . Look at yourself through your baby's
eyes and you will see yourself as good and warm and loving, worthy
of all this devotion and with plenty of your own to offer."[2]

Leach's views reach millions of mothers. Her books, most
notably, *Your Baby and Child,* are perennial best-sellers and have

been published in twenty-eight countries. Her cable television show, *Your Baby and Child with Penelope Leach,* airs several times a week on Lifetime Television. Unlike most of the other authorities, she is not a pediatrician, but has a Ph.D. in psychology.

Her passion for children explodes from the page; she writes lyrically and sensitively about life as they see it. She crusades, admirably, against corporal punishment and child poverty and for extended parental leaves and greater work flexibility. Leach offers a creative and appealing vision of a society with institutions that support children and families—community centers in which mothers of young children could congregate and children could gather after school, networks of telecommuters based at home who introduce children to the world of work, and companies that do not penalize women or men who take time off to stay at home with their children.

Leach's ideas would go a long way toward assuaging the anguish of many mothers whose hearts are at home while their bodies are at work. Leach pays lip service to the idea that mothers of young children have a right to their own needs. She acknowledges that some mothers will want to work and that mothers cannot build their entire lives around their babies because most adults need other contacts, too.

Though she insists that she is not telling any mother what to do, her true feelings break through. When her writing gathers force, when her anger and indignation build, you know she is writing from her heart. And in her heart, she cannot understand why any good mother would really want to work while her children are young because working is so obviously not the best thing for children. She scolds those mothers who do not comply, as would the British nanny she so despises, her tone reproving and self-righteous.

If Leach had her way, mothers who were not willing to stay home with children for two years would not be allowed to produce them: "With excellent contraception and liberal abortion laws, couples who do not want children need not have them. For those that do, a two-year commitment for each child is not very long."[3]

Yet Leach seldom acknowledges the possibility that an attuned, devoted mother, a mother who responds in the sensitive way that she advocates, could also be a mother who wants or needs to go to work when her children are young. There is little room in Leach's world for women like Donna King, a mother of four who works as a hospital laboratory supervisor. Donna speaks openly and easily about her love for her children, but she is equally candid about her need for work. When she had her fourth child four years ago, she said her husband urged her to quit, but she wanted to go back to her job.

"If people say we're doing it for the money, I say not really," Donna said. "I think you need a little bit of self-gratification, of going out and doing something. When I see these women on *Oprah,* the stay-at-home moms shouting at the working moms, I feel like, 'Tell the truth, lady, those kids are driving you nuts.' You love them so much. But children are children, and they will get on your nerves. There are days when if someone wants something from me, I'm just going to explode. Then I think if I were a stay-at-home mother, it wouldn't be too good for the children. I feel like I can give more of myself to my children because I do work . . . and to my husband."

To Leach, parents who make any arrangements for surrogate care are only thinking selfishly of themselves: "They need to realize that they are making the decision for themselves, not for the baby."[4] The baby, Leach maintains, will see the mother's absence as a devastating abandonment. Leach's language is calculated to punch a hole through a mother's heart. "You may not be able to prevent him minding, prevent him from tearing you apart by crying and holding up his arms to you as you leave for work," she writes.[5] A substitute must try to be a "life raft when the mother's absence would otherwise leave her [the baby] drowning in a sea of deserted despair."[6] There is no hint here that a baby who howls when a mother walks out the door may be gurgling and smiling a minute later.

In Leach's eyes, the working mother will pay even if she is conscientious enough to find a life raft. She will cede her influence to whomever she pays to look after her children, and she will miss the precious, irrecoverable "firsts" of childhood. "If you are not there when a toddler's first rhyme is spoken, you will not hear it or see her face as she hears what she has made. Magic moments happen when they happen and the painful truth is that the ones that are missed are gone forever."[7]

Leach could have been writing in the 1950s. In 1953, a mother featured approvingly in a *Ladies' Home Journal* article titled "I Can't Afford to Work," wrote of her decision to stay home: "I don't want to give Linda over to a stranger. I'd be thinking of her . . . with a sore finger to be fixed by a kiss . . . out walking and waving at a bird with shouts of joy. . . . I want to be there for all of it."[8]

If the modern mother braves Leach's talk of abandonment and loss and insists on working, Leach has another round to fire. In *Children First,* she rips into virtually every kind of surrogate care for young children, taking potshots at the mother all the way. Nannies may be convenient and even stable, but they are simply paid to provide the loving the mother will not: "But who is going to want to fill, as a job, the role with someone else's child that the mother does not wish to fill with her own?" she asks.[9]

Unsupported by evidence or most other child-rearing authorities, Leach declares unequivocally that any form of group care for children under three years old is always damaging. Speaking of parents, she writes, "Why do they believe that daycare is OK? What sad and subtle subtext tells them that money earned away and spent on their children is more important than time at home spent with their children?"[10]

Leach gives grudging approval to family day care, in which children are cared for in someone else's home, because these women are not driven by filthy Mammon but "mostly look after other people's so as to be able to go on looking after their own."[11]

What if, despite Leach's dire warnings, your baby actually seems all right? You played Russian roulette and survived—this time: "If the day-care arrangement they find works out, if the baby settles and does not seem upset, if his basic relationship with the parents seems still secure, then they have got away with it."[12]

Leach's attitudes were forged partly from her own experience.

When her son was two years old and Leach was working (part time) as a researcher in child development, he almost died from an attack of viral meningitis. Leach, like many of the women she writes about, was pressed to return to work before she felt ready. In a 1994 interview, twenty-three years after her son's illness, she still felt its power keenly enough to tear up. She told the interviewer that she left her son with a nanny, "knowing perfectly well the only person he was OK with was me." Sure enough, picking up on her grief and conflict, her son grew emotionally shaky: "You could reduce him to tears playing peekaboo."[13]

Leach quit her job some months later. She had endured a terrible trauma, one that must have sharpened her sensitivity to the many women who are forced back to work before they are ready. It is always tempting to apply personal experience broadly. Not all women, though, are reluctant to return to work after the birth or illness of a child.

Leach's stand on work is part of a broader problem, one that permeates her philosophy of child rearing and harkens back to the powerful, persistent ideal of the sacrificial mother. She assumes that if mothers only understood how babies felt and why they behave as they do, they would find joy in submission. Although she is right that knowledge of child development helps mothers respond appropriately to their children, she leaves no room for the give-and-take of real life.

In Leach's world, mothers are constantly helping their babies do things the babies will learn anyway, like uncurling their fingers to show them how to drop objects once they clasp them. Or they are busy whipping up educational toys with pieces of string. Her list of playthings mothers can make themselves is daunting even to think about: putting marbles in used detergent bottles; tying playthings to the crib with knitting wool; threading elastic through bulldog clips and hanging it over the crib so you can constantly change the items the baby sees; cutting faces from foil plates; threading rings on a rod; pushing a Ping-Pong ball through a cardboard tube and letting the baby look at it go up and down. It's all so purposeful, so portentous, so intense—and so remote from most mothers' real-world, imperfect mothering. It's also controlling. The baby never gets to experience anything without the mother's interference.

Leach never tells you it will be all right—at least once in a while—if you just plump the baby down on the rug while you try to sneak a glance at the paper and flash smiles his way now and then. That's obviously not how you should conduct all your communication with a child, but Leach never acknowledges that all grown-ups, and all kids, need to tune out sometimes to store up enough energy to tune in.

What Leach misses is any sense of what the mother thinks and feels about this experience—and how the mother's thoughts and feelings, in turn, will affect her child. Worst of all, Leach seldom acknowledges the legitimacy of the dark side of motherhood—the resentment, rage, and self-doubt chronicled by countless mothers, from Adrienne Rich writing of the 1950s in *Of Woman Born* to Nina Barrett writing of the 1990s in *The Playgroup*. About the closest Leach comes to acknowledging such feelings are sentences like "A brand new baby is neither lovable nor loving," and her admission that mothers may experience "furious irritation at his crying" or feel "swamped in claustrophobia."

Her remedy is, essentially, to soldier on: "Understanding your own importance is both the prevention and the cure. All the vital developments of these months are waiting inside your baby. . . . You can help him develop and learn or you can hinder him by holding aloof. . . . Like it or not, you are a family now."[14]

Note that Leach is not suggesting that the mother should go out for a walk; hand the baby to someone else; or, heaven forbid, return to work even part time. Nor does she concede that these feelings may be valid. They simply get in the way of the baby's development, so change them. It's a lethal cross of stiff upper lip and hectoring that makes the feelings seem taboo, almost criminal.

THE CULT OF THE BABY

Leach is only the latest of a parade of experts who have offered wildly contradictory advice to parents. In the 1920s, John B. Watson insisted that babies would thrive only on rigid schedules; his was a view of a baby fit for the assembly-line age. As scientists absorbed the ideas of genetics in the 1930s, they began to see the child emerging from the womb as less malleable, more a distinct personality, programmed to go through certain developmental stages at set times. Arnold Gesell, a leading proponent of such views, told the mother she did not have to mold her child; rather, she should accept the baby and try to accommodate to him or her.

Then, as popular Freudianism reached a cultural apogee during the 1950s, the experts turned their attention to children's inner lives. Rather than applaud as their children passed through Gesell's developmental milestones, mothers had to ensure that their children would successfully navigate Erik Erickson's stages of trust and autonomy. Whereas mothers once had only to frog-march their children through Watson's schedules, now they had to be attuned to their emotions. Benjamin Spock was one of the first experts to urge temporizing the strictness of the past with a new concern for children's points of view. Nonetheless, he advocated a far firmer hand at home and paid far more attention to parents' needs than Leach does.

Leach's books match a new zeitgeist that dawned in the 1980s, just after the first edition of her book *Your Baby and Child* was published in 1977. A baby boomlet was hatched in the 1980s and grew into a full-fledged boom by 1989. In that year and for several years afterwards, more than 4 million babies were born—the highest birthrate since the baby boom. As the children of the first post–World War II baby boom began having children en masse, they brought to parenting the same level of intensity, scrutiny, and narcissism that many had previously devoted to protest, relationships, and careers.

The result was a fascination with babies that borders on the obsessive. Just as we had supermom, that flawed and impossible standard, we now have superbaby, the optimally stimulated, optimally nurtured child who requires a full-time mother at his side.

The 1950s cult of domesticity prompted a consumer explosion that targeted the mother as the chief purchaser of products that would help her be a better cook, cleaner, and helpmate to her husband. The recent cult of babyhood has produced another flood of products, this time aimed straight at babies but with parents' purses in mind. The possibilities for purchase are endless. Knee bumpers to protect baby's precious little knees as she learns to crawl (only $9.95 a pair). A "boppy" for $29.95 to brace your infant to prevent her falling over in the approximately four weeks it will take her to learn to sit up properly. A $79.95 dolphin float for the little one in the pool, complete with its own sun umbrella and built-in baby bottle holder.[15]

Too many parents, desperate to give children every advantage, end up treating them as trained seals. Too many working parents spend their weekends frantically compensating for their absence during the week, rushing children from zoo to puppet show to museum, cramming in stimulation when many children would prefer to lounge around in their pajamas until noon.

Anucha Browne Sanders, a Maplewood, New Jersey, mother of two who works in marketing for IBM, said she made that mistake at first with her oldest son, who is now five. "I see this guilty mother syndrome—my kid's got to excel," she said. "What happened to just letting them play? I learned that the hard way. I put too much emphasis early on with Roy learning the alphabet and sounding out words. Now I say, 'Let's go look for worms.' Let them go out for walks in the rain."

Fueling this syndrome is Burton L. White, a Harvard psychologist whose inflexibility and arrogance on the subject of working top even Leach's. He says flat out that mothers should not work—an opinion he puts forward as scientific because it is based on his research observing how families raise children. Yet he offers no evidence in his book that he systematically compared objective measurements of how children of working mothers and children of mothers at home turned out.

He plays right into the craze for intellectual stimulation in his popular book, *The First Three Years of Life*. The book comes complete with lists of games and toys that every mother must offer to her children at specific stages in their lives to make sure they learn crucial concepts like object permanence.

White, too, acknowledges that more conventional research does not necessarily support his opinions. Aiming straight at super-achieving parents, he tells the mother, maybe the research can't detect any particular harm. But if you aren't at home, if you aren't doing what I told you, your child won't be as smart, won't be the very best that he can be.

At the other extreme lies the earth mother school, best exempli-fied by *Mothering* magazine. The magazine is much warmer and more supportive of mothers than Leach and the mainstream experts. Its articles bracingly urge mothers to ignore the experts and do what they feel is natural. *Mothering* often carries enlightening features like one about the importance of "benign neglect," asking children to fend for themselves at times.

Several of the causes that *Mothering* champions, though, do not help mothers understand that they have a right to draw lines for their own sanity. A prime example is the magazine's attack on experts who tell mothers to let their babies cry it out at night. The editors at *Mothering* are acting as the defenders of mothers' instincts; it is excruciating to listen to a baby cry in the middle of the night and not to respond, and many mothers guiltily ignore the advice because they cannot bear to carry it out. Yet allowing a baby to wake up several times a night for months or even years does nei-ther the child nor the mother any good.

As the mother of two infants who never learned how to sleep through the night on their own, I can attest to the transformation of my life when I finally forced my children to do so. I had to wait in the bathroom, with the water running, to block out the sounds of crying. Hard as it was, the reward was that for the first time in months, I could sleep for more than two hours at a time, an infusion of energy that made me a more joyous mother.

The cult of the baby threatens to eviscerate the baby as well as the mother. The superbaby is a possession to cultivate, an asset to show off. What is most troubling is that the superbaby syndrome places the highest value on the pursuit of genius, not on trying to understand and celebrate who an individual baby is. A baby who is not a prodigy is deficient, and the mother is the culprit because she failed to stimulate the baby properly. New brain research has given this craze for stimulation an added urgency; the research suggests that a child's early years are crucial in forming the actual structure of the brain and determining intellectual ability. Early stimulation is undoubtedly critical, but there is a real danger that parents will underestimate the equally crucial needs of a baby for emotional contact.

The superbaby syndrome is not only bad for the baby, but it can leave little room for the mother. She is the mobile dangler, the flash-card shuffler, the one whose sacrifice produces the superbaby. Critics denounce a cultural narcissism that seems to them to honor the mother's needs at the price of the baby's. Yet those adults who heed the experts, at least, are far more conscious of children's feelings than were many parents a generation ago. The experts coach parents to echo back children's emotions, to empathize, to discuss decisions with children. All are admirable in moderation, but the advice too literally followed can produce parents who fail to convey a reasonable degree of authority that reassures children they are not in charge.

BERRY BRAZELTON

For years, T. Berry Brazelton—like Spock before him—believed that children of working mothers would be psychologically damaged until his own daughters challenged him and he changed his view. Brazelton is a far cry from the excesses of Leach, but he is just as guilty of making arbitrary pronouncements about how long mothers should stay home and just as prone to exaggerating the stresses of work while underestimating its rewards for women.

Brazelton declares that mothers should stay home a minimum of four months, and he has made countless appearances on television saying that a year or longer would be even better. Brazelton, like Leach, bases his belief that mothers and children need a concentrated and uninterrupted relationship on a psychological theory called attachment, which suggests that if a mother leaves a child in the early months, they will not form a healthy bond. His edicts have inspired countless other self-appointed experts to make similarly arbitrary pronouncements.

Unlike Leach, Brazelton is not in danger of forgetting about mothers; his books and cable television show address them directly and compassionately. In *Infants and Mothers,* a classic since its publication in 1969; in his 1985 book, *Working and Caring;* and on his cable television show, Brazelton offers a number of specific suggestions about how to combine working and mothering so children's best interests are served.

He includes several tips about handling the return home at the end of the workday, selecting high-quality child care, setting aside one-on-one time with each child, and understanding that "quality time" is more likely to mean low-key shared moments than special expeditions. He acknowledges that research shows that a woman who is happy at work is more likely to be a successful mother than one who is unhappy at home. And he admits that even loving mothers will find child rearing oppressive at times.

Nor does Brazelton blame mothers who find the early months of infancy rough going; *Infants and Mothers* offers several case studies of mothers driven to distraction by demanding or hard-to-soothe infants. He avoids laying down rigid rules, urging parents to trust their own instincts and be guided by their own baby's temperament.

Yet Brazelton's undeniable concern for mothers is sometimes overshadowed by the detailed and exhaustive treatment of the problems that working mothers face: bad child care, sick children, and the frenetic rush to combine child care and household chores. When mothers return home from work in the pages of his books, they are exhausted and stressed—not so happy to see their children that they shed some workplace tension and put work in its proper, and separate, compartment. Working mothers, he says, are so tired that they find it harder to deal with the negativism of the toddler years—with no concession that they might find it easier to put that negativism in perspective if they've had a break from it during the day.

No one can deny the hardships of working mothers, particularly those who work because they must at grueling, unrewarding jobs. Almost nowhere in his book is there mention of the compensations that even hard-pressed working-class mothers have said they enjoy: a sense of self-sufficiency, social contacts with other adults, and the satisfaction of setting an example of the work ethic for their children.

Brazelton talks and writes often about the pain that mothers feel leaving their babies prematurely, and he has used his celebrity to lobby tirelessly for a longer paid family leave policy and other policies to ease the conflict between work and home. Yet he also believes that women who do not feel that way are in denial, that they prevent themselves from attaching to their babies because they are so afraid they will not be able to leave them. It's an interesting example of the way experts have always labeled such "unnatural" mothers deviant or disturbed.

Diane Crispell hardly fits the stereotypical portrait of a career-consumed professional; she works regular hours and almost no nights or weekends. Nor does she seem a stranger to her own emotions. She was not ravaged when she returned to work eight weeks after the birth of both her children. She is the executive editor of *American Demographics* magazine, and her husband works seasonally in construction jobs. Eight weeks was all their family could afford to go without her salary.

"I had no feeling of 'Oh, I have to do this; this is terrible and I wish I could be home,'" said Diane, who was thirty-six when we spoke in the spring of 1996. "I guess part of it was financial necessity. I am the primary breadwinner in my household, and, in that sense, there was no choice. I don't just work for the money. I love my job. The whole concept of challenging your mind was a very positive concept in my family. My mother made the choice to do it at home; I made the choice to do it in the labor market. It's a matter of making your choice, feeling good about it, and accepting that about yourself."

Many mothers who return to work willingly, though, find it hard to leave their children. Many might feel a lot better about doing so if they believed that their babies would not suffer in their absence. Unfortunately, Brazelton compounds that guilt by his own mixed messages. You can pull this off, he tells mothers, but at the same time, perhaps you shouldn't.

In his introduction to the revised edition of *Infants and Mothers,* he writes: "Inadvertently, I may have added to mothers' feelings of guilt when they were not able to stay at home throughout the first year. This has not been my intent, for I have seen how critical it was to many young women to include a job in their daily lives."[16]

Later in the book, he suggests that such attitudes might change if women only understood just how crucial a job being a mother is: "My bias is that a woman's most important role is being at home to mother her small children, but I have learned that there is a time when a mother's awareness of her needs is critical to her and to their adjustment . . . an understanding of the importance of their role as mother, as well as a realization of its potential in their developing families, should help them to see mothering as a goal that is as important as anything they can achieve in their professional life."[17]

In Brazelton's introduction, he describes a "typical" mother. She was a counsel for a women's rights organization and, she told him, "had bought completely into their beliefs." But after she had a baby, she knew she had to go back to work but did not want to. "I couldn't eat or sleep or think of anything but my baby. I don't care about work any longer. I realize I'm a woman without a culture. I can't believe in the women's movement in the same way I did in the past."[18] He says that he wrote this book for her. It's not likely to reassure her.

Brazelton and many other baby care experts are often outwardly hostile to feminism; he, Spock, and Leach want to restore the dignity and intellectual challenge they believe feminism stripped away from the task of motherhood. That is one reason why he and the others dwell in such often-intimidating detail on the complexity of child rearing; they need to demonstrate how worthy it is of a woman's full attention.

Yet there are other experts, equally devoted to the ideal of putting children first, who suggest that the level of intensity

Brazelton and Leach hold out as a model of interaction with children is unnecessary. "Even the average lovely mother, whose baby is well cared for most of the day, is not going to be engaged in the way you read in Berry Brazelton," said Dr. Donald Cohen, a child therapist who is the director of the Yale Child Study Center. "If you have a few minutes now and again when Mommy and baby are really enjoying themselves together, that's fine."

Again and again in his books, Brazelton states unequivocally that if a mother does not stay at home long enough—he arbitrarily picks four months—she will not have enough time to learn to know her baby and will cede her authority to someone else.

"If someone else, in a secondary caregiving role, helps the baby through this period, or if the baby begins to smile, vocalize and play games for another, new parents will never feel competent or truly attached to their baby," he writes in *Working and Caring,* describing the first four months of life.[19]

As cautionary tales, he includes in the book the tribulations of two mothers—a lawyer, Carla Snow, and a typist, Ann McNamara. The voice of Brazelton comes through in the repeated haranguings of Carla's mother, who keeps telling her she doesn't know her baby well enough and is delegating too much to the nanny. Sure enough, when the nanny has a family emergency, Carla has to stay home and feels incompetent. "If only she could have stayed home longer in the beginning, she might have felt more secure now."[20] When a day care worker asks Ann McNamara to describe the baby to her, she fumbles. Because Ann had to return to work at six weeks, Brazelton wrote, "she had no time to see Tim as an individual."[21]

Brazelton's authority to make these blanket statements is based, he says, on his research. Brazelton has certainly observed many families, both in his pediatric practice and in his travels around the country. But these observations are not supported by most of the existing studies on mothers' attachments to their children. How can Brazelton say with such assurance that a mother will "never" gain this confidence? Learning to become a mother takes time, and each mother will find her own way. Gaining that knowledge takes a lifetime, not four months.

A New Vision: Mother as Expert

Not all the advice books annihilate the mother or fall into well-meaning muddles. What a welcome contrast to Leach is her fellow Englishwoman, Sheila Kitzinger. Kitzinger is best known for her works on pregnancy and birth, particularly *The Experience of Childbirth,* first published in 1965 and still in print. Her broad cross-cultural perspective as a social anthropologist has freed her from prescribing any one way to mother or, indeed, even elevating the Western ways as the best ways. Experts are just as culture bound as the societies they live in and the child-rearing fashions of the day and just as blind to those influences.

Parents, Kitzinger writes, should be "wary about the advice given in books on how to prevent children's emotional deprivation, how to ensure that you meet their psychological needs, or how to raise a more intelligent child superior to all the other mis-managed children of unenlightened families."[22]

Her travels around the world observing mothers in Jamaica, Africa, Israel, Eastern Europe, Russia, Mexico, Fiji, and New Zealand have convinced her that most Western mothers are peculiarly and painfully isolated. The idea of the mother as singly responsible for the way her children turn out exists primarily in Western cultures—and is a recent, largely middle-class phenomenon at that, she says. Other societies embrace the idea that many other people will help rear children, be they relatives, neighbors, or hired helpers.

As many anthropologists have pointed out, such communities help shield women and men in traditional societies from the kind of severe depression or chronic anxiety that afflicts many people in modern cultures. In hunter-gatherer societies, mothers could combine family life with work, so they did not have to give up one to enjoy the benefits of the other. Moreover, because women in traditional societies raise children encircled by networks of relatives and friends, they do not have to endure the exhausting, repetitious, and draining moments of child rearing by themselves. They have other hands to spell them, and their children have the benefit of other adults with a range of personalities and interests who could supply what their mothers cannot.

Indeed, a new group of scholars, known as "evolutionary psychologists," who trace the evolution of the human mind and emotions, have focused on the psychological ailments stemming from the mismatch between the modern environment and the one that prevailed at the dawn of evolution. These psychologists say that the June Cleaver home, held up as the right way to live, was neither natural nor healthy. Isolation in rapidly growing suburbs often cut mothers off from their extended families and even from neighbors.[23]

Kitzinger understands that such isolation, combined with the inevitable strains of motherhood, can produce dark emotions that shame many mothers. Her five daughters were born in fewer than seven years (including a pair of twins who were born one year after the birth of her oldest daughter). She is no stranger to the dark side of motherhood. Rather than lecture mothers to think of their baby and banish all those ugly, unnatural thoughts, Kitzinger reassures mothers that such feelings are normal and virtually universal. "If having children is all about love," she told me, "it's also about passion, and once you have passion, there's always this other side—of feeling desperately frustrated, perhaps feeling depressed, angry, all the other side of the intensity of love. But we romanticize a mother's relationship with her child."

Kitzinger takes direct aim at the ideal of the perfect mother, acknowledging that ambivalence is inevitable and two-sided. "No mother loves her baby all the time," she writes. "Your baby probably has similar conflicting feelings about you. . . . You are often a goddess, and sometimes a witch."[24]

No mother, she reminds us, can meet the exacting standards promulgated by women's magazines, parenting manuals, and hectoring experts. "Gurus and mentors who have forgotten, or never known, what it is like to be with a baby for twenty-four hours and to carry the sole burden of responsibility for another life call for impossible standards of maternal devotion and the total surrender of self," she writes in *The Year After Childbirth*.[25]

Liz Forest spent months after her second daughter was born reproaching herself for feeling that life at home with two children under age two was an ordeal, not the joyous relief from juggling a career and children the experts had promised her. She left her job as an economist when her second child arrived just seventeen months after her first. She loved her job, but it demanded unpredictable hours and offered no realistic part-time options. When we spoke in spring 1996, Liz had been at home for six months, and she was still shocked at how grueling and emotionally taxing the days were.

"They're on opposite schedules during the day now," she said. "I don't have a break all day long. I can't write a letter. I can't do anything anymore. I'm a result-oriented human being. Now I am counting my accomplishments on a daily basis. I made three meals for two days. I changed umpteen diapers. They both had baths. I vacuumed both bathrooms. I have to keep reminding myself that all that is very important."

Liz does not want to go back to work. She says she can no longer believe that anyone else would be able to give her children the same level of intellectual stimulation and emotional sensitivity. But because her decision to quit cut her household income in half, she cannot afford the relief a baby-sitter might bring.

"Perhaps I feel a little guilty thinking that things would be happier here if I had somebody coming in a few hours a week," she said. "The whole point of this was for me to be more with the kids. But it's the truth. I had an unrealistic expectation of what I can actually be as a wife and mother and individual, and something's going to have to give here. Or else I'm going to lose myself totally."

Above all, Kitzinger defends mothers' needs to stay true to what they feel, rather than what others tell them they should do. "It is not just a matter of a mother performing an action, such as breast-feeding a baby, but of how she *feels* about what she does— and whether or not she behaves in an easy, spontaneous and above all self-assured way may be a good deal more important than the system of child rearing she adopts."[26]

It is that recognition of the crucial missing psychological link that sets Kitzinger and her small band apart. It will do no one good to list all the special toys a mother can make or pronounce that breast is best or that four months is the absolute minimum time for attachment unless the mother's experiences are taken into account, as well as the baby's, because those feelings affect the baby intimately and directly.

Marilyn Heins and Anne M. Seiden, a pediatrician and a psychiatrist, also understand that truth. These mothers, who held jobs long before most others did, searched in vain for a book that reflected their personal and professional experiences: that parents ignore their own needs at their children's peril. So they wrote one, *Child Care/Parent Care,* which is now unfortunately out of print. They actually begin their book with a chapter on the importance of parents taking enough time for themselves, for their hobbies, their marriage, and their other interests. "Parents cannot effectively give to children what they do not have to give," they wrote. "When parents are too stressed, or too unfulfilled, or too guilty to take their own needs into account, the children suffer."

Even more than what Kitzinger and the others of this breed of experts say is their calm, matter-of-fact tone and the assumptions that tone implies. Mothers can learn to be mothers, but there are no hard-and-fast rules. Mothers and fathers will make mistakes, lose their tempers, feel rage and loneliness, even fail at times—and these behaviors and feelings are understandable, forgivable, and utterly common. Children are resilient, although they deserve and should command our best efforts. Motherhood is not a grim contest to produce a poster child, and mothers do not have to lose themselves along the way.

PART TWO

SCIENCE WEIGHS IN

The Perils of Psychology

In February 1991, I sat at home with my five-month-old, watching the Gulf War on television, another war raging inside me. As the months of my maternity leave had passed, I became forced to admit that this was far from the blissful communion, the respite from the routines of work, that I had anticipated.

My days had become increasingly desperate exercises to fill up the lonely hours, to find company and distraction. I tried the one form of domesticity I do enjoy, cooking. I bundled my daughter into the carriage for a several-block walk to the best butcher; I combed through recipes thinking my hours at home would enable me to prepare a good dinner for a change. But my efforts produced only frantic stabs at stirring and basting while my daughter, afflicted with colic, screamed whenever I put her down.

I tried reaching out to other mothers. I joined a play group of warm and friendly women, all of whom but me were staying at home for the duration, but I increasingly felt like an alien or, worse, a fraud. When they talked about relishing the time spent home with their children (although they all had full-time nannies who gave them invaluable freedom to come and go), I mumbled excuses about needing the money to go back to work. I was too ashamed to tell them I was aching for the intellectual stimulation, company of adults, and sense of engagement with the outside world that work means to me.

Even as I longed to reenter the world of work, I was terrified about my daughter. Would our bond survive my leaving her for hours every day? My worst fears were fanned by a long cover story that month in the *Atlantic Monthly,* describing the ideas of two psychologists, John Bowlby and Mary Ainsworth, who elevated the importance of the mother-child bond to heights unimagined even by Freud.[1]

Bowlby and Ainsworth are the developers of attachment theory, which has become one of the most pervasive and influential ideas not only in psychology, but in society as a whole. That theory has helped give scientific legitimacy to the idea that mothers who work when their children are young risk damaging their bonds with them.

Attachment theory teaches that the quality of children's first loving relationship lays the foundation for the rest of their emotional lives. If their first attachment is secure, children are on track for emotional health, self-confidence, and good relationships; their early experiences teach them how to love themselves and others. But insecure attachments can cloud the rest of children's lives, crippling their self-esteem and their ability to make friends or form any bonds of trust and affection.

To Bowlby and Ainsworth, as well as some of their followers, the importance of early attachments means that mothers should stay at home for at least the first few years of their children's lives. They believe a mother who is gone for several hours every day is not able to know her children well enough to read them with the sensitivity that will ensure a secure bond.

As I read the article, I began to lose my moorings, swept away by the passion of their beliefs as well as their undeniable concern about children. I found myself thinking, *It's obvious that the first year of life is important. Maybe it wouldn't be such a terrible sacrifice to stay home to make sure that I am as attuned, as sensitive, as I can be.*

That is a message with great resonance today, one trumpeted by attachment purists and popularizers who sometimes distort the theory's ideas. That message reflects a grave shortcoming with a whole range of psychological theories—they tend to see a mother as existing solely to love her child, not as a separate person with her own emotional life and her own dreams. Attachment theory, and psychology in general, tend to focus far too much on whether a mother works, rather than on how she behaves toward her child. The experts pronounce what would be best for children without considering how a mother's state of mind affects those children.

THE ATTACHMENT CREED: MOTHER, HOLY MOTHER

Attachment theory crops up everywhere. It informs the work and opinions of Penelope Leach and T. Berry Brazelton, who have helped popularize its ideas to millions of parents. It has guided the thinking, research design, and testing of many of the most important and widely cited studies on the impact of child care and maternal employment on children. Religious right and centrist policy-makers quote it chapter and verse to justify calls for mothers to stay at home. Criminologists cite it to explain juvenile delinquency. Judges use it to help decide custody battles. College textbooks, like one used by an undergraduate I interviewed at Western Michigan University in 1995, rely on it when they declare flatly that children should not go to day care before the age of one year so they can form bonds with their mothers. Attachment theory pervades the everyday assumptions of working mothers and those around them.

The many popularizers of attachment theory tell the public that mothers who work when their children are young are putting those children at risk—of emotional trauma and lifelong damage if they are lucky and of creating psychopaths who love and trust no one if they are not.

Attachment theory is invoked to justify all sorts of pronouncements, from the moral fiber of our children to the future of our democracy. "If the proper bonding and subsequent attachment does not occur—usually between the child and the mother—the child will develop mistrust and a deep-seated rage," thundered Dr. Ken Magid and Carole A. McKelvey in their book, *High Risk,* which foresees a "national time bomb" of young psychopaths.[2]

Jean Bethke Elshtain, an influential political theorist at the University of Chicago, warned that disrupting children's early attachment to their parents could undermine democracy. Because children "need particular, intense relations with specific, beloved others," she wrote, placing children too early "inside anonymous institutions that minimize that special contact and trust with parents" could produce children unable to relate to others and unable to see themselves as members of a wider democratic community.[3]

With varying degrees of sanctimony and self-righteousness, many members of the attachment camp insist that what they have "proved" may be out of political fashion or hard on the mother, but that it is better for the child. This is a powerful club to wield: What mother wants to expose herself as someone who puts her selfish interests above the needs of her child? Furthermore, unlike Freud's theories, attachment ideas have been "tested" in countless studies, lending them an aura of science and empiricism.

Yet science and culture are inextricably bound—particularly the social science of psychology.[4] It is culture that determines which theories escape the confines of the laboratory and capture the imagination of the public. Attachment theory has become so popular, in part, because it seems to offer scientific explanations for something that many people intuitively believe to be true: It is better for mothers to stay at home with their babies.

Just as Bowlby's ideas caught fire after World War II, when psychologists and government authorities were trying to shoo women out of factories and into the home, attachment theory meshes well with today's residual uneasiness over the sweeping changes in women's roles and American families. Some of the most ardent popularizers of attachment are political conservatives who use it to justify their attacks on feminism and on working mothers.

Jerome Kagan, the Harvard psychologist, calls attachment theory "a morality play," one that holds out the sanctity of the mother-child bond as a kind of balm for twentieth-century ills. "Every society needs some transcendental beliefs to keep them going," he said. "In the 19th century, Americans believed that knowledge is good, progress will happen, marriages are loyal. All of these have gone by the boards. We're down to a very small number of life rafts. One of them is that babies should have their mothers. If a baby could be raised by anybody, that is really threatening."[5]

JOHN BOWLBY AND THE BIRTH OF ATTACHMENT THEORY

Despite the impressive stack of studies it has spawned, attachment theory, like any other theory, is at heart a belief system, one you can buy into or not. Its ideas are shaped by the personal experiences and convictions of its founders, and its research studies are devised and carried out with these convictions (or biases) in mind.

John Bowlby, like many other upper-class British children of his time, was raised at physical and emotional arm's length from his parents. According to Robert Karen, a clinical psychologist and author of *Becoming Attached,* a history of attachment theory, who based his account on interviews with Bowlby's wife and associates,[6] Bowlby's daily care was given over almost entirely to a crew of servants: a head nanny, a succession of young undernannies, and a governess. He was not allowed to eat with his parents until he was twelve, when he could join them for dessert—at least during the infrequent occasions he was home from the boarding school he entered when he was eight. His parents were apparently remote and, when not indifferent, critical or bullying. Some of the rare warmth that came his way emanated from a young nanny, but she left, and left him desolate.

It is hardly armchair psychologizing to surmise that Bowlby's memories of a loveless childhood, absent parents, and the departure of a beloved nanny shaped his ardent conviction that mothers should be not only warm but physically present, his skepticism about any but a mother's care, and his sensitivity to the impact of separations on children.

With these early experiences as emotional baggage, Bowlby

developed his theory about children's crucial need for attachment—in essence, mother love—and his belief that the quality of
these early attachments colored children's emotional lives forever.
He drew on existing psychoanalytic theory, the relatively new field
of ethnology and animal behavior, and on his own observations of
children in orphanages and hospitals, as well as a group of juvenile
delinquents he studied in the late 1930s.[7]

He traveled through Europe in 1950 observing war orphans, children who had been sent away to escape wartime bombing, and children given up for adoption. He also reviewed psychological studies of
disturbed and institutionalized children. What he found was horrifying. He saw listless and dazed children, infection prone despite being
well fed and sheltered. The children were unable to trust or befriend
anyone. They usually had low IQs and could not perform physical or
intellectual tasks normal for their ages. Several older children were
aggressive, deceitful, and unable to concentrate in school. They
seemed unreachable either by kindness or punishment.

The condition of war orphans was remarkably similar to the
depression he saw in children who had to spend long stretches in the
hospital and were either denied any visits from their parents or allowed
to see them only one hour a week.[8] They reminded Bowlby of the alienation displayed by forty-four young thieves he studied, all of whom had
endured losses of their mothers or long separations from them.

On the basis of these extreme cases of separation, abandonment,
and deviance, Bowlby built his case against mothers leaving their
children, even for a short time. Many years later, critics would show
that it was wrong to attribute the shocking conditions Bowlby had
witnessed entirely to the absence of mothers. The children Bowlby
saw were separated not only from their mothers, but also usually
from their fathers, their siblings, their friends, their communities,
and the familiarity of their homes; their entire world had been
overturned. Once they entered orphanages or hospitals, they often
received antiseptic, impersonal care. Some were cared for by as
many as fifty different people, and few infants were held or provided with any intellectual stimulation. Many of their symptoms
could be attributed to that kind of neglect.[9]

In a huge leap of logic, Bowlby argued that daily separations from a mother can be just as traumatic to children as the catastrophic, prolonged, and unpredictable separations of wartime, death, or illness. Even in a normal home, "partial deprivation"—when a mother was not there either physically or psychologically—could wreak havoc on a child. In a list of why families fail, Bowlby included "fulltime employment of mother" along with "death of a parent," "imprisonment of a parent," and "social calamity—war, famine."[10]

When Bowlby wrote these words, he was in tune with a world glorifying domesticity after the horrors of World War II. His voice was one of a chorus of experts haranguing mothers to stay at home; fulfill their biological destinies; and stifle their unwomanly, neurotic yearnings to compete with men. Bowlby held fast to his belief that mothers of young children should not work even as the world changed around him and working mothers became the majority. In 1989, a year before he died, he told Robert Karen: "This whole business of mothers going to work, it's so bitterly controversial, but I do not think it's a good idea. I mean women go out to work and make some fiddly little bit of gadgetry which has no particular social value, and children are looked after in indifferent day nurseries."[11]

Bowlby sketched out a life plan for women that is uncannily similar to the one mothers are being urged to follow even today: stay home until the youngest child is three and then work part time, but make sure to be home when the children return from school. In a medical analogy that is revealing because it places working motherhood on a par with smoking, with its scientifically proved ravages of death and disease, Bowlby said: "I mean people don't smoke; they used to. I think women will realize that if they have children, then they have responsibilities, and if they want to have happy relationships with their children in later life then it's important to do a lot of work with them when they're small."[12]

Psychology and Mother Blaming

Bowlby's comments are typical of a dismissive and punitive attitude toward women that runs through psychology in general.

"Attachment theory rubs out the mother as a human being and as an individual in and of herself," said Dr. Stella Chess, a child psychiatrist who is one of the most eloquent critics of mother blaming in psychology. "She doesn't have a name or a personality."

This faceless mother plays a star turn as the villain when it comes to assigning blame. "I believe we give to women a magical quality that they can give to their children," Jerome Kagan said. "A bad mother can make a killer and a good mother can make a genius."

For all the scorn that feminists have heaped on Freud, he actually didn't say all that much about mothers; they didn't figure in his case studies. Only later in his life and in his last book did Freud begin to speculate about the role of the mother, who he believed was more important in the psychic life of girls.[13] It was Freud's followers and popularizers who zeroed in on the mother's influence. In classic psychoanalytic theory, and even more so in the pop Freudianism that permeated American cultural life in the 1950s, the mother looms large and menacingly. Some of Freud's interpreters were just as guilty as attachment theorists of casting the mother as the handmaiden to the child, rather than as a subject in her own right.

Just as the mother in attachment theory exists mainly to respond to the child sensitively and help develop a sense of trust, the mother in psychoanalytic theory exists to help the child negotiate among the demands of his environment, the pangs of conscience, and his instinctual needs. Many psychoanalysts believed that sharing a child's care with another figure could disrupt the child's bond with the mother, distorting a child's sense of self and damaging her ability to control aggression and develop a conscience.[14]

In the eyes of many Freudian popularizers of the 1950s, who reduced subtle and complex ideas to absurd dictates, women were, in fact, fulfilled only if they became mothers. Then they would be able to overcome their penis envy because having a child replaced the penis girls could never have. Only if they became mothers could they regress to a childlike state and repair the earlier damage. Therefore, women would meet their own needs by meeting their children's.[15]

A mother could do no right. If she took her motherhood responsibilities too seriously, she was overprotective and suffocating. Or she was negligent, letting her children practically waste away from lack of "tender loving care."[16] Psychologists in the post–World War II years blamed mothers for a bewildering array of psychological and even physical problems. A mother's "primary anxious overpermissiveness" caused colic.[17] Mothers were uniformly fingered for mental illnesses that have now been proved to have biochemical origins. "Refrigerator mothers" caused children to retreat into autism, Bruno Bettelheim declared.

Chess, who had been a practicing psychiatrist since the 1930s, finally exploded about mother blaming one day in 1964 after receiving a letter from a patient's guidance counselor. The child had been brought to her for a consultation, and she had asked the counselor to send her information. "To meet Johnny's mother," he wrote, "is to understand his problem."

More than thirty years later, Chess still vividly recalls her reaction to that letter. "I was fuming about it," she said, when she got a call from the editor of the *American Journal of Orthopsychiatry* asking for an editorial on a controversial subject. He got her wonderfully pointed essay, "Mal de Mère" (in French, *mal de mer* is seasickness; *mal* means bad, but *mère* means mother).

The real problem, Chess wrote, was that psychologists never looked further than the mother in trying to assess children's problems. She described the case of an eleven-year-old boy who challenged the teacher's authority and tended to storm out of the room if his parents criticized him. A psychologist asked him to draw a picture; he identified it as a boy of seven. It so happens that when he was seven, his mother returned to her work at a magazine. "The discussion is now centered upon assumed maternal rejection proved by maternal 'desertion,' " Chess wrote. The answer was psychotherapy for the boy, coupled with "discussions with the mother concerning her ambivalence toward the maternal role, which she should resolve by stopping outside work." When Chess looked further into the case, she found that the boy had, in fact, acted in this tempestuous way since infancy, long before his mother even considered returning to work. He had an intense temperament, not a long-simmering sense of abandonment.

What Chess described in 1964 still happens with depressing regularity today. A therapist I know told me about a child who was having considerable trouble at school; the school insisted that the problem was that the mother was working and suggested that she think about quitting. The mother had her child tested and discovered neurological difficulties.

Kathy Klema, an investment banker, told of an encounter with her daughter's nursery school teacher. Her older child had an adventurous personality and had no trouble separating when he started nursery school; in contrast, her daughter had a tough time. The head teacher, rather than seeing Kathy's daughter as a child who struggled with transitions, instantly blamed Kathy's frequent travels for work (even though she was usually gone no more than a night or two at a time). "It's much more complex than that," Kathy said. "But my child was having difficulty in school, so they immediately alighted on that."

In the 1970s, Chess was one of many to raise the alarm about the resurgence of the idea of infant-mother bonding—just as the feminist movement began to flower and more mothers began to work. This theory, which has since been roundly discredited by scientists, proposed that if a mother and child did not "bond" in the first hours of life, their relationship would be forever affected.[18]

This emphasis on bonding in the first few hours, as well as the broader ideas of attachment theory, struck at the very premise of adoption, and it has been revived in the discussion of "attachment disorder," which gained currency during a widely publicized trial in 1997 of a mother who killed her adopted daughter. Her defense: The child's time in a Russian orphanage had deprived her of the ability to trust anyone and created a monster who provoked the mother until she snapped. Although it is true that researchers following some children who spent years in particularly deprived circumstances in foreign orphanages before they were adopted have detected some behavioral and emotional problems, the notion that children who do not have a mother's care in the first few months of life will never be able to form close relationships does not square with the experience of many adoptive parents. They found their ties with their children strong even if they adopted them when they were several months old, or even older.

Over the past thirty years, new research, as well as intense criticism of mother blaming, has managed to mute some of psychologists' exaggerated claims and prompt experts like Spock and Brazelton to soft-pedal their initial opposition to working mothers. Bad fathers—violent, sexually abusive, neglectful, alcoholic—now play a large role in the psychological literature, amid wide and growing concern with the ill effects of the absence of good fathers from children's lives. Biological and genetic explanations for mental illness and personality are on the rise.

Yet mothers are still blamed in studies and textbooks for an astounding array of psychiatric problems. Janna Malamud Smith, a clinical social worker, quoted a 1987 textbook describing a "typical psychosomatic mother" as "domineering, overly involved and intrusive, excessively demanding, and clinging and smothering" and held her responsible, at least in part, for bronchial asthma, ulcerative colitis, anorexia nervosa, peptic ulcers, hyperthyroidism, and eczema. Indeed, Smith wrote, "In the dozen years I have worked in an outpatient psychiatric service at a hospital, I do not remember ever having heard a clinician suggest that a patient had a really terrific mother."[19]

The simpleminded and single-minded sense that the mother is the problem remains an assumption so deeply rooted that it defies even medical knowledge to the contrary. Dr. Harold S. Koplewicz, a psychiatrist at Long Island Jewish Medical Center who treats hyperactivity and attention deficit disorder, told the writer Katharine Davis Fishman of his medical students' reaction after seeing a videotape of a child and mother. "The child was running around playing with sixty-one different toys in ten minutes. The mother was frustrated and yelled at him. The students all said, 'If I had a mother like that, I would be running around also. What's wrong with that mother? She's intrusive, she's not following the kid at all, she doesn't say anything nice to the kid.'"

Then Koplewicz showed the students a second tape, after he had prescribed Ritalin, a commonly prescribed medication for attention deficit disorder. The child sat quietly playing with the toys. The students said, "What did you give the mother? Valium? Thorazine?"[20]

Cheryl Moorefield, a labor nurse in North Carolina, voiced the plaint of many mothers. "It used to be that kids were bad because they were bad," she told me. "Now it's somebody's fault. Usually that somebody is Mom. We just want them to tell us we're not messing up big time, that our kids are turning out fine and we did a good job."

MARY AINSWORTH AND THE SENSITIVE MOTHER

Despite Bowlby's Olympian pronouncements on working mothers, his theory never pinned down just why a short, predictable, and routine separation from a child would be just as harmful as the prolonged separations he had observed. Many attachment theorists believe that missing link is provided by the work of Mary Ainsworth and the stack of empirical studies her disciples conducted.

Ainsworth conducted detailed observations of mothers and children in their homes in Uganda and Baltimore in the mid-1950s and mid-1960s. She found that the babies who seemed the most secure had mothers who were quick to pick them up when they cried; held them longer; were sensitive to their cues; adjusted to the babies' own rhythms, rather than insisting on a rigid schedule; and were emotionally open to them. In contrast, children who seemed clingy, angry, or emotionally withdrawn often had mothers who rejected them or reacted unpredictably.

Ainsworth's observations proved to hold up remarkably well over time (as long as nothing else changed in the children's lives). In extensive follow-up studies the children she had categorized as securely attached often flourished, and the ones she had classified as insecure often faltered. Ainsworth hypothesized that most children use the reassurance of their mothers' presence as their "secure base."

Only when assured of that first attachment, secure in their mother's love, can they explore the rest of the world.[21]

These assumptions are, on some levels, reasonable enough. Certainly, there's no doubt that children are influenced by early experiences (to what degree and how inalterably is still debated). And certainly, a sensitive, warm, responsive style is inherently a good thing for children. Where I part company with the important insights of attachment theory is the unproved assumption that working makes it difficult or even impossible to nurture a child in the sensitive way Ainsworth described. Ainsworth is far less rigid in her public pronouncements about working mothers than Bowlby was, but she believes that it's not possible for a mother to develop a sensitive, nuanced responsiveness to a baby if she is gone for several hours five days a week. Yet Ainsworth's work does not directly prove Bowlby's assumption that separations themselves cause insecure attachment. Instead, that is the conclusion that some attachment theorists draw from their research, one that has been called into question by the largest, most comprehensive study conducted to date.[22] The idea that working imperils the mother-child bond is, essentially, a hunch—but it has often been presented to mothers as scientifically verified fact.

ATTACHMENT THEORY UNDER FIRE

The ideas of attachment remain important today, decades after Bowlby developed them. But the results of new research, as well as generations of critics, have called into question Bowlby's nearly exclusive focus on mothers, his insistence that even short separations damage children, and his conviction that early childhood irrevocably shapes children's futures.

Bowlby saw separations as inevitably wrenching, precisely because he believed that children would develop one strong, preferred attachment relationship, almost always to their mothers. Deprived of their mothers, children would be at sea without an emotional anchor; no one else would do.

Yet study after study, including those by attachment theorists themselves, has demolished the idea that children can form only one attachment relationship. Bowlby singled out mothers instead of seeing them as part of a far broader and more complex array of influences on a child. These influences include the other people in a child's life, a child's temperament, a family's income, the schools a child attends, and the kind of community she lives in.

Many researchers, including the British child psychiatrist Michael Rutter and the American psychologist Michael E. Lamb, have argued that Bowlby overlooked the crucial role of fathers in children's lives. A large and growing body of research is suggesting that children's security is fostered not exclusively through one person but through a network of attachments—to fathers, relatives, friends, and others who look after children.

Critics of attachment theory have also argued that Bowlby was wrong to conclude that separations always have to inflict a psychological toll. As Rutter pointed out, if separation does not affect a mother's behavior to her children, then the children will probably not experience separation as traumatic. Separation is damaging only if it causes stress, fear, or disruption in a child's usual relationships.[23]

Years of research have also called into question the widespread belief, at the heart of both attachment theory and psychoanalysis, that what happens to a child in the first few years of life will mark his life forever. There is no question that early childhood is a crucial time, and recent neurological studies have confirmed that early experiences actually help determine the chemical wiring of the brain, influencing aptitude for foreign languages, mathematics, and music, as well as emotions. There is evidence that there are critical periods after which it is harder for children to develop those skills or even, perhaps, to change emotional patterns and learn to regulate anger. The research is sobering, and it suggests that working parents must be conscientious about selecting care for their children. Yet there are also studies indicating that some of these early effects—even those that involve the wiring of the brain—can be reversed at later points in children's lives.[24]

Although the early years are undeniably important, researchers

caution against seeing them as all-important. A wide array of studies has found and a number of leading researchers have concluded
that children's experiences in their first years do not reliably predict
how they will turn out later in life. For one, few children's circumstances stay exactly as they were when they were infants. As children grow, other influences, including teachers, friends, and neighborhood, become more powerful.[25] If children can form deep and
satisfying bonds with a few people simultaneously, if separations do
not have to be traumatic, and if the early years do not set in stone a
child's life course, then Bowlby's argument against mothers working essentially collapses. Over time, some of Bowlby's followers
have softened his absolutism about working and refined or modi-
fied some of his other tenets. Just as not every Freudian still believes
that women have children as a replacement for the penis they
wanted but never had, not every attachment theorist working today
supports Bowlby's strictures on working mothers, either. "I don't
know too many people now who are invoking Bowlby's notion of
pathological responses to extreme separations as a direct analogy to
what's happening with brief separations," said Dr. Lawrence Aber,
a developmental psychologist and attachment theorist at Columbia
University. "Doing clinical work tempers theoretical zeal."

As many studies have found, it is the mother's actual behavior
with her child that matters, not whether she works or not. Dr.
Cathryn L. Booth, an attachment researcher at the University of
Washington who participated in the largest child care study to date,
said, "You get just as much variety in mother care as you do in child
care. You get mothers who think they should stay at home but don't
want to who are frustrated and angry. You get mothers at home
who want to be there and are wonderful."

THE ASSAULT ON NURTURE

Not only attachment theory but all other psychological theories that
emphasize nurture are under increasing attack from the champions of
nature. For many years, mothers were held responsible for everything
that happened to their children; now, in an abrupt pendulum swing

typical of the extremes of the debate, they are being told that they have virtually no influence, that we are all at the mercy of our genes.

A large and growing body of psychological and biological research has challenged some of our most cherished beliefs about families' influence on children's personalities. These studies have shown that infants are not blank slates. Instead, the studies have suggested, babies are born with distinct biological, genetic, and temperamental qualities—qualities that limit, though do not eliminate, the power of mothers or fathers.

One of the major challenges to Bowlby's work came from Chess, who observed and documented what so many mothers knew intuitively—that her own four children had dramatically different temperaments. Chess and her husband, Alexander Thomas, believed that mothers were being wrongly blamed and were blaming themselves for children's behavior, when these children had demonstrated distinct temperamental types since earliest infancy.[26]

Instead, Chess and Thomas found evidence in their work that certain behaviors were part of a child's innate temperamental style. Their work on temperament has transformed the advice given to parents, who are now generally told that different children need different kinds of handling to thrive.

Chess and Thomas argued that much depends on what they called goodness or poorness of fit, the match between a child's temperament and a parent's. Some children have temperaments that suit their parent's: a quiet child and a reflective mother or an active child and an exuberant father. The temperaments do not have to be the same, of course, but when they grate against each other, that can spell trouble. It is not just that the mother isn't doing something right; it is that her natural rhythms and her child's don't fit. Chess recognized that from the outset, infants contribute to shaping the relationship with their mothers and fathers.

Jerome Kagan's research on children with an "inhibited" temperament—shy, timid, or fearful—has gone even further in suggesting that some characteristics are inborn.[27] Parents cannot change these children's shyness and fearfulness, but they can handle them well or badly, helping children to flower or to fade.

The strongest and most unsettling confirmation of the power of genes and biology has come from widely publicized studies of identical twins who were raised separately. Researchers around the world have found astonishing similarities in personality and habits among identical twins who grew up with different families in different places. These findings suggest that personality may be shaped by genetic heritage.

Researchers now point to biology for a host of afflictions that psychiatrists once blamed on bad mothering: hyperactivity, manic depression, schizophrenia, and obsessive compulsive disorder (such as constant hand washing). They have found genetic components in smoking, insomnia, suicidal tendencies, and even whether and when twins marry and divorce or how they choose their careers and hobbies. Researchers have attributed neuroticism and what may be called a tendency to melancholy to genes.[28]

Some experts have gone even further and suggested that genes program children to create and alter their environments, the way a smiling baby tends to evoke warmth and affection. In effect, this means that no matter where these children live or who raises them, they are likely to act in certain ways that evoke responses that will shape their lives.

Sandra Scarr, a leading researcher, argues that unless a parent is destructive and abusive, a parent's style and child-rearing techniques have little impact on a child's intelligence, interests, and personality—though they may influence values, principles, and other crucial components of a child's inner life.

Yet many experts, including Chess and Kagan, say that family does matter. Parents can help channel or tame temperamental excess—and the way they handle children can cause physiological changes in the heartbeat and hormone levels that, in turn, affect behavior. "Of course families have an influence," Kagan said. "It's not as simpleminded as the nursery-rhyme stuff we see in the magazines. Families have an effect on your values, on the standards that you have."

Kagan and other experts take issue with a common vision of the child as immensely fragile and forever vulnerable. Instead, they see a child's nature as far more robust, one in which bad experiences do not necessarily have to be permanently damaging and good experiences early in life do not magically shield the child from the impact of later tragedy.

A NEW MODEL

While the geneticists chip away at the influence of families, a new wave of psychoanalytic thought is challenging the conventional view of the mother-child relationship. The classic psychoanalytic view, built on the work of Freud, his daughter Anna, and a later camp of object relations theorists, placed the mother at the center of the child's emotional development. But the mother was usually considered only as far as she met or failed to meet her child's needs. Her own feelings—feelings that would necessarily affect her child—were neither discussed nor even considered.

Instead, the mother is supposed to be the facilitator of the child's developmental struggles. Different theorists have identified different tasks for the mother to guide her child to emotional health. One of the most widely endorsed tasks, developed by Margaret Mahler, is that a mother teaches her child to learn first that he is separate from her physically, and later that he is separate psychologically.

The influential work of Dr. Daniel Stern offers further evidence that infants are more active partners in shaping their relationship with their mothers than most psychoanalysts had thought. Stern videotaped the everyday interactions of mothers and babies for the first two years of their lives. Stern conducted his research with mothers, though his insights could apply as well to fathers or other caregivers. By slowing the tapes down, Stern was able to trace each gesture and response by the mother and baby, revealing duets as subtle as the meeting and aversion of a gaze or a mother's shimmy of her shoulders in response to a baby's excited grab at a toy. His work offers a window into the precise physical gestures and rhythms that determine whether mothers read babies well or badly.

Stern called such synchrony attunement, and his observations suggested that babies suffered if mothers consistently misread them. Some babies became fearful and dependent, some became passive, and some became anxious; it depended on what cues the mother missed. Stern believes that it is through these repeated daily encounters that babies learn that others can share their feelings. The quality of these encounters, he argues, helps shape how children will relate to others throughout their lives.

The attachment camp has hailed Stern's work as further evidence that if attunement is so subtle and complex, naturally mothers have to stay at home for a long while to be good enough at it. Stern makes a slightly different argument, saying that mothers need time at home with their babies to deepen what he calls the "motherhood constellation," the way a mother's concerns, fantasies, and relationships with others change after childbirth to revolve around the baby, to a greater and lesser degree, forever.[29]

"The best system for the baby, the best system for the mother and the parents, is if one of the parents can actually stay home with the baby for quite a while," he told a 1996 conference at Teachers College in New York. "That is my prejudice that I work from."

Like most of the baby care experts who agree with him, Stern is speaking from conviction, but not hard evidence. Several studies have shown that mothers at home and mothers at work appear to read their babies equally well. Stern simply cannot imagine, the way many other experts cannot imagine, that a mother who returns to work can still place her child at the center of her psychological life.

Interestingly enough, Stern's work itself can be read to challenge the classic psychological idea that a mother exists only to serve her baby. Stern himself has emphasized the reciprocity and mutuality of the relationship between mother and child. His research has detailed the ways in which mother and child affect each other.

Building on Stern's work and that of feminist psychoanalysts like Dorothy Dinnerstein and Nancy Chodorow, the psychoanalyst Jessica Benjamin has outlined a bold new vision of the mother-child relationship. In many cases, these ideas can apply to the father-child relationship as well, but with one crucial difference: No one assumes that the father has to sacrifice everything for his child, and Benjamin assumes that mothers do not have to either. This new approach honors both the centrality of relationships and the idea that a mother has a right to an independent existence—one that will not harm, but can actually enrich, her child. Trying to correct psychology's exclusive focus on the child, Benjamin argues that separation is an important, but insufficient, landmark of children's development. It is not just that children have to see themselves as separate people, but that, in the process, children also have to recognize that their mothers are independent beings with their own needs. Benjamin calls this concept "mutual recognition." Her idea of mutual recognition could also apply to fathers who share the task of child rearing.[30]

In the earliest months of life, an infant glimpses that separateness when a mother fails to guess what he wants or mismatches his emotional intensity. These miscues signal a baby that she is not part of the mother anymore. But as a baby grows, he also comes to understand the joys of connection with another person. When a baby shakes a rattle and sees her mother's (or father's) joy reflected in the shimmy Stern described, the baby begins to grasp that pleasure can be shared.

The next step, which is commonly called the terrible twos, is when children find that they and their parents do not always share the same view, that they cannot always get what they want. Gradually, as babies become toddlers, they move from a naturally self-centered world in which their emotions reign and their every demand is satisfied to one that must take account of others' feelings and needs.

As one illustration of how children learn to see their mothers as individuals, Benjamin describes an experiment with two-year-olds who were asked to pretend they were their mothers saying goodbye. At first, the children acted out their own experience in a kind of gleeful retaliation: "I'll do to you what you did to me."

Slowly, though, they developed empathy; they began to understand their mothers' feelings: "I could miss you as you miss me."

Eventually, they grew to accept their mothers' independent existence: "I know you could wish to have your own life as I wish to
have mine." As Benjamin puts it, the children come to recognize
that "the leaving mother is not bad but independent, a person like
me."[31]

This recognition of others' needs has long been hailed by psychologists as a necessary developmental step, the discovery of empathy. But Benjamin emphasizes the mother's role in a different way:
Empathy toward others has its roots in a child learning empathy
for—not just from—her mother. The child has not just learned she
is separate; she has also learned to respect someone else's right to be
separate.

The new psychoanalytic theories challenge the old way of seeing the mother as a mere adjunct to the child, and the latest
research strikes at the heart of the blame-the-mother ideology. The
bond between a mother and child does matter. Declaring that
working destroys or disrupts that bond, however, is not only
wrong, but feeds into an ideological crusade with a long and
shameful history.

5

The Day Care Wars

For all my bravado as I marched back to work and all the evidence that my children were thriving, I was never really quite sure. I remained skittish, easily thrown off balance by even one study suggesting that children of working mothers had fared worse on some measure than those of mothers at home. I worried that my children might grow up marred in some way, less secure, less content, and even less intelligent than if I had stayed at home with them.

My fears were stoked by a steady stream of publicity about studies that seemed to find problems with children whose mothers worked. I kept hearing that working mothers were raising a new generation of passive, amoral children or insecurely attached, aggressive, and even violent troublemakers. Commentators linked working mothers with all kinds of social ills, from latchkey children to the rise of juvenile delinquency.

They brandished research to justify stepped-up attacks on leaving children with anyone but their mothers. A prominent day care researcher recanted his earlier optimism, saying that new studies showed that placing infants in day care put some at risk of lifelong emotional damage and increased aggression at school. New research on the brain proved that experiences in the early years affected the chemical wiring of the brain. The obvious conclusion: Better stay home to fashion the optimal brain.

The religious right also invoked the mantle of science to support its crusade against day care. The Rockford Institute's *Family in America New Research* newsletter, for example, issues monthly bulletins about the "plagues" suffered by children in day care. Each disease sounded more ominous than the last: otitis media, astrovirus, cytomegalovirus, gastroenteritis, rotavirus, croup, and conjunctivitis.

The truth is, of course, far more complicated than the alarming headlines. Children in day care centers do have a greater risk of contracting illness than children at home, because they have greater contact with other children in an enclosed space. Yet few children escape bouts of most of these relatively common and usually benign illnesses, which, translated from medical jargon, mean ear infections, colds, stomach flus, diarrhea, severe coughing, and pinkeye.

The way research on working mothers and their children is publicized tends to be as intellectually dishonest as it is inflammatory. Either experts broadcast alarm or they trumpet relief. I could dismiss the prophecies of disaster, but I did not trust the blithe assurances that everything was fine, either.

In fact, a careful review of the major studies on child care shows that the fears are overblown: When a mother works and places her children in the care of another, most children will thrive if that care is good. We should not be worried because so many mothers work, but because so much of the child care in the United States is terrible. Moreover, the studies consistently suggest that the most important influences on a child's life remain the family—its income, the education level and emotional health of the parents—not whether a child's mother works.

Yet there remains a great deal we simply do not know. Many of the studies were woefully incomplete. They did not measure how good the child care was. They focused on children's bonds with mothers, not fathers. They did not examine a wide range of children, and they did not take account of the influence of families themselves. Many studies are suffused with the bias of classical attachment theory against working mothers. Few studies followed children over time, and even fewer reported any results for children past elementary school.

What is even more important, most popular descriptions of child care research do not explain how to interpret studies—how to understand what they tell working parents and what they do not. Without a guide, many mothers remain, as I did, at the mercy of the polemicists.

THE ASSAULT ON DAY CARE

The American public has always distrusted day care. For a brief time, though, from the mid-1970s to the mid-1980s, researchers reassured working parents that day care did not harm their children. Now a stepped-up assault is under way. The attacks rely heavily on attachment research, and the attackers argue that studies show that children of working mothers have weaker bonds with their mothers than those who stay at home. Mix that insecure attachment with the findings of some studies linking day care to aggression, they say, and the brew will yield disruptive, even delinquent, children.

In 1986, Jay Belsky, an eminent attachment researcher, rocked the day care world when he argued that children who were placed in day care as infants for more than twenty hours a week were at risk of insecure attachment and aggressive behavior. Belsky's thesis, later elaborated in a 1988 paper drawn from five studies, ignited a firestorm. "Is Day Care Bad for Babies?" asked *Time* magazine in its June 22, 1987, issue. "Day Care for Infants Is Challenged by Research on Psychological Risks," the *Wall Street Journal* told its readers on March 3, 1987. "Brave New World: How Day Care Harms Children," ran the headline in a seven-thousand-word article in the spring 1988 issue of *Policy Review,* published by the conservative Heritage Foundation. A *Washington Post* story on April 23, 1988, began, "All right, working parents, get ready for more worry and guilt."[1]

Belsky built his case on several studies conducted in the 1980s that turned up more ratings of insecure attachment among children whose mothers returned to work when they were infants than those whose mothers had stayed home.[2] His ideas met instant and furious opposition from many other child care researchers. Experts clashed bitterly over the significance of the results. They pointed out that day care critics wrung the most alarmist possible interpretation out of every research finding. Although the studies at that time did find that children of working mothers were more likely to be rated as insecurely attached than children of mothers at home, the differences were by no means dramatic—anywhere from about 3 percent to 8 percent more of the children of working mothers had insecure bonds. In every study, the majority of the children of working mothers were securely attached to them. Nor did staying at home ensure secure attachments—almost one-third of the children of mothers at home were rated insecurely attached.[3]

If the differences between the two groups were slight and if the majority of children of working mothers were securely attached, a mother's employment alone could not explain why some children were rated insecure—though that important point was generally lost amid the hysteria.

Belsky countered that even small differences in insecure attachment could yield large social disruption. If mothers working during infancy produce just one more child misbehaving per classroom, he said, that result multiplied in classrooms across the country equals widespread turmoil. Belsky has raised some important issues, most notably the question of whether day care can pose some risks for certain vulnerable groups of children. He believes even now that he has been vilified because he dared to challenge a political orthodoxy among day care researchers.

Yet many of the studies that Belsky and other critics cited were built on the flawed biases of attachment theory. One particularly egregious example is a study by Peter Barglow, Brian E. Vaughn, and Nancy Molitor, which reads as if John Bowlby himself had written it in the 1950s at the height of the hysteria over maternal deprivation. In their report, the researchers stated flatly that they chose to study mothers with one child because women with more than one child would want to stay at home with them: "It is consistent with our intuitions that a married, middle class woman with two or more young children would elect to remain at home working as a caregiver."[4]

Those unnatural mothers who returned to work, they speculated, could be suffering from some unresolved trauma in their past: "It may be the case that some mothers of young infants who return to work are responding to a conflict rooted in their own infancy and early childhood."[5]

The researchers found that more of the infants whose mothers returned to work were insecurely attached than were those of the mothers who stayed at home. Their data do not explain why they found the result, but the researchers had an idea straight out of attachment theory: They suggested it was because those babies experienced "maternal absence" as a profound rejection. The problem was that their own data did not fully support that interpretation; since the majority of children of working mothers were securely attached to them, they wrote, there must be other factors that alleviate the impact of separation for many babies. They did not choose to explore what those factors could be or how babies could thrive even if separated from their mothers.

The studies Belsky cited were limited in other important ways. Most did not measure the quality of care children received, so it was impossible to tell whether that factor had any bearing on the results. Many studied fairly small groups of children, most of them middle class. And, worse in the eyes of the critics, most relied on only one test of emotional health given to toddlers: an observation of mothers and children at a laboratory, called the Strange Situation, developed by the attachment theorist Mary Ainsworth.

The researchers based their dire predictions that children in day care were at risk of lifelong emotional damage from this twenty-minute test, which was devised thirty years ago when most middle-class mothers stayed at home. This test has become the most popular, and controversial, tool in developmental psychology.

Ainsworth developed the Strange Situation to measure attachment in children aged twelve to about twenty months old. The test was deliberately designed to put the children under increasing stress so that researchers could judge the strength of their bonds with their mothers. During the twenty-minute test, a mother and her child are brought to a laboratory playroom with toys. A stranger enters the room while the mother is present. Then the mother leaves the child with the stranger. The mother returns, and then both adults leave the room. The stranger reappears, and finally the mother returns.

Ainsworth found that the children who cried when their mothers left and refused to be comforted by the strangers, but calmed down once their mothers returned, were the same children whose mothers had been most sensitive and responsive to them when she observed them at home. She classified these children as securely attached.

Children who were insecure fell into two broad groups. One group, whose mothers tended to be unpredictable in their behavior, were "ambivalent": They were very anxious when their mothers left, but alternately reached out for them and pushed them away when their mothers returned. The other group, whose mothers tended to be cold, rejecting, and angry, was "avoidant": They did not seem to care when their mothers left or returned. Later attachment researchers noticed that these avoidant children were acting just like the children Bowlby had observed who had suffered long separations from their mothers; their surface calm masked depression or anger.[6]

More than twenty years of studies following children who were categorized as secure or insecure in the Strange Situation found that secure children did better in school, made more friends, showed more persistence, and were generally better adjusted well into their teens. Children with insecure attachments, however, appeared anxious or defiant, had more trouble making friends, and were rated as more difficult by their teachers.[7]

Researchers like Michael Lamb, however, have questioned these results; Lamb's analyses show that the relationship between early attachment and later behavior held true over time only if family circumstances or child care arrangements stayed the same, and such circumstances often change.

The Strange Situation has come under heavy and sustained fire from several prominent researchers. These researchers argued that when Ainsworth devised her test in the 1960s, most middle-class mothers were staying at home. Ainsworth expected that the normal reaction would be for children to cry and then seek comfort from their mothers. Children would find separation stressful because they were not used to separation. The critics argued that the test may not have the same psychological meaning for children whose lives do not resemble those Ainsworth studied thirty years ago—children whose mothers go to work.

The most devastating, and telling, complaint is that the Strange Situation has often been the only measure of emotional health that researchers have used. This test would give a far more nuanced result if it was coupled with observations at home and alternative measures of attachment. To check whether early predictions of trouble are actually borne out as children grow, follow-up studies could include such indicators as teachers' reports, peer relations, and academic achievement.

THE BEST NEW STUDY

As experts divided into camps and parents agonized over what to do, twenty-five of the country's leading experts began in 1991 to collaborate on a massive new study of child care tracking more than one thousand children from birth to age seven. The study's formal title is the National Institute of Child Health and Human Development Study of Early Child Care; it is widely known as the NICHD study.

With more money to work with and the luxury of hindsight, the NICHD researchers have been able to address many of the limits of earlier studies. The new study includes more children from diverse backgrounds—poor as well as middle-class children; children from two-parent and single-parent families; and white, Hispanic, African American, and Asian children—and has covered every kind of child care, measuring how good or bad the care was.

The researchers left the shelter of the laboratory and ventured into the home, videotaping children playing with their mothers at regular, though brief, intervals. The home visits also allowed them to make important assessments of family characteristics and the home environment, so they would be less likely to attribute a result to child care that might have stemmed instead from family background. The researchers evaluated children's temperaments, their parents' psychological adjustment, mothers' sensitivity to their children, mothers' attitudes toward work, and families' social stresses and supports. Because the researchers are following the children from birth, they can gain insights into what motivates the families' child care choices.

Their plans to track children until age seven will also allow them to see how results bear up over time. Attachment will not be the only criterion of how children fare; the researchers will also evaluate children's physical health, their cognitive and language skills, and whether they get along well with classmates or act aggressively. These findings should clarify many continuing debates in the field.

The results of this giant new study so far have defied the doomsayers and contradicted the earlier studies that Belsky cited to make his case against day care. The hue and cry about the small differences in attachment security between children of working mothers and those of mothers at home did not hold up when a more complete study was conducted. The study found that the number of hours children spent away from the care of their mothers made no difference in whether they were securely or insecurely attached to her at the age of fifteen months. Nor did it make a difference in how well children scored on language or cognitive skills tests at age three.[8]

None of the concerns that were raised in the debate about day care—how many hours children were in care, what type of care they were in, how good or bad that care was, how young they entered care, how many times the care changed—appeared to affect infants' trust and sense of confidence in their mothers. Researchers also found that the Strange Situation test proved equally reliable with children whose mothers worked and those who stayed at home, at least on two specific measures they used.

The findings are immensely reassuring: Working mothers do not have to fear that they endanger their relationship with their child by working. The main issue, the results suggest, is not whether or not a mother works; it is whether or not she is sensitive to her child. "I think this study is pretty clear: being in nonparental care isn't necessarily a problem," Michael Lamb said. "Having an insensitive parent is."

Indeed, the researchers found that when mothers handled their babies sensitively, their babies were more likely to be securely attached to them. They also found, as previous studies had, that mothers' emotional health appears to affect their bond with their babies. Mothers who were the best adjusted psychologically had the most secure infants.

Despite encouraging results, no one should feel complacent. When this book went to press, the researchers had not yet analyzed data from older children. The early findings that children's security was not affected by their mothers' work could change over time.

The NICHD study made it clear that when mothers handle their children insensitively, their children are more likely to be insecurely attached to them. Some examples of what researchers call insensitivity include mothers who did not respond to their children's questions or who were often angry at them.

The study's results suggested that for some vulnerable children, child care—particularly low-quality child care—could aggravate other problems in their lives. Children whose mothers handled them insensitively were more likely to be insecurely attached if they were also placed in bad child care, stayed longer than ten hours a week, or changed child care arrangements more than once a year.

True to the way that bad news plays better than good news in the child care wars, many articles emphasized a finding that appeared to suggest that working, particularly when children were very young, could make mothers less sensitive. But a closer examination of that finding shows its importance was exaggerated in some popular accounts. The study found that when children spent more hours in child care, particularly those who started child care before they were six months old, their mothers were slightly less sensitive and slightly

more negative toward them. These children also displayed somewhat less affection for their mothers. That result, however,
depended on the quality of child care. When children were in high-
quality care, their mothers were more sensitive to them.

Even more important, the researchers found that the impact of
child care on a mother's sensitivity was extremely small. The number of hours in child care accounted for just one-half to one percentage point of the differences in a mother's sensitivity. Far more
important were other factors, such as whether or not a mother was
depressed, whether a child lived in a two-parent household, the
family's income, the level of a mother's education, and the child's
own temperament.

Finally, the slight differences in sensitivity the study found did
not translate into insecure attachments, at least through the age of
fifteen months. It is not clear at this point in the study whether
those differences in sensitivity could affect children's behavior in
the long run.

Belsky said that he saw no reason to be alarmed about the
study's findings regarding mothers' sensitivity. He believes, however, that the study proves his claim that day care can be a risk for
some children and that it is most likely to spell trouble in combination with other problems, such as low-quality day care for a child
from an already stressed family.

Most previous studies have found that working does not cause
mothers to treat their children any differently than do mothers who
stay at home. Several studies that observed mothers and children in
the home found that employed mothers and mothers at home inter-
act similarly with their infants.[9]

Another finding that intrigued the researchers, who are still
trying to make sense of it, was that more time in child care posed
some risks for boys, but less time was potentially risky for girls.
Boys who were in child care for more than thirty hours a week, but
girls who were in child care for fewer than ten hours a week, were
slightly more likely to have an insecure attachment to their mothers. No differences were found, however, between boys' and girls'
language or cognitive abilities at age three.

Overall, however, the results of the NICHD study reinforce what the skewed debate about day care all too often ignores: Whether or not a mother works is usually beside the point and does not usually affect her bond with her child.

AGGRESSION: FUTURE SOCIOPATHS?

The results regarding attachment are just one part of the case against mothers working. Belsky also suggested that infant day care produces more insecurely attached children, who then grow up to become more disruptive in classrooms and less popular among their peers—exactly as attachment theory would predict. As evidence, he pointed to several studies that have linked placement in day care with increased aggression in children.

"I think we've got twenty years of evidence showing that early, extensive, and continuous care is associated with increased rates of aggression and noncompliance," Belsky said. "It's not all child care related. There is divorce. It's because the social fabric is not so well put together that we should be concerned because we have amplifying effects here. I start to wonder, are we polluting human capital?"

Belsky argued that like attachment, the effects of day care on aggression would be heightened by what he calls multiple risks—for example, if parents placed children in day care before they were a year old, kept them there for a full workday, and continued the care for several years.

The research evidence to support his case is mixed. Some studies have found connections between early day care and aggression; they have reported that children placed in infant day care were more aggressive in preschool classes and in elementary school, although their behavioral problems lessened or disappeared when they grew older. Other studies have found links between infant day care, poor peer relationships, and poor adjustment to school in kindergartners in Missouri, Indiana, and Tennessee and third graders in Dallas. All the aggression reported was in the normal range; the children were not classed as extremely violent or unmanageable.[10]

Other studies have found almost exactly the opposite results. The NICHD study found no strong, consistent relationship between infant day care and aggression, as did another important study by one of the field's leading experts, Carolee Howes. Another study found that children who were placed in day care as infants behaved better than those who stayed at home, and still another reported that mothers who worked full-time had more compliant children.[11]

The NICHD study of children through the age of three found that the way a mother handled her child, not whether or not a child was in infant day care, best predicted whether that child became aggressive in preschool.

The key to the puzzle may be the quality of care that children receive. Extensive studies by Howes, who observed children in preschool and kindergarten, and Deborah Lowe Vandell, who observed the same children in preschool and then when they were eight, found that children in high-quality care who had good relationships with their day care teachers were less aggressive and had superior social skills than did children in poor day care.[12] The NICHD study did find that being in low-quality day care increased the chance that the child would be aggressive at the age of two or three, but the quality of care did not matter as much as family background or a family's disciplinary style. These studies suggest that contrary to attachment theories, it was not the separation from a mother and the subsequent insecure relationship with her that led to aggression, but poor-quality day care and an insecure relationship with a teacher or caregiver.

Indeed, most of the studies that have found links between day care and aggression could not measure quality of care because the researchers observed the children in school and then found out whether they had been in day care in the past.

In some cases, children in high-quality day care fared even better than children reared entirely at home by their parents. Two studies followed children through ages eleven and thirteen in model day care centers in the United States and Sweden. They found that children who had spent more time in day care as infants had more friends, were less aggressive, and were rated by teachers as emotionally healthier than those who spent fewer hours in child care or, in the case of Sweden, spent the first year at home.[13]

Most researchers in this field believe that one answer to the problem of aggression is to seek out day care that emphasizes teaching children how to resolve conflicts. Several studies have indicated that children in such care were more skilled at getting along with their peers later on in school.[14]

"Day care does not have to be seen as a risk to society," said Alison Clarke-Stewart, a leading researcher who has often squared off against Belsky in the past. "It could be seen as an opportunity to improve society. You can teach them some social skills or negotiating skills right along with the alphabet."

The NICHD study has only analyzed results for children through the age of three and may offer further clues when the researchers study older children. For now, experts like Vandell, whose studies Belsky cited as evidence of the link between day care and aggression, offer a measured stance. "I worry about being an alarmist because it's not a social role that I feel real comfortable in," Vandell told me when I asked her how she would evaluate the case linking day care and aggression. "Do I think there's a lot of poor-quality care out there? Yes. Do I think that being in poor care undermines peer relationships? Yes. So what it leads me to do is to recommend things like appropriate standards across the fifty states for child care. I think there are things we really need to do. But that's not a statement that child care is bad for peer relationships."

CRIME

If a child manages to escape day care unscathed, though, working mothers are not off the hook: The evils of premature sexual activity, drug use, and juvenile delinquency lie ahead, critics warn. When Brenda Barnes resigned, one columnist in Des Moines wrote, "Barnes clearly wants to do what she can to ensure that her children don't end up on some police blotter."[15]

The conservative Rockford Institute bombards working mothers with shards of studies, with headlines almost worthy of the tabloids: "Employed Mothers, Promiscuous Daughters"; "Employed Mothers, Fornicating Sons"; "Fearful Children of Unavailable Mothers"; "Unsupervised Delinquents." A former chief justice of West Virginia, Richard Neely, wrote in the *Wall Street Journal* that his state had low crime rates because West Virginia has the lowest percentage of working women in the country.[16] In addition, the Heritage Foundation, a Washington think tank that helps shape conservative thinking in Congress and beyond, issued a long background paper examining the roots of crime and charging working mothers with some of the responsibility.[17]

The author, Patrick F. Fagan, wove together arguments from attachment theory and day care studies to conclude that children with working mothers are at a higher risk for delinquency than are other children. He used the same argument, in effect, that Bowlby did in the 1930s—that juvenile delinquents often had weak attachments to their mothers. Fagan quoted the eminent criminologist and political scientist James Q. Wilson as saying that "the extended absence of a working mother from her child during the early critical stages of the child's emotional development increases the risk of delinquency."

When children grow older, the risk of their having working mothers does not lessen: Fagan argued that working mothers will not be at home to prevent their teenagers from getting into trouble. As evidence, he pointed to studies showing that poor parental supervision increases the risks of delinquency and drug use. He quoted two criminologists, Stephen Cernkovich and Peggy Giordano, who said that "maternal employment affects behavior indirectly through such factors as lack of supervision, loss of direct control and attenuation of close relationships."

That theme is also sounded by the religious right. In a Family Research Council briefing paper on youth crime, Robert L. Maginnis wrote, "What contributes to the upsurge in the number of young murderers?" His answer, in part, was working mothers. Working mothers are more likely to have unsupervised children, he stated, and teenagers of working mothers are more likely to become delinquents. Being neglected as a child increases the risk of

delinquency, and teachers and law enforcement officials believe
that the lack of parental supervision at home contributes to violence
in schools. Maginnis did not specify what neglect means, but the
implication is clear: Working is a kind of parental neglect.[18]

Some of these statements are technically accurate. There is evidence that poor parental supervision increases the risk of delinquency, and if a mother works, there is a greater chance that her
children may be alone after school until she (or the father, who is
never mentioned or studied as a possible source of supervision)
returns home. Yet the critics exaggerate the links between working
motherhood and delinquency and make the risks seem ominous
and inevitable instead of preventable.

Many criminologists and experts on juvenile delinquency challenge the belief that mothers working increases the risk of delinquency. "I think that's a conclusion that's really not appropriate,"
said Cathy Spatz-Widom, one of the country's leading experts on
juvenile delinquency, who has found strong links between child
abuse and future delinquency. "In some people's research, maternal
employment is a protective factor in delinquency. If you're living in
a community where there's a lot of poverty, maternal employment is
a good thing, as opposed to being on welfare." Robert J. Sampson, a
professor of sociology at the University of Chicago, and the author of
an influential study on juvenile delinquency that Maginnis cited as
part of his evidence, also rejects the link between mothers working
and rising crime rates. "There's nothing about maternal employment in and of itself that would lead to delinquency," Sampson said.

When Sampson and John H. Laub reanalyzed one of the largest
and most ambitious studies of juvenile delinquents ever undertaken, from the late 1930s through the late 1940s, they did not find
any direct relationship between mothers working and delinquency.
In fact, maternal employment was not related to many measures of
how well the family functioned, including how well children were
attached to their mothers or fathers.[19]

Sampson and Laub did find that if the mothers worked, the
boys were less likely to be supervised. Less supervision often led to
delinquency; in fact, 83 percent of the boys in the low-supervision

category were delinquent. Children whose mothers arranged for other adults to look after them, however, did not become delinquents.

Spatz-Widom and Sampson both noted that the lesson to be drawn from their research is not that mothers working is a risk, but that parents must look after their children. "It's not work, it's a question of how you take care of kids," Spatz-Widom said. "For some kids, it's OK to be left at home after school. For other kids, it's not. Lots of responsible parents who are working provide supervision for the kids even though they're not home."

In fact, many studies have shown that whether they are physically present or not, parents can make a big difference by monitoring their children's friends and whereabouts. Teenagers' friends play a far more significant role than their families in determining whether they become delinquents, said Gary Melton, director of the Institute for Families in Society at the University of Southern California. "There is a fair amount of evidence that kids' peer groups are orchestrated by the parents," he said. "Mom says, 'Why don't you invite so-and-so over for the weekend,' or 'I heard about this group doing this—interested?' It's structuring opportunities for kids to have positive relations with peers. It really is, 'Do you know where your kids are?'"

The real problem for all parents is how to protect, influence, and watch over their children in an increasingly menacing age. The real culprits, Sampson stated, are the breakdown of community and the failure of employers to grant parents enough time away from their jobs to spend with their families. Sampson and other criminologists point to some sobering statistics. Several studies have found that between 3 P.M. and 6 P.M.—the hours, typically, when children are out of school and before their parents arrive home from work—is when teenagers are most likely to commit crimes, experiment with drugs, or have sex.

LATCHKEY CHILDREN

Instead of asking why society has provided so little opportunity for children in any kind of families to gather together in constructive, well-supervised after-school activities, critics blame working mothers for another scourge: children staying home alone. Newspapers and television shows recount tales of young children cowering at home, taught to dial 911 before they can even read, accidentally setting fires, or taking advantage of their freedom to get into trouble when they are older.

The U.S. Bureau of the Census estimated in 1987 that 7 percent of children between five and thirteen years old stay at home unsupervised by an adult at least part of the time they are out of school, and several studies have indicated that these children are at risk for social, academic, and emotional problems.[20] No one counts the number of teenagers who are at home alone because officially they are not a problem; they are deemed old enough to look after themselves. Yet the statistics on crime, drugs, and sex offer plenty of evidence to worry about them, too.

Although there is reason for concern about children who are left home alone, studies about such children present a far more subtle picture, one that offers working parents important guidance and even hope. For one, researchers are finding out more about who is typically left alone and for how long. Contrary to stereotypes about poor parents being negligent, for example, studies have found that these parents were far less likely to leave their children alone than were upper-income suburban white parents. Poor parents and African American parents usually arranged for children to be looked after by relatives, neighbors, or older siblings.[21]

Nor are children typically home alone for a long time during the day. Vandell and her researchers called children periodically over the course of one year and asked them to report what they did every fifteen minutes during the time they left school. Most children who spent any time by themselves were actually alone for an average of thirty to forty-five minutes, Vandell found. "Very, very rarely would you see a child alone for hours," she said.

Although some studies have shown that latchkey children suffer from emotional and behavioral problems, what is most surprising is that several studies have found no differences between latchkey children and children who are cared for at home by mothers—not in behavioral problems, classroom achievement, adjustment to school, self-esteem, or reports of being afraid or lonely. These studies were conducted on third, fourth, fifth, and seventh graders in poor urban neighborhoods and middle-class suburbs.[22]

The results even surprised many of the researchers. Vandell said, "I sort of went into it assuming this would be a bad thing." Instead, she found that as they grow older, many children push their parents to allow them to be at home unsupervised, and that some concessions to children's growing independence are probably necessary.

Yet she said that these results do not mean that children should be left alone. "If you are looking at middle schoolers to high schoolers, some supervision is called for," she stated. "I say this as the mother of a sixteen-year-old boy. Exactly where are you going to be? Children need some increased autonomy. But make sure it's within appropriate boundaries."

In fact, Vandell and other researchers found that the key factors are the age of the child, the type of latchkey arrangement, and how well parents monitor children. In a follow-up study to her earlier research, Vandell looked at four kinds of "self-care" arrangements: at home completely alone and unsupervised, at home with an older sibling, at home with an older teenager or a teenage baby-sitter, or with peers and unsupervised. Children who were left alone in third grade suffered persistent depression, fear, and loneliness; the symptoms were noticed by teachers and parents and continued through the fifth grade. Fourth and fifth graders who stayed at home by themselves, however, did not report being afraid or lonely. In fifth grade, children who were left alone began misbehaving. Children who were allowed to hang out with peers, from third grade on, also had behavioral problems. There were no problems associated with being left at home with an older sibling or older teenager.

Lawrence Steinberg's study of fifth through eighth graders in Madison, Wisconsin, found that the children who were at a higher risk of delinquency, drug use, or sexual promiscuity were those who were allowed to hang out with friends at a mall or outside the home or to visit friends' homes after school with no adult supervision. If parents took some steps to supervise the children from afar—calling home regularly or establishing a set schedule of chores or activities that could even include watching television—children were better off. Those children who stayed at home alone after school in such cases fared no differently on any measure—risk of delinquency, school grades, or psychological adjustment—from those who were at home with their mothers. "We thought it was very good news for working parents," Steinberg told me. "There are things that you can do. Just because a mother is working doesn't mean her children are unsupervised."[23]

Many mothers know this intuitively. When Shawn Rhea was growing up in Detroit, she chafed under her parents' regimen, but she admits, from the perspective of adulthood, that their vigilance worked. Both Shawn's parents worked in medical equipment sales, and from the time she was eleven, she was allowed to be at home after school with her brother for about an hour until one of her parents arrived home.

"Even when they were not at home, my parents were in control of the household," Shawn remembers. "Within fifteen minutes of the time we should be home, we would be getting a call. I remember getting put on punishment because I was not home. It would be, 'OK, you're home, now start your homework.' If I would want to go somewhere else, it was 'Give me the number. A person is not your friend if I don't know their parents and if I don't have their phone number.'"

Shawn believes that part of her parents' success in raising three children while working was a sense of community that infused her mostly black, mostly middle-class Detroit neighborhood. There, her parents were surrounded by family and friends who knew and kept track of each other.

"About being home after school, I thought it was so unfair and arbitrary," Shawn said. "But it was for a very specific reason. My mother and my father knew they couldn't keep a twenty-four-hour vigil. At times my girlfriend and I would try to sneak and do things, but our mothers knew each other, and I'd get caught. There was always that fear. And it stopped me from doing a lot of things."

The Brain, Intelligence, and Achievement

Just when it seemed that working mothers did not have to worry that their children would emerge emotionally damaged or delinquent, new fears were raised about the link between working and children's intelligence. Newspaper headlines, magazine cover stories, television specials, and even a White House conference in spring 1997 trumpeted an accumulating scientific consensus: Children's brains are shaped mainly during the first year of life, and the ability to think and succeed in school depends, in large part, on how many words infants hear during that first year.

New brain research shows that most of the connections between neurons that make children smart and creative are formed by the time children are a year old. That means that parents—or whoever they choose to look after their child in their absence—may shape a child's intelligence far more than any school or teacher can.[24]

Experts shook their heads and solemnly intoned that they weren't going to tell women what to do, but the subtext was clear: Why risk your child's entire future when you can ensure it by staying home during the crucial first year to shape your child's brain? Can you really leave this task in the hands of a day care center? An immigrant baby-sitter?

Undeniably, the first year of life is a critical time for babies; the scientific evidence is overwhelming. Yet the research is often presented to the public as if the only responsible choice is for a parent, preferably a mother, to stay at home with her baby during the first year of life.

In a 1992 opinion piece in the *New York Times,* Andrew Cherlin, a respected and influential authority on the family at Johns Hopkins University, cited a study on children's language development to argue for a family leave bill. In the article, headlined "Too Young for Day Care," Cherlin pointed to "evidence that full-time day care, as against having a parent home, may harm children under the age of 1." Cherlin was citing a study of three- and four- year-olds whose mothers worked in the first year of their lives. Those children scored lower on a word-knowledge test that tends to predict how well children do in school than did children whose mothers stayed at home for the first year. I understand why Cherlin waved that study before the public: To convince politicians to act, it is often necessary to make the case that children will suffer if they do not. Indeed, President Clinton signed a family leave act when he took office.

The study Cherlin cited, however, does not prove that day care hurts children's language abilities. Poverty is the more important culprit. The difference between children of working mothers and children of mothers who stayed at home was very small—a matter of two or three points on the test. Working accounted for only a small portion of that minor difference in scores, said Jeanne Brooks-Gunn, one of the study's authors.

In fact, like many other previous studies, the comprehensive new NICHD study found no difference in language or intellectual ability between children of working mothers and those of mothers who stayed at home, at least through the age of three. Children of working mothers scored just as well on language and school readiness tests, no matter how young they were when their mothers started working or how many hours they spent in child care. In other words, babies who were placed in child care during that crucial first year of life were not damaged; those crucial neural connections were apparently formed even without a mother being there twenty-four hours a day.

In this study, as in previous ones, when those who were taking care of the children talked to them and answered their questions, the children scored higher on tests of their language and cognitive ability. The quality of child care mattered: Children in high-quality day care, in which caregivers tended to talk to them more, scored higher. The type of child care also made a difference: Children in child care centers scored higher than did those cared for in family child care homes or by nannies.

Yet child care itself had relatively little impact on children's intelligence (1.3 percent to 3.6 percent of the differences in scores) compared to other factors, including family income, a mother's vocabulary, and the stimulation of a child's home environment (5 percent to 41 percent of the differences).

In one study that showed just how important family background can be, researchers recorded every word spoken for one hour a month over a two-and-a-half-year period. The children of professional parents heard an average of 2,100 words an hour, compared to 1,200 words from working-class parents and 600 words from welfare parents. Children of professional parents continued to outscore the other children throughout elementary school.[25]

Several other studies of children aged three to twelve echoed the NICHD findings. These studies showed no differences in achievement scores between children whose mothers worked when they were infants and those whose mothers stayed at home. In some cases, when children were placed in top-quality day care centers, they scored higher on academic, social, and behavioral measures than did children who spent their early years at home.[26]

The NICHD study, however, has not addressed one important lingering question about intelligence because the researchers have not yet broken down the results by income levels, comparing poor to middle-class children, for example. A few studies have indicated that middle-class children, boys in particular, may score somewhat lower on cognitive tests if they are placed in child care when they are young. In two studies, these children scored lower on verbal, reading, and mathematics tests if their mothers worked when they were infants.[27]

One of the few studies of high school children that has been conducted found slightly lower high school grades, particularly for boys from middle-class or upper-middle-class backgrounds, whose mothers had worked when they were babies. Girls scored the same if their mothers worked in high school, but lower if they had worked during infancy; boys scored lower if their mothers worked at any time.[28] The findings do not hold true for poor or working-class children; several major studies have found that these children score higher if their mothers hold jobs.[29]

These results do not mean, in the opinion of experts I interviewed, that middle-class mothers, particularly mothers of sons, should not work. Rather, they suggest the importance of selecting high-quality substitute care. Researchers suspect that one reason some middle-class children score lower may be that middle-class homes are often very stimulating, and the vocabularies and educational levels of middle-class mothers may be higher than those of the people who care for their children. So when parents examine a child care center or interview a baby-sitter, they should look for someone who talks to children and understands the importance of stimulating them.

THE GOOD NEWS ABOUT WORKING

Almost buried under the hail of accusations about working mothers is the fact that most studies that have followed children over time—as opposed to predicting their futures based on measures like the Strange Situation—have found virtually no differences between children of working or at-home mothers.

Several extensive reviews of the existing studies on maternal employment all concluded that there were few consistent differences between the children of working or at-home mothers.[30] Another review found no convincing links between mothers' work (or divorce or illegitimate births) and such important outcomes and social indicators as children's educational achievement, crime rates, drug use, or pregnancy outside marriage.[31]

One of the most extensive studies was conducted by Adele Eskeles Gottfried and W. Allen Gottfried, who followed middle-class, mostly white children from age one through age twelve. Gottfried and Gottfried gathered a wide range of data: from academic achievement tests, IQ tests, assessments of how well children solved problems without resorting to conflict, teachers' evaluations, and mothers' responses to questionnaires about their children's temperament and behavior with friends. They measured how warm and stimulating the children's homes were, what methods of discipline were used, and whether fathers were involved with their children. They also included mothers' emotions: their attitudes toward employment, satisfaction with their roles, and stress on the job.[32]

After twelve years, the Gottfrieds found no significant differences that lasted over time between children of mothers who stayed at home and those of working mothers on any of the ratings or even between boys and girls in intellectual achievement, teachers' ratings, academic motivation, behavior, or home environments. There was no consistent link between mothers working and children's achievement or adjustment.

What did matter over time were the socioeconomic status of the families, the quality of the children's home environments, and the children's gender. The Gottfrieds found that the children who did best had an intellectually stimulating home environment, involved fathers, and stable child care. Tellingly, these successful children also had mothers who were satisfied with their roles, either at work or at home, and who experienced less stress.

The Gottfrieds' study is rich with subtleties that inevitably elude a researcher who takes a onetime snapshot of a mother and child in a laboratory. For example, at various ages, there were moments when either the children of employed mothers or at-home mothers were doing better or worse, but these advantages and disadvantages did not persist over time.

One of the most important influences on a child's achievement was the level of a parent's job, a finding that has been upheld in several other studies. If a mother or a father had a high-status job, the child tended to score better on intelligence, academic achievement, school performance, and academic motivation. There was no link, however, between a parent's job status and a child's emotional or behavioral adjustment.

Contrary to received wisdom, the Gottfrieds did not find any negative effects of long parental work hours on children's achievement or adjustment. In contrast, Lois Hoffman's review of the literature suggests that some mothers who worked more than forty hours a week were more anxious and less sensitive, some children were more anxious about separating from their mothers in kindergarten, and some children scored less well on adjustment measures. In general, the Gottfrieds found that in two-career families, the fathers tend to spend more time with the children, so that the total parental time with children tended to be similar to that in families where the mothers stayed at home.

The study's findings do not quiet all doubts. The Gottfrieds began their research in 1979, before the surge of concern about infant day care (and when fewer mothers were working during their children's infancy), and did not even begin observing the children until they were a year old. There is no information, then, about how many mothers worked before their children were a year old or what impact working might have had. Only three of the mothers in the study have worked continuously, and it is not clear whether that made a difference.

The Gottfrieds' study is the latest of several to suggest that it is absurd—and ideologically driven—to think that a mother's work, by itself, is going to seal a child's fate. Although most research shows that working makes little difference in and of itself, several studies have also found benefits to children when mothers work outside the home. Some studies have shown benefits to children of mothers working, although the overriding research finding is that working makes little difference in and of itself. Several studies, however, have indicated that children of working mothers, particularly poor children and girls, are more socially adjusted; perform better in school; and have greater self-reliance, higher career aspirations, and more egalitarian views of sex roles.

In her review of the research, Alison Clarke-Stewart stated that children in group day care often score better on tests of verbal fluency, memory, and comprehension; they often string beads, write names, and draw shapes earlier than do children who are reared at home. In addition, their speech is more complex, and they are able to identify other people's feelings and points of view earlier.[33]

An eighteen-month study by the psychoanalyst Patricia Nachman also found evidence of precocity in toddlers whose mothers worked. Compared to a group of children of at-home mothers, the children of working mothers showed earlier evidence of abstract thought and related earlier to other children. In most cases, though, children who are reared at home catch up once they enter kindergarten.[34]

CHILD INDICATORS

Regardless of evidence to the contrary, many Americans share the belief that children are worse off now than in the past because more mothers work. Many commentators from Sylvia Ann Hewlett to David Gelertner link working mothers to troubled children.[35] "American children are doing badly," Gelertner wrote in the February 1996 issue of *Commentary*. "From drug use to suicide rates, from academic performance to the perpetration of violence, the numbers tell us that they are failing. . . . The decline that so many have noticed did not happen overnight. It coincided, roughly speaking, with the surge-tide of a Motherhood Revolution. . . . Could there be a connection between these two sets of facts?" Yet there is no evidence to support this widely-held idea. Researchers have repeatedly examined virtually every indicator of worsening child well-being and have found no direct links to mothers' employment.

"The evidence is not there," said Nicholas Zill, who has conducted some of the most extensive research on child well-being and whose papers are widely cited in the field. "Many people have searched for these negative relationships and not been able to find them. I don't know how many regressions I've seen of the data: Maternal employment didn't do anything to account for variations in children's well-being."

The public hears little about this conclusion, though. One reason is that arguments like Gelertner's seem intuitively right to many people. Another is that academic journals do not tend to publish research that does not find statistically significant links.

Zill pointed out that in many ways, children's lives have improved over the past thirty years. Children enjoy better physical health, and the death rates for infants and teenagers have fallen. Children live in smaller families, so parents have more time for each child. They start school earlier and stay in school longer. There are more opportunities for minority children. More children score at or above proficiency levels in mathematics, reading, and science, and more complete high school. Finally, parents, particularly mothers, have higher levels of education today than they did in the past. Most of the studies show that a mother's education level affects her child's success far more than whether or not she works.[36]

These bright spots aside, there is sobering evidence that children are worse off now than they used to be. The percentage of children in extreme poverty has doubled since 1975, to 10 percent of all American children. More children are living in single-parent homes, either with divorced or unmarried parents, and children in single-parent households are at a higher risk for a wide range of problems and are more likely to be poor. The number of children getting psychological help nearly doubled between the late 1960s and the late 1980s. The teenage homicide and suicide rates have both tripled since 1960. More teenagers are sexually active, and more are giving birth to children of their own. Rates of drug use and smoking have risen, particularly since 1992, though they remain lower than in the early 1970s. Tests show declines in high academic achievement, although there have been important gains among minority children.[37]

None of these problems is directly tied to mothers working, although in a few cases, there are some indirect links. Poverty is one of American children's worst afflictions and the factor associated more strongly than any other with how children fare. In many families, only a mother's work protects her children from poverty, although her job often does not pay well enough to move them out of the ranks of the working poor. One out of every eight American children in two-parent families in 1988 was either living in a family whose income was under the official poverty line, despite his or her mother's employment or would have been living in poverty if the mother was not working, according to Donald J. Hernandez, the former chief of the marriage and family statistics branch at the U.S. Bureau of the Census and now study director of the National Research Council.

There is no relationship between working mothers and high suicide rates or child abuse. Most of the reported rise in children's emotional troubles seems to stem from the trauma of divorce or family strife, not whether mothers are employed. Furthermore, working mothers' children are no more likely to repeat a grade or be suspended from school, and in one study, Zill found that working mothers were more involved in their children's schools than were mothers who stayed at home.

Conservatives have often charged that because more women held jobs, they felt freer to leave marriages, thus subjecting their children to the trauma of divorce. Zill and other scholars have found no direct evidence to support that claim either. Indeed, the problems commonly attributed to working mothers—crime, drug and alcohol abuse, and premature sex—are really related to whether children are properly supervised.

THE LIMITS OF RESEARCH

We still know little about how mothers working affects children. Studies are designed to offer limited information about a specific number of variables. No study can guide any one family because no study can replicate the web of individual circumstances in a particular family.

In general, it's hard to separate the effect of child care from the background noise of so many other influences in a child's life: the family's income, the mother's educational level, the birth and spacing of siblings, parental depression, the type of discipline parents use, and the child's temperament, to name but a few.[38] Parents at home who hear the latest research results often have no clue whether the study trumpeted as a warning against working is even a particularly well-designed one. Parents need to know how many children researchers studied, how diverse a sample the study included, what other comparable studies show, and whether researchers are comparing similar kinds of children (as Lamb noted, early studies compared children from different socioeconomic and ethnic backgrounds, but attributed differences between them to child care).

It is also crucial to remember that studies may find a "correlation," but that does not prove cause and effect. A study may demonstrate that there is a connection stronger than random chance would dictate between, say, a mother's work and a child's test scores, but that does not prove that her work affected the child's scores. Even if studies find a correlation, it is important to know how strong that connection is; popular accounts of studies seldom spell that connection out.

Most of the studies about the impact of working on children are also distorted by our cultural biases about motherhood. Almost no studies have compared the quality of mother care with that of any other care. We have so romanticized the mother at home that we imagine everything goes well behind those walls, and we assume that every mother at home is a good mother.

For fifty years virtually all studies about mothers working were framed by one stated or implied question: How will it hurt children? Belatedly, researchers are beginning to ask the more neutral question: What effects on children can be observed?[39]

Notice that the question remains how children will fare if mothers, not fathers, work. Although it is true that, in most cases, mothers are the ones who take primary responsibility for raising children, few studies have examined the relationship between working fathers and their children.

Generations of children have cited their fathers as lifelong mentors and crucial shapers of their values. And generations of children have also decried fathers as distant workaholics who swooped down only to administer spankings or take them on occasional fishing trips. There were many different kinds of relationships between working fathers and their children. No one suggested that just because fathers worked they were disqualified as sensitive or dedicated or even skillful parents. Yet mothers are still the target of most studies, even though the body of research on fathers is growing.

THE USES OF RESEARCH

As a society, we are so stuck on debating whether child care damages children that we ignore the crucial question: How can the research be used to reduce the risks? The studies offer several clues.

As the pioneering research of Stella Chess and Alexander Thomas showed, parents can study their children's temperaments and choose the kind of care accordingly. "Difficult" children—those who cry intensely and often, sleep irregularly, and adapt poorly to change—may do better with care that is more individualized, more structured, and more predictable. Children who are shy and withdrawn will also resist change and need a particularly warm, unpressured atmosphere. Physically active children need time to run around, not a program that forces them to sit quietly and write in workbooks.[40]

Though the evidence is still sketchy, there is research suggesting that boys are more vulnerable than girls in a number of ways. Boys tend to be more aggressive, so parents need to be careful to select child care that stresses social skills.

Parents of infants also need to pay particular attention to quality if they are considering placing their babies in group care. Good group care for infants means that one adult should not have to care for more than three babies at once. Babies need especially flexible and responsible handling, and that is impossible if a child care worker has to watch over too many at a time.

Several studies have also shown that children in day care suffer from more ear infections and illnesses in general; they are hardier when they are older. Toddlers, too, are vulnerable because their stormy moods and litany of no's often inspire rage in those who look after them. Studies have shown that they fare better in small groups.

Several unnerving studies of child care suggest that parents are poor judges of its quality; parents were satisfied with care that researchers rated as mediocre to poor. States regulate child care, but many allow conditions that researchers believe can stunt children's development. Studies have found that children do better when groups are smaller, the ratio of adults to children is smaller, and caregivers are sensitive. Children need space to run around and a predictable day, with a mix of structured teaching, such as circle time, and free play. What is most important, young children need continuity; a high turnover of child care workers makes it difficult for children to feel safe and to develop trusting relationships.[41]

WHAT'S THE VERDICT?

How seriously, then, should we take the warnings that working mothers produce children who are emotionally damaged at best and criminally sociopathic at worst? A careful review of the evidence shows that whether a child has a mother who works or one who stays at home is usually not the issue. What does matter, the studies indicate, is sensitivity and responsiveness on the part of both parents, coupled with good supervision and an ability to set limits. The research suggests that working mothers are just as able to provide such care as mothers who stay at home.

Because the percentage of mothers who work when their children are infants has soared over the past decade, the battles waged over infant day care have been the fiercest. Most researchers in the field, however, believe that the concerns have been overblown and ideologically loaded.

In a comprehensive review of virtually all known day care research that runs for nearly two hundred manuscript pages, Lamb concluded that day care need not harm children, although it can. Others would go further. Howes, a respected researcher whose previous studies found links between day care and aggression, believes that "this early child care entry really is a dead issue." Her latest study on aggression showed no links with child care; it is one of many others that has cast doubts on how long lasting the effects of early child care really are.

Lawrence Aber, the developmental psychologist at Columbia, said that most mothers would run no increased risk of insecure attachment if they returned to work. In fact, he said, his own wife went back to work when their son was five months old and their daughter was three months old. "People wondered why I, as an attachment theorist, thought this was a fine idea," he said. "I felt it wouldn't increase the risk for us. One, it shouldn't be a foregone conclusion that she should be the one who shouldn't go back to work. One of the things my wife said was 'I'm not going to be very good for my kids if I don't do some of these things.'"

Yet I believe Belsky is right on one crucial point: Because most child care in the United States is poor to mediocre, it could pose risks for children. Several surveys of child care, however, have found that the worst care is often the one available to working- or middle-class children because much care for poor children is subsidized and of higher quality.

I think there is a credible argument that there are children in bad day care who have a higher risk of developing insecure relationships with their caregivers, becoming more aggressive, and failing to receive the intellectual stimulation they need to become successful in school. That risk may well be compounded, as the NICHD study suggests, if children are receiving poor care at home, too.

Yet far from the laboratory, real-world women are making excruciating choices. Most women have to work to earn enough money to survive, and many of the women who are most strapped for cash (divorced women, single mothers, and poor women) have the least money to buy good child care.

Particularly if the choice is between work and poverty, some mothers' decision to work may well be the right one for their children, even if they have to put them in second-rate child care. Poverty has far more devastating, more powerful, and more clearly demonstrated effects on children's lives than does day care.[42]

"Last time I looked, income still had a lot to do with how kids turn out," said Aber, who is also the head of Columbia University's National Center for Children in Poverty. "Many women are making very rational choices for themselves and their children. If I get back into the workplace, I increase economic security and can purchase quality care for them or education for them."

Rather than raise honest questions about potential social problems, most of the day care debate ends up condemning working mothers out of hand. The critics essentially say that it would be safest for all women to stay home until their children are at least a year old—or even through their teenage years—to prevent an explosion of young criminals.

There is a more sinister consequence of our obsession with "maternal absence." Blaming mothers diverts attention from the many other factors that studies indicate can have a far more important effect on children's lives: poverty, social and emotional support for mothers, and mothers' own attitudes about working.

We should be concerned about children because, unlike many other industrialized nations, the United States has not made a commitment to providing high-quality child care or allowing working parents far more flexible working hours or helping parents find good after-school care.

Personal responsibility is and must be at the heart of any flourishing society; parents are responsible for making the best arrangements for their children that they can manage. Yet if good care is too expensive for all but the wealthiest parents to buy, if poverty wreaks far more havoc with children than the worst day care center, then mothers are not to blame; society has failed its responsibility to children.

Are You My Mother?

Whenever I told other mothers that I was writing this book, they asked me the same questions that haunted me when I returned to my job: How can I be a mother when I am gone for much of the working day? Will my children, like the baby bird in the classic storybook, spend their lives metaphorically asking everyone they meet, "Are You My Mother?"

For many mothers, judgment day comes when their child calls someone else "Mommy." That is the dreaded, the expected, punishment for abandoning a child. Gary Bauer, an influential leader of the religious right, says it was after their two-year-old daughter called their baby-sitter Mommy that he and his wife had an epiphany, and she decided she could not continue working.[1]

It can be a heartrending moment, as I know. A few months after my son was born, my daughter, who was then four, began crying nearly inconsolably when her beloved baby-sitter left for the day. She told me that she wanted her baby-sitter to live with us and never leave, that her baby-sitter could be the mommy and I could be the baby-sitter.

I was rattled, though I tried not to show it. I comforted myself that I had evidence of something extremely important, without which I would never feel comfortable going to work. My daughter loved her baby-sitter; I had picked someone who was meeting her needs.

Over time, I also came to see what lay behind my daughter's words. My son's birth had forced her to confront just how anyone could love more than one person at once. I loved her; I loved her brother. Could I love them both at once? She loved me; she loved the baby-sitter she had known since she was six months old. Could she love both these mother figures at once, or was she betraying one to love the other? Was I betraying her by loving her brother?

After a few weeks, the crying jags stopped. My daughter was at peace, and so was I. She had learned it was all right to spread her love around, and I learned that my fears of being displaced were unfounded.

Indeed, research completely debunks the idea that working means surrendering the chance to shape a child's fate and values. Instead, the studies show that the family remains the overwhelming influence on a child. The mountains of studies do not explain, though, how children can form enduring connections with mothers or fathers who are gone for many hours a day.

Few studies have explored what seems to be going right when a child forms a secure bond with a working parent. Even fewer have looked to the mother's emotional life for clues because traditional psychological theories have either ignored the mother's feelings altogether or relegated the mother to a supporting role to the child.

The studies that exist point to the centrality of a mother's emotions. They suggest that a woman's satisfaction, her sense of effectiveness and accomplishment, are more important to her children than whether she holds a job or not. And an accumulating body of research offers evidence that when women want to hold jobs and rear children, they and their relationships with their children can thrive.

WHOM WILL YOUR CHILDREN SEE WHEN THEY WAKE?

Undeterred, social commentators prey on the false but disturbing idea that mothers will be usurped by the very people who help them care for their children. The experts intone that a mother who works not only damages her bond with her child, but gives up her influence as well. They base their warnings on what is often a distortion of attachment theory, the notion that a child needs the constant presence of a mother to thrive and that sharing the task of child rearing means abdicating it altogether.

James Dobson affects a kindly, almost fatherly demeanor, but his advice column speaks directly to mothers' anxieties: "Whom will your child pattern himself after? Whom will he see when he wakes? When he experiences the rushes of good feelings from being fed, changed or bathed, who will be indelibly etched in his mind, you or a caregiver? . . . Mom, your children's identity will be indelibly stamped with the identity of the significant caregiver. His security and self-esteem will be permanently affected by his setting, especially if he has to establish himself in a crowd of other little folks all clamoring for attention, recognition and regard."[2]

This theme is echoed across the ideological spectrum. In his book, Amitai Etzioni, the influential founder of the centrist communitarian political movement, declared flatly that modern-day caregivers, unlike nannies in the antebellum South, are replacements for parents. Penelope Leach told parents that a child's "attitudes, discipline and education will be as much in his caretaker's hands as yours."[3]

There is an element of retribution in such comments, a sense that if mothers do dare to hold jobs, that is the price they must expect to pay. Cheryl Moorefield, the labor nurse in North Carolina who had to support her two children after her divorce and before her remarriage, said, "In day care, who's teaching them values? When I was a single parent, I think that helped take some of the guilt off. But I did still feel a pull—I'm not the one raising my children."

SHARING WITHOUT SURRENDERING

Despite parents' worries, the results of studies are virtually unanimous: Children's relationships to other caregivers do not surpass the one with their parents in emotional intensity or influence. Study after study has found, with only rare exceptions, that children overwhelmingly prefer their parents to their caregivers. A vast body of research in the United States, Israel, England, and elsewhere completely rebuts John Bowlby's premise that a nanny or anyone else will steal away a child's primary allegiance.[4]

The new NICHD study offers the latest and most comprehensive evidence that the quality of family life outweighs virtually all other factors in shaping children's emotional and intellectual lives. Even if children were in child care full time, factors such as their family lives and their mothers' vocabulary accounted for far more of the difference in their scores on language and cognitive ability tests than did the effect of child care. Nor should working mothers fear they will lose their influence over their children. The NICHD study compared children whose mothers stayed at home with children who spent at least thirty hours a week in child care and found no evidence to support that accusation.

"The average mom should know that what goes on at home, when she's home, matters a lot more than what transpires in child care," said Jay Belsky, one of the study's researchers. "If you're a mother and you need to work, even when a child is in care full time, you still matter," said Sarah Friedman, the study's coordinator. "Family matters. Don't think that if your child is in fifty hours of care, there is no family for that child."

The results of this research are also echoed in the less testable yet suggestive insights of psychoanalysis. One psychoanalyst I know told me, "The housekeeper [by which she meant the nanny] never shows up in the material," her patients' dreams and associations. The ones who loom large in her patients' emotional lives, the ghosts who crowd the consulting room, are parents.

The studies suggest that children may have a close relationship with another caregiver without detracting from their bonds with their mothers. Yet working mothers do have to allow other people into their children's lives and, therefore, other influences. Prominent researcher Michael E. Lamb said that if the mother is the only one raising a child, then 100 percent of all a child's love relationships are with a mother. If a father shares in the care, a mother's relative influence is less, as it is when parents hire a different caregiver.

Mothers who work outside the home have to relinquish a certain amount of control; they cannot be there to insist on what would be impossible in any case, that another caregiver should handle every incident exactly the way they would. Indeed, one study by Rita K. Benn found that mothers who saw their caregivers as partners had more secure relationships with their children than did those who saw them as rivals.[5]

Going to work does mean accepting that your children, if you are lucky, will come to love someone else passionately, to cry for that person when they are hurt. To include someone else in a child's care is to share something precious, and it is hard to do. It is natural to feel threatened, to worry that somehow the other person will mean more to your child than you do.

Yet working mothers do not have to dread sharing their children; doing so can be a boon for both of them. Just as one parent can comfort a child when the other parent has not been able to help the child, other influences can broaden and fortify a child's world. Research studies have confirmed the value of "multiple mothering." Learning to trust more than one person is a source of resilience for children. No one person can ever meet all a child's needs; if more than one person helps raise a child, the odds are better that the child will find what he or she needs.

"If you have a couple of adults with different developmental histories, the chances of getting something right for the child at different stages go up," said Lawrence Aber, the Columbia University psychologist.

Any individual mother has limits of character, personality, knowledge, and past experience, so that it is unwise to allow one person complete power over a child's life, argued Ann Dally, a British psychoanalyst. "Exclusive care means there is no escape and the child has no opportunity to rectify the situation or find satisfaction that his own mother cannot supply," she wrote.[6]

A MOTHER'S EMOTIONS: CRUCIAL BUT NEGLECTED

One clue to how the bonds between working mothers and their children endure is to examine the neglected mother's end of the relationship, to see how her emotions, needs, and aspirations shape the dialogue between mother and child.

Again and again, studies have found that working mothers who are satisfied with their child care arrangements, comfortable with their decision to work, maintain frequent social contacts, and enjoy social support tend to have secure bonds with their children.[7] Rita Benn's study found that mothers who had secure relationships with their sons were most confident about working and child rearing, most sensitive and warm in their handling of their children, most willing to see their children's caregivers as partners, and most psychologically healthy. The women who were most conflicted about working, most uncertain of their skills as mothers, and most likely to see the caregivers as better mothers than themselves were the ones who tended to have insecure relationships with their sons.

The best measure of mothers' bonds with their sons, Benn concluded, was not whether they held jobs or stayed home, but their "underlying emotional state." That was also the finding of the NICHD study: Women who were the most well-adjusted psychologically had the most secure babies.

Benn also found that 70 percent of the mothers who had scored only moderately well on her psychological tests also had secure bonds with their sons. These were mothers who were ambivalent and frustrated about motherhood, more emotionally distant, and less likely to choose good child care. They were, however, clearly "good enough." This study raises some important and little-explored questions about the standards we hold mothers to. To read the work of many psychologists, you would tend to think that the mother has to be a paragon, responding instantly and accurately to the minute signals that Daniel Stern recorded in his research on attunement to have a healthy relationship with her children.

If mothers are dissatisfied—either with working or staying at home—that picture changes. Several studies found that guilt and anxiety about working were associated with insecure attachments. These studies suggested that working mothers who do not want to work or feel guilty about working may have strained bonds with their children. In one study, women who were more anxious about separating from their children had less secure babies. They tended to have a more intrusive style, hovering over their babies; interrupting what they were doing to direct them to do something else; and injecting themselves and their needs into the interaction, rather than watching their babies and responding to their signals.[8]

In general, though, studies have found that the unhappiest women, and the ones whose unhappiness appeared to have the greatest impact on their children, were women who wanted to work but stayed at home. One study of forty-three children found that more than half experienced changes in attachment once their mothers returned to work. Some bonds deteriorated, but many improved. "It raises the fairly obvious observation," said Lamb, one of the authors of the study, "that for some kids, they are much better off not being at home with somebody bored, trapped, resentful, unstimulated."

The work of other researchers supports what some have dismissed as a feminist rationalization. Several studies have found real costs if mothers are unhappy at home: irritability, depression, lower self-esteem, and dissatisfaction with their child-rearing skills. These feelings translated into problems for children. Mothers who stayed at home unwillingly were less responsive to their infants. Their children had lower grades in school and scored lower on tests of creativity and persistence.[9]

The researchers speculated that children of dissatisfied housewives had more exposure to their mothers' unhappiness because those mothers were at home.[10] In another study, mothers at home who wanted to work scored higher for depression than mothers at work who wanted to stay home.[11]

Mothers' depression, researchers know, can damage children. Several studies have found that infants whose mothers were depressed began to seem depressed themselves as early as three months old. These infants were less attentive, fussier, less active, and babbled less often. Depressed mothers tended to view their babies more negatively, to be less attached to them, less affectionate with them, and less sensitive to their needs than were other mothers. By the time they are a year old, infants of depressed mothers often have delays in development. When they are toddlers, they tend to show more sadness, speak less, and explore less. Many children of depressed mothers are argumentative, refuse to accept limits, and throw severe tantrums.

In addition to the obvious risks that understimulated babies will become less intelligent, researchers believe that, over time, such children do not learn the skills they will need for social interactions, such as perception or emotional expression. Moreover, such problems do not have to result only from a serious, prolonged depression; one leading researcher, Tiffany Field, found similar problems among infants of women who scored high on depression scales but not high enough to rate as clinically depressed.[12]

The broader point is not where women are, at home or at the office; it is where they *want* to be. One recent study found that more mothers of toddlers who worked full time were depressed than were those who worked part time or stayed at home. Yet only 35 percent of mothers who liked their full-time work had depressive systems, a rate comparable to the rate of depression among at-home mothers. Of the mothers who were unhappy with their work, 67 percent suffered from depression.[13]

These studies undercut the arguments of those like T. Berry Brazelton who say that if mothers understood how important it is to give their children a good start, more of them would not begrudge the few years to stay at home. The research suggests that if staying at home does not make a mother happy, then leaving a job she likes is not going to be better for her child.

WORKING AND THRIVING

The champions of mothers staying at home argue that because most women feel that motherhood is their most important role, holding jobs will deny them the very satisfaction they need to forge strong bonds with their children. Most mothers today are miserable, they say, because their jobs tear them away from their children, leaving them too stressed and exhausted to act like mothers when they arrive home. As countless authors and studies have documented, many women are overloaded at work and at home, unfairly expected to shoulder a double burden.

Unfair as the second shift may be, the research suggests that most women are far from collapsing under the stress. A federal study of heart problems found that working women were not showing any increased coronary symptoms. In daily "stress diaries," women reported more stress than men, but they handled it better. Another study found that most married working women experienced strain balancing their domestic and professional lives, but less than one in five of them were unhappy about how they coped with those pressures.[14]

In a four-year study sponsored by the National Institute of Mental Health, Rosalind C. Barnett observed three hundred families in which the husbands and wives both worked full time. Most women were in good health and did not show signs of depression or anxiety, even though most of them reported feeling stressed. They were satisfied with their relationships with their children. Many women, from working class to upper middle class, found unexpected compensations in their work. They told the researchers they were grateful that they and their husbands both had full-time jobs because they were free of debilitating worries about economic insecurity.

Several studies have found that taking on more than one role can act as a buffer against depression. Critics have tended to dismiss accounts of depressed women who stay at home with babies as so much feminist propaganda. There is no definitive proof that housewives suffer disproportionately from depression, although there are strong indications that they do. About half the studies have found that mothers at home are more depressed than working mothers and half have found no difference. In extensive reviews of research on mothers' employment, Lois Hoffman, Faye J. Crosby, and Rosalind C. Barnett all reported that most studies found higher levels of satisfaction among employed mothers than among mothers who stayed at home.[15]

That finding held true for blue-collar workers, as well as middle-class ones: Tellers and clerical workers who were juggling roles as wives, mothers, and workers were not more depressed or anxious than those who were not married or rearing children. Waitresses, factory workers, and domestic workers told the researchers in a 1987 study that they would not leave the workforce even if they did not need the money.[16]

One reason for this unexpected resilience may be that satisfaction in one sphere of their lives may help keep women going when they encounter disappointments in another, according to studies by Crosby and several other researchers. These researchers found that the more dissatisfied a woman was with her home life, the more depressed she tended to be. Working women, on the other hand, felt less depressed about troubles at home than did housewives.[17]

The sobering exception is women whose work offers them little control or authority, particularly those who toil in low-level, repetitive jobs. Several studies have suggested that they are the working mothers to be worried about. These mothers report higher levels of emotional distress and more trouble with their children.[18]

In fact, examining the type of work mothers do is proving a far more rewarding avenue of study than merely asking whether working hurts children. Increasingly, researchers are finding that the kinds of jobs mothers and fathers have are more important than how many hours they work or whether they work at all. One study found that the greater mothers' control over their own decisions at work, the fewer behavioral problems in their four- to seventeen-year-old children. The researchers found no links between how many hours parents worked and their children's behavior; what mattered was whether parents' work intruded into their home lives. Those parents whose jobs did not disrupt their psychological involvement with their children had better-behaved children.[19]

WHAT ABOUT THE KIDS?

Even though there is no conclusive evidence that children are harmed when their mothers work, I, and every mother I know, wonder how working looks through the eyes of children. It would be absurd to pretend that there are any definitive answers, because so much depends on the personality of individual mothers and children and on the conditions of their lives. In most families, different children have different perceptions of the same set of parents; it is almost as if children grew up not in one family, but in several. When children have resentments or they believe their mothers have let them down, they may blame the fact that their mothers worked, but the problem is likely to be broader and more complex than that.

I thought about interviewing a large number of children for this book, and when I first started talking to working mothers, I asked to talk to their children, too. I found that young children were blindly loyal to their mothers and had no alternative to hold against the experience that they accepted as normal. In contrast, teenagers were at once pulling away from and clinging to their mothers, and it was hard to separate their mothers' work from the rest of their adolescent baggage.

A poll of teenagers I worked on at the *New York Times* in 1994 offered me an object lesson on the difficulties of assessing what children think of working mothers. The poll asked whether it would be better for children to have both parents working or to have one parent at home. At first glance, it seemed as though the results confirmed the criticisms of working mothers. Fifty-four percent of all the teenagers preferred to have one parent at home, while 42 percent said it would be better to have both parents working.

That answer changed, however, when the responses of teenagers who lived in two-earner households were counted. The opposite held true: Fifty-one percent of the children of working mothers replied that children would be better off if both parents worked, and 44 percent said that one parent should be at home.

The poll also asked whether the teenagers believed their parents were too busy to be available to them. The results were no different whether their mothers worked or not: 8 percent said their parents were often unavailable, 33 percent said sometimes, 41 percent said hardly ever, and 18 percent said never.

I pursued the question in several follow-up telephone interviews, talks that exposed the subtleties behind a yes or no answer. Some of the teenagers contradicted themselves within the course of a ten-minute conversation. "When I do want to talk, they're around, but it seems like nobody really has time," said sixteen-year-old Kourtney Monroe from Chicago, whose mother was unemployed. A moment later, without any further prompting from me, she said, "My parents are definitely there." And later on, after she had talked about how she believed she was more cautious than most of her friends, who called her a "Goody Two-shoes," she said, "My mother—we talk every day. We make sure we have a daily conversation."

Sometimes the mothers one would expect to be around for their children are not, even if they are at home. Jennifer Hester, a sixteen-year-old from Mississippi, said, "They're usually going somewhere or are somewhere. They're not necessarily at the house. My mother doesn't work. She shops a lot."

And sometimes it was clear—as I believe is the case most of the time—that whether a parent works or not was largely beside the point, that the family had established a tone of either closeness and affection or of distance and alienation.

One sixteen-year-old boy who wanted to be known only as Aaron M drew a picture of a lonely life. His mother worked at a refrigerating and air-conditioning company, and his stepfather managed a bakery. "Even when they are here, it's like they're not because they don't have any time," he said. "They're busy working or relaxing from work. Sometimes it can get to me. A lot of times I don't really care. We never do anything. We never go out to dinner. We used to do it all the time when we were younger. Now that everyone's older, no one really does anything together anymore."

Intrigued, I asked him whether he thought things would change if his mother was not working. "I don't know," he said. "For a while she wasn't. It was sort of the same because she was always doing other things. It's stuck the way it is."

Some children had mingled pride and regrets, like a boy from Chicago who did not want me to use his name. He longed for more time with his parents, but still felt nourished when they were together. "My parents are hardworking," he said. "My dad's a trucker, and my mom has a second shift. Now that I'm fourteen, I can handle most of the stuff by myself. It's OK now. Around school time, I wanted them around more. It's OK." Asked what was his most precious possession, he replied, "My family and my house. I feel pretty close. We do things as a family. We go out to some amusement parks. This July Fourth, we'll go to the Wisconsin Dells."

And some children felt loved and cared for despite the demanding jobs of both their parents. Cristina Smith, a sixteen-year-old from Chicago whose mother works for Illinois Bell during the day and whose father works for the post office at night, said: "I get a lot of attention. Sometimes I'd say too much. Sometimes I feel like my mom is unavailable to me because of the job that she has. Sometimes they send her away for a week at a time. But if there was anything I needed, I could just ask her for it. She's never far away. I feel close to my parents. That's why I feel I can talk to them about anything. We go to church every week. We go shopping. We go to Great America. We travel a lot. We play games. We watch movies. We eat supper together."

An essay I read by a Queens high school student, Amelia H. Chamberlain, stands as an eloquent tribute to the dedication of her working mother, as well as a measure of her resentments. Amelia wrote about going to her mother's room to wake her up at 10 P.M. so her mother could prepare for her night job.

I turn to go back to my bright room, when she asks me to make her a cup of tea. I swivel around, and a spark of anger flicks through my eyes. The guilt quickly replaces it. How can I be angry? Every day she gets up and goes to work on four or five, sometimes only two hours of sleep.

I watch her from the door in wonder. How does she do it? How does she always remember to give me $3.60 for school? How does she always remember to tell me that she loves me? How does she work all night and do errands all day? How does she raise me and my sisters on her own? She never gives up or says, "I can't go today." She never, ever doesn't get up, no matter how little sleep she's gotten.[20]

What is the truth, then, about working mothers and their teenage children? Cristina Smith's tightly bound family or Aaron M's lonely one? Amelia Chamberlain's flicker of anger or her words of admiration? The only honest response is that there is no one truth, that mothers working is but one element among the many that make up the mystery of family life.

LOOKING BACK

There is no one truth about working, either, for adult children of working mothers, who may offer the best glimpses into the experience of growing up with working mothers. Even the portraits I offer here, though, are inevitably skewed. Not only are they arbitrary selections on my part, but they cannot reflect the experience of today's children. Any adult child of a working mother today grew up in a time when mothers working was far less common and was regarded with even more suspicion than would be the case now.

Some of the adults I interviewed spoke of regrets. One successful professional woman, happily married and thinking about having children of her own, reflected on growing up with a well-known mother who was a member of the pioneer generation of working mothers in the 1960s and 1970s. "I grew up uncritically," said the woman, who asked not to use her name because she did not want to hurt her mother's feelings. "It was such a thrill to have my mother come home at the end of the day. It was only later in life that I wondered if her presence had not been so precious and so special, I would not have felt I needed to make the most of every moment and perform. There was not a lot of downtime."

Her mother loved the family rituals so celebrated by the promoters of family values. They always ate dinner together, and holidays were marked by readings and family discussions. Yet in a mark of how the meaning of rituals depends on the emotions that accompany them, her daughter remembers those family times as highly charged. "This is your time to get it all in," she recalled. "What if I didn't have something to report? There was a lot at stake in family holidays and not a lot of tolerance of things going wrong. There was no room for conflict."

As she spoke, I wondered whether she was really talking about working or about the costs of living with celebrity, parental accomplishment, and high expectations. The longer we talked, the more I felt that some of the issues lay in the personality of the mother—perhaps a lack of reflectiveness and flexibility—and the demands her children felt she made of them.

"My mother is an unconflicted person," she said. "I don't think she gave me a model of grappling." She resolved that when she had children, she would probably work, but would try to send different messages. "I really want to feel available in an unconditional way," she said. "You don't have to make my time worthwhile. You don't have to tell me about five achievements." Despite her reservations, this daughter remained close to her mother and spoke of her with great tenderness.

Others I interviewed talked about their lasting bonds to their mothers and their mothers' enduring influence on their lives. Jenifer Schweitzer and Elesha Lindsay, for example, grew up in different worlds—Jenifer in the wealthy enclaves of New Canaan, Connecticut, and the Upper East Side of Manhattan and Elesha in a rural North Carolina town where her parents worked hard to provide the basics. They shared a sense of their mothers' presence and a conviction that working can confer its own gifts on children.

Jenifer Schweitzer

Jenifer Schweitzer drew strength and confidence from her enormously accomplished mother, who was one of the first group of executive women in the 1960s and 1970s. "No one I know whose mother worked feels abandoned or unconnected," said Jenifer, who was twenty-seven when we spoke in winter 1997. "When I was younger, I didn't know, care, or notice that my mother wasn't around—it was my impression that she was around a lot."

That was an impression that Jenifer's mother, Sandra W. Meyer, worked hard to foster. An executive in several companies, including General Foods and American Express, Sandra said she realized early on that she could arrange her workday "to move in and out in such a way that you are there a great deal."

When her children were babies, her office was not far from her home, so if a meeting was canceled, she would go home and have lunch with the children. As the children grew, she marked school plays on her calendar just the way she would schedule meetings and left for them unapologetically. She used her salary to pay for live-in nannies and other household help to do chores that would otherwise take away her time from her children. And she realized if she organized her work efficiently, she did not have to stay as late as the men around her.

"I wanted to be home for dinner, and I could do that because I cleaned up all the routine stuff," Sandra said. "I took everything I could read home with me to do when they were asleep. I didn't take things home on the weekend unless it was a crisis. And about three nights a month, I stayed until midnight."

As the children grew older, she taught them to use the telephone, and they checked in with each other during the day. While some working mothers believe that they need to separate their work from home to shield their children from its stresses, Sandra said she had learned that it made more sense to show the children her world, so they would understand that they both had responsibilities, and her children would be able to share their world with her.

Jenifer's parents divorced when she was young, and she, her sister, and her mother formed a tight-knit, if unconventional, family for the times. "We did not have, by any stretch of the imagination, a Martha Stewart household," Jenifer said. "Why spend time stringing popcorn—that was time she might spend with the kids."

The closest they got to Martha Stewart was when her mother decided they should all eat macrobiotic foods, and they would spend weekends together making bread for the coming week. Jenifer remembers that her mother did not like doing many of the things her friends' mothers did, like going shopping together; that was a task she left to Jenifer's grandmother.

"She thought that was not how we bonded," Jenifer said.

"When I would go after school to a friend's house, her mother would be there, but she would be on the phone; she was not with us. When my mom was home, she was with us. She went out of her way to figure out who we were, so we would always be having real conversations. I always appreciated that my mother noticed a lot of stuff about me. If she hadn't, that would have made me really feel abandoned."

Sandra dismissed the idea that working would interfere with her bonds with her daughters. "Those are really straw men, issues like will I be able to be as connected with them? I quickly realized that with my kids, with whom I connected very strongly even in the hospital."

When Sandra returned to work, she said, she thought hard about how her children would feel secure. Part of the answer, she said, was to offer them predictable routines and structure and to make sure that the women she hired to help look after them did so as well.

Jenifer remembers her nannies fondly, but she never saw them as replacing her mother. "The second nanny we had, I called her Mama Louise," Jenifer said. "I had my mommy and Mama Louise; it was my way of expressing affection. I think one thing that mothers have trouble with is that kids are going to love other people. But they always will, whether you're home or not."

There were times when Jenifer wished her mother was more like her classmates' mothers; she remembered in fourth grade complaining that her mother did not pick her up after school the way the other mothers did. Yet she did not offer any example of a lasting grievance.

When Jenifer talked about her mother, she did so with a sense of detachment and pleasure that suggested that she was not praising her out of reflexive loyalty, but that she had thought about their relationship from the perspective of an adult. She and her mother remained close; they talked several times a week.

As Jenifer looked forward to her own wedding, then a few weeks away, she did not know whether she would lead a life like her mother's. She had recently left a law firm because she decided she hated corporate finance and was searching for a job in advertising. Jenifer said she might be tempted to spend some time at home when she has children, but not at the price of feeling marginalized at work. She admires her mother, but feels free to find her own way, in part because her mother, by being an individual, had shown her how to be one, too.

"My mom not only equipped us to go into the real world," Jenifer said, "she allowed us to see her always as someone who had her own life—whether or not we wanted that life."

Elesha Lindsay

Elesha Lindsay is a breadwinner from a tradition of breadwinners. Her mother never had the luxury of staying at home, and her mother's example inspires her as Elesha raises her own daughter. "She knitted us together," Elesha says of her mother. "My closeness with my mom, I just think it's family values. She always worked and she's still working."

Elesha remembers a household full of purpose and structure, with clear rules and responsibilities for everyone. "Mama got us up. There was breakfast on the stove. My father was coming home from his third shift when she was leaving. We all had assigned chores after we got home from school. Mine was to empty the trash cans, sweep the hallway, and vacuum the living room and den. I remember when Mama came home, if she sat down in the den and relaxed, I felt good. I'd made it a little easier on her. By the time she got home, my dad would have left for work and we would eat dinner and talk. We'd go over homework together. I think that's where I got that from, talking to my daughter about everything."

Elesha works long hours balancing a full-time job as an administrative assistant in a hospital with college courses three nights a week. Though she spends many hours away from her daughter, who was four when we spoke in spring 1996, Elesha is engrossed in every detail of her life, at school, at home, and at church. They go over her Bible study together, and Elesha puts her college homework aside if her daughter needs her help with schoolwork. "One day she got in the car with her writing paper and said, 'I can do better than this,' Elesha recalled. I turned in an assignment late. I apologized, but I said my daughter was upset and I needed to spend time with her on her writing skills."

Though the classes cut into her nights with her daughter, Elesha believed she was investing in her daughter's future. A college degree, Elesha understood, was her only chance for a better income and management responsibility. "I want to make sure I'm financially able to offer her school and a good start in life," she said. "I don't want her to struggle just to start."

Her long days are possible because Elesha can draw on her close extended family, who share in her daughter's care. Elesha's sister picks up Elesha's daughter at her nursery school and brings her home to her two cousins. She bathes her and puts her in pajamas, and when Elesha arrives around 9:30 P.M., her daughter falls asleep during the forty-five-minute drive to their house. "She's not really away from me that much, and when she is, she's still with my family," Elesha said. "She just thrives there. She just thinks she's there to tell them what to do."

Elesha believes her daughter's life is richer because so many people around her are watching over her, too: Elesha's mother and father, the sisters who bring her daughter with them to choir practice and watch her until Elesha returns from work, and her church school teachers. She has been particularly grateful for that help since her divorce a few years ago. Indeed, her parents pressed her to move in with them, but Elesha felt that would have been admitting defeat.

As a divorced mother, Elesha has no choice but to work, but she enjoys her job, too. She relishes the financial independence, the social contacts, and the chance to achieve her goals. "I don't have fear that I'm alone in this world," she said. "Being totally dependent on someone scares me most of all. I don't want her to see me that way as a person dependent on someone else."

Elesha is now trying to decide if she will take fewer classes so she can spend more time helping her daughter at night during her first year in elementary school. She does not want her daughter to repeat what Elesha now sees as her mistake, taking a job right out of high school. "I'm going to be active in the PTA," Elesha said. "I did fine in school; I was an honor roll student. But I didn't have any push or know-how. I thought my parents had done a darn good job and they didn't even graduate from high school, so I didn't push for college. I want to make sure I'm very active in school to make it as easy as possible on her."

In one way, Elesha has been lucky; she did not have to do battle with the traditional ideal of the good mother. She saw working and sharing her child's care as normal. "I don't think being a good mother has anything to do with your job," she said. "It will depend on the type of person you are. It will depend on what you instill."

THE MYSTERY OF BONDING

As I and many other mothers and their children have found, our bonds can survive hours or days apart, even if the research says little about why and how they do. I pressed experts to explain, and I got back answers that were more or less sophisticated variants on the idea that somehow children sense when a parent is—or is not— committed to them.

Lamb said that parents' influence is pervasive even if they are gone much of the working day because decisions they make continue to shape their children's lives in their absence. Parents select and arrange a child's home environment: whether there are books present, for example, or what kind of videos or television children are allowed to watch. They choose who cares for their children when they are gone. In many cases, too, baby-sitters or child care workers change over time, but the parents remain a constant.

Psychologists, from Freudians to attachment theorists, drawing on their clinical and research experience, use the same words and phrases over and over. A child has to sense that the parent is in charge, that he or she has not ceded responsibility to the caregiver, that the parent may delegate, but is looking out for the child.

Precisely how a child understands this is a mystery. Part of the answer lies in the child's experience over time, if she repeatedly gets comfort and reassurance from her parent. Some psychologists talk about what they call the internalization of the parent, the way that a child gradually, with accumulated experiences of dependability and the growth of skills like memory, is able to carry a mental picture inside her of the parent and to use that image as a source of solace. Patricia Nachman, a psychoanalyst, found that children of working mothers she observed for nearly two years used dolls, play, and words to conjure up their mothers.

"What you want is her to have that internalized presence of you during the day; when somebody hurts her feelings, you want her to feel some calming presence of Mommy," said Dr. Donald Cohen, the child therapist and director of the Yale Child Study Center. "This internalization is a wonderful process God gave us. What allows us to survive as a species is the internalization of the behavior, feelings, style of the people we can say, 'This is who I will be like when I grow up.' The people who can't do that develop the serious problems and come to see people like me."

We have long recognized that this process takes place with working fathers. But unlike mothers, fathers have not been told that working automatically disqualified them from transmitting values or forging bonds. The family-values advocate David Blankenhorn quotes Xavier McDaniel, a basketball player with the Boston Celtics, talking about his father, who worked two jobs, one loading and unloading trucks, the other as a janitor, to support his six children. "Some days our family didn't even see our dad," McDaniel told a newspaper reporter. "I saw him in a situation where he didn't give up, so why should I give up?"[21]

Blankenhorn rightly points out that McDaniel talked in the same breath about not seeing his father and seeing him. McDaniel's father was an inspiration to him, no less present to him because he was not physically there. While I was writing this book, a colleague of mine and father of three, Nathaniel Nash, died in a plane crash. In response, another colleague, John Darnton, wrote an eloquent essay about the death of his own foreign-correspondent father when he was eleven months old. The father he had never known lived on inside him to shape his ideals and his choice of a career. We allow fathers this power from a distance, even death, but we say that mothers forfeit it if they spend eight to ten hours a day apart from their children.

My deepest joys as a mother have come when my children have shown me that somehow, through this mystery of internalization, I live in their hearts as they live in mine. When my daughter was four, I told her one night that I had to leave for an interview early the next morning while she was still asleep, so I would not be there to kiss her as usual when she woke up. "I'll come in and kiss you quietly," I told her. "I know," she said. "You always do." I didn't always, in fact, but what mattered was that she thought I did.

PART THREE

PUTTING CHILDREN FIRST

Politics, Policy, and the Law

What Do Women Want?

The longer I worked, the more confident I became about my ability to hold a job and rear my children. The bogeymen created to frighten me back into the house vanished one by one.

I discovered that I loved my children with a passion I could never plumb even though I did not act like the good mother I carried inside my head. I learned that I was allowed to give my children and myself some breathing room, that I did not have to tend them with the fevered intensity of a Penelope Leach to tend them well. I realized that my children knew I was their mother and that we shared a close and durable bond, despite their loyalty to their longtime baby-sitter. I found that I did not have to worry that my children would be dogged by emotional, intellectual, or behavioral handicaps.

Yet I could not dodge the feeling that I was somehow out of step, that I did not want what other women wanted. Other women, I kept hearing and reading, did not want to work, or certainly not full time. Even mothers with rewarding, creative jobs were bailing out. Why didn't I want to go home or even cut back? Perhaps I was a holdover from some other time, lost in the wrong decade? Even though I am a journalist, skeptical by trade, it was often hard for me not to be convinced by what I read and the anecdotes I heard.

When I applied my reporter's training, though, I found that what women really want was far more complicated than the words others were putting in their mouths.

WORKING MOTHERS: ON THE WAY HOME?

When Brenda Barnes, one of the most prominent women in American business, declared that she was leaving her job as head of PepsiCo North America to spend more time with her family, her decision became a public cautionary tale: You can't have it all. "Pepsi Exec Decides to Put Family First," ran one of many typical headlines.[1]

A flood of articles and television shows followed, featuring women who had left the fast track and working mothers who wished they could afford to make the same decision. The publicity focused on the grueling tradeoffs of the executive life: Barnes rose at 3:30 A.M. to start work before her children woke up; she and her husband lived in different cities for nine years. In an interview on the *Today* show, Katie Couric asked, "With Pepsi, you missed an awful lot of birthday parties. Did you?"

Barnes struggled to make a different point. "I did miss things. But I have to say that I had the joys and rewards of many things, both with family and with work. So I can't say that I had an agonizing time while I was working. It was a wonderful career, and I had a wonderful time with my children. I think it's just a matter of this stage in life, focusing, instead of 100 percent career and family, maybe shift a little bit more to family."[2]

Her attempt to inject subtleties was generally lost amid the breast-beating about the stresses of working on families and the implication that many women either would, or would like to, follow Barnes's lead.

It was merely the latest sighting of a "trend" that business magazines first heralded several years ago. Working mothers, they pronounced, were dropping out. Stressed-out, burned-out, guilt-ridden, they were going back home. In 1994, a version of that story was hard to escape in any newspaper or magazine, even though the trend was based on the predictions of a single research analyst, backed up by the merest statistical tic.

In fact, the percentage of mothers in the workforce is not drop-ping. For a few years in the early '90s, it stayed the same, and then began to rise again. But analysts gleefully seized on even that tem-porary halt to declare that working mothers were beginning to see the error of their ways.

The story of the great sea change that wasn't began when a *Barron's* reporter picked up on a projection made by Richard Hokenson, the chief economist at Donaldson Lufkin & Jenrette. Analysts make their living by trying to spot trends that may influence stock prices and guid-ing investors accordingly. Hokenson had noticed data from the Bureau of Labor Statistics showing that after three decades of robust growth in the number of women flooding into the workforce, those rates had slowed between 1989 and 1991, risen a bit in 1992, and then flattened out again in 1993. The percentage of women aged twenty to twenty-four who were working or looking for work actually dropped about one percentage point from 1989 to 1993. The percentage of women aged twenty-five to thirty-four who were working or looking for work stayed virtually the same over that period.

These changes coincided with two other economic trends that Hokenson believed would enable mothers to stay at home with their children: lower interest rates, which translate into lower home mortgage payments; and stagnant real wages, which meant that women might not consider it worth their while to hold jobs, because their pay would not increase very much.

Building on these modest changes (the most dramatic decline was, after all, a drop of one percentage point), Hokenson trumpeted the beginnings of a "demographic sea change": mothers flocking back home and the resurgence of the one-paycheck family. Maggie Mahar wrote in *Barron's* that Hokenson foresaw "stores filled at midday with stay-at-home mothers, rolling serenely from aisle to aisle, comparing prices and ounces." The article "Working Women: Goin' Home," which appeared on the cover of *Barron's* March 21, 1994, issue, was illustrated with pictures of a 1950s housewife with apron and dress displaying a freshly baked pie, loading a washing machine, and pouring her husband a cup of coffee.

To flesh out Hokenson's numbers, Mahar interviewed women

who had left the workplace for home. Naturally enough, those women who decided to quit their jobs painted a grim picture of the stresses of the working life and voiced fears that they had neglected their children.

The *Barron's* article was quickly picked up and repackaged by news services and newspapers across the country. Religious-right leaders like James Dobson quoted it approvingly in a newsletter to the faithful; *Christianity Today* mused about the impact on church donations and volunteerism. In a cursory computer search, I found several articles that built on Hokenson's thesis within several months of the *Barron's* article, from the *Arizona Republic* to the *St. Louis Post-Dispatch* to *Advertising Age*. The Gannett News Service and the Newhouse News Service ran articles. Like the *Barron's* story, these articles were based largely on one source, Hokenson, included one or at most two interviews with women who had left jobs to rear children, and contained scant evidence for the trend they proclaimed. That didn't stop the sweeping generalizations.

"Superwoman has had enough," the Gannett News Service proclaimed. "The one-paycheck family appears to be a growing trend," Newhouse News Service declared. *Advertising Age* quoted the vice chairman at the McCann Erickson advertising agency as saying that his own studies had revealed "a significant portion" of upper-income women were returning home; he had to concede, however, that "we have no statistics."[3]

There was only one problem: It wasn't true. "There is no evidence of a massive reversal," Howard V. Hayghe, an economist in the Bureau of Labor Statistics' division of labor force statistics and a leading expert on working women, told me. Hokenson had focused on the drop in younger women, saying they were critical because age twenty-five is the average time for women to form families and bear children, so if fewer women this age were working, this trend could accelerate.

Hayghe pointed out that there was a far simpler explanation why fewer of these women were seeking jobs: At a time of economic recession, more were boosting their educational credentials. School enrollment, in fact, rose from 20 percent in 1989 to 26 percent in 1993.

The proportion of two-earner families did drop from 1991 to 1992, and there was a rise in the proportion of traditional one-paycheck families, in which the fathers were working and the mothers were not. This was a one-year movement; in fact, the trends were exactly the opposite from 1990 to 1991, with two-earner families increasing and one-earner families decreasing. Hayghe believes these fluctuations reflected the turmoil in the job market stemming from slow economic growth and corporate downsizing. In fact, a sharp increase occurred over this same period in a different kind of one-paycheck family: one in which the mother, not the father, has a job. Moreover, just as stagnant wages could have convinced mothers to stay home, they could just as reasonably have pushed mothers into the workforce because their husbands' income might not rise enough to keep pace with expenses.

Sure enough, as time went by, the much-touted exodus from the workforce never materialized. Data from the Bureau of Labor Statistics made it clear that mothers were not fleeing jobs; quite the contrary. More women, more mothers, and more mothers of young children were working each year. After 1993, the percentage of women in the workforce resumed its rise, with mothers accounting for the increase. The percentage of mothers with children under the age of one who held jobs continued to increase, from 54.6 percent in 1994 to 58 percent in 1997.[4]

THE PERILS OF OPINION POLLS

Maybe mothers aren't leaving the workforce in droves after all, but they really want to. That, at least, is what many commentators want the public to believe, and they brandish public opinion polls as evidence. Most commentators cite only the polls that bolster their case, while conveniently ignoring the polls that undermine it. From Gary Bauer of the religious right to Elizabeth Fox-Genovese, an academic and recanted feminist, polemicists point gleefully to polls suggesting that public disapproval with working motherhood is on the rise, and mothers' own discomfort with working is, too:

- The polling firm of Yankelovich Clancy Shulman asked employed mothers if they would consider giving up their work indefinitely if they didn't need the money; the percentage who said yes soared 18 points in one year, from 39 percent in 1989 to 57 percent in 1990.[5]

- A 1990 Times-Mirror poll found that 73 percent of all Americans believe that too many children are being raised in day care, up from 68 percent in 1987.

- Fifty-five percent of adults in 1990 believed that children are more likely to suffer if mothers work outside the home, a jump of eight points from the 48 percent who thought so just a year earlier, according to the *Washington Post*.

- On the eve of Mother's Day 1997, a Pew Research Center poll found that 56 percent of women surveyed thought their mothers were better parents than they were. Less than 30 percent thought that two parents who were both working full time could do a good job raising their children.

Indeed, most polls show that many Americans continue to believe that mothers should not work if their children are younger than six; nearly half of those surveyed believe that to do so harms young children, according to Janet Elder, who conducts polling for the *New York Times*. It would not be surprising if more Americans are worried now about mothers working. As years of stagnant wages forced more mothers into the workforce to pay the bills and spasms of downsizing reduced Americans' sense of economic security, families became afraid to rely on one income, so many more mothers are working now because they must, not because they want to. Attitudes have also doubtless been swayed by the flood of bad news about working mothers: the horror stories about day care, the scare tactics about broken bonds, the suggestion that any woman who can afford to is getting out.

For every poll purporting to prove that mothers just want to go home, though, there are polls indicating the opposite.

- A 1994 Louis Harris & Associates poll found that more mothers would choose to work if money was no object, either full time (15

percent) or part time (33 percent). The percentage who said they
wanted to stay home dropped from a 1981 poll. Roughly equal
numbers of mothers wanted to trade places, too: Twenty-three percent of homemakers said they would rather be in the workforce,
and 25 percent of employed mothers would rather be at home.[6]

- A separate Harris poll in 1992 also found that most women
  wanted to work, either full or part time.

- A 1992 poll in *Redbook* magazine, hardly a bastion of feminism,
  found that 57 percent would work even if they didn't need the
  money.

- A September 1997 CBS News poll found that more women
  wanted to work outside the home (50 percent) than stay home
  (42 percent), reversing the trend found in a 1995 poll.[7]

Polls have consistently found that most working mothers, professional and blue collar, believe they are setting a good example for
their children, value the independence their incomes buy them, feel
proud of their role as providers, and would not want to give up
some of their responsibilities. At the same time, polls have also
shown a divide between college-educated women, who usually prefer to work and raise children, and hourly employees, who would
stay home if they were given a choice.

Yet when I interviewed women across the country, even working-class women in jobs they hated, I was struck by how much they
saw work as a form of power. In winter 1996, I sat in a room full of
mothers in central Michigan. Most of them were in their late thir-
ties and forties. Some were married, and some divorced.
Kalamazoo is hardly a hotbed of feminism, but the conversation
became electric when the women began talking about the precious
independence and financial security that work brought them.

They talked so fast I could barely take notes. Many of these
women began in traditional marriages, but soon discovered that
they needed to work. Kay Greene had worked before she married,
but she and her husband agreed she would stay home with their
children. They quickly had three, but her husband left when the

youngest was two months old and the oldest, two years old.

"Then I was divorced with three kids and didn't have any money to support them," Kay said. "I don't want to have to marry somebody; you need to take care of yourself."

"Me, too," said Laurie Gildes, who was working as a secretary while raising her three children.

"I want to be independent," Kay said.

"Not to depend on any man," said Paulette Xamplas, who has been married for twenty-seven years, has two children, and is now majoring in biology and English at the community college.

"For ten years, while I stayed home, my husband kind of repressed me," said Robyn Rhan, a twenty-nine-year-old mother of four who is majoring in computer information systems. "He always had an excuse for me not to be doing what I wanted to be doing. It's my turn now."

A thorough examination of the results of polls suggests that women do not want to abandon work; the picture is far more complex. Women and men (when pollsters bother to ask them about these issues) seem to be rethinking the role of work in their lives and yearn for alternative arrangements that would allow them more time with family.

There are women who want to stop working, but many others would actually prefer part-time work or work with flexible hours. Many women are loath to give up the financial and emotional rewards of work, yet many find work as traditionally structured too stressful. There is little evidence that most women want to return to the breadwinner-homemaker household of the 1950s.

The Virginia Slims Opinion Poll has been charting women's attitudes for twenty-five years. A 1995 poll did suggest some important shifts in the public mood. It recorded a seven-point drop in the percentage of women who believed that the most satisfying lifestyle is for both parents to work and share child rearing, from 57 percent in 1985 to 50 percent in 1995. That trend also held true for women working full time; 73 percent of them thought the most satisfying life was an equal partnership in 1985 and 61 percent of them thought so in 1995.

Yet there was no corresponding rise in the percentage of

women who opted for the husband working while the wife stayed at home; that figure was 37 percent, the same as in 1985 and 13 points lower than 1974.

Although most women still say they prefer to combine work with raising a family, that percentage also dropped, from 63 percent in 1985 to 55 percent in 1995. The percentage of women who wanted to marry and have children but not work did not increase.

More working mothers reported feeling stressed balancing work and family and guilt about the lack of time they had with their families than in 1990. And more women believed they would be better mothers if they did not work; that figure jumped from 15 percent in 1985 to 22 percent in 1995.

Women may be more unhappy with combining work and motherhood because more of them are doing so unwillingly; for the first time in the poll, a majority of women said their work was necessary to support their families; in the past, most women said they worked to earn extra money.

The results suggest a pervasive dissatisfaction with the stresses of work. They do not signal a mass yearning to stop working. A substantial percentage of mothers who were working full time did not want to change their schedules.

When pollsters ask the same questions of men, though, they find that many men want what women want. Men and women find their jobs draining, and men and women want more time at home. The 1994 Harris poll found that just as 33 percent of women would prefer to work part time, 28 percent of men would like that option. And what is perhaps even more surprising, 20 percent of the men who were polled would prefer to stay at home full time with their children, compared to 31 percent of the women.

As this poll and others show, many women (and smaller but still substantial percentages of men) want to restructure work. They want more flexible hours, the option to work part time or work at home, and on-site child care.

Yet any conclusions drawn from polls must be tentative ones. The pundits who fling about poll results seldom bother to admit the limits of polls as evidence. As any polling expert knows, just as statistics can easily be manipulated, the results of polls can and have turned on how questions are phrased or how the results are combined.

It is extremely difficult to assess trends in the results of polls because few polls ask exactly the same questions over time. Michael Kagay, who directs polling for the *New York Times,* warned, "If there is one lesson every pollster learns over and over again, no conclusion should ever depend on one question, or one question over time. I'd like to see multiple pieces of evidence for any given conclusion."

PART-TIME WORK: THE NEW NIRVANA

Many women, it is clear, want to work part time, although many cannot afford either the lower salaries or the loss of benefits. Most of the women I interviewed, and the majority of women in several public opinion polls, said they would work part time if they could afford to; very few wanted to stay at home full time. Many mothers I talked to, as well as several of my own friends, have thrived working part time.

The drumbeat is deafening: Stepping off the full-time track is the ideal solution for women who are torn between their jobs and homes. *Sequencing* is the new buzzword: slow down or stop working when children are young and then pick up the pace as they grow older. This is the way, women are told, that they can really have it all—over a lifetime, not all at once.

Yet the glamorizing of sequencing and part-time work as the only respectable and responsible choice for mothers can be just as dangerous as telling women that their only path to success lies in working just as insanely hard as men. Part-time work offers rewards, but it also entails risks, and few of the glowing reports on the joys of part-time work spell out its potential economic and psychological costs. Just as part-time work can offer women with drive and credentials a rewarding way to have the best of both worlds or even open up entirely new worlds, it can consign other women to professional oblivion and permanent financial straits. Mothers may be more than willing to pay this price to spend more time with their children, but before they embrace part-time work as a panacea, they should understand the potential consequences.

Writers like Barbara Whitehead and Sylvia Ann Hewlett talk about dividing up tasks between men and women fifty–fifty over a lifetime, rather than in any given day. Fathers could emphasize careers while mothers of young children put their jobs on hold; women would take on more work as their children grew older, and men could pull back in return.

The problem with this scenario is that such decisions often have lifelong ramifications, as Rhona Mahony pointed out in her book, *Kidding Ourselves.* If the man is earning more money, his job is more important to the household economy and usually stays that way because he usually continues to advance while the interruptions to the woman's career mean she will lag behind him in earning power. That means that the woman must often continue to make career sacrifices, even when it is supposedly her turn to race ahead, because the man's job contributes so much more to the household. The person who earns less often has less bargaining power at home, too.[8]

Economics researchers have found that particularly for women in professional jobs, choosing to work part time may mean paying a substantial price in lower salaries and fewer opportunities to advance. A study by two business school professors compared 128 women who had never had a gap in their employment with 63 who had taken time off and returned to work full time by 1987. The women had not been away from their jobs for that long; the average time off was close to nine months. But after adjusting for differences, such as years of experience, the study found that women who had taken time off earned 17 percent less in 1993 than did the women who had worked continuously. Sixty percent of women who had not taken time off had reached upper-middle management ranks or higher, compared to 44 percent of those with gaps in employment.[9]

Solomon W. Polachek, an economist at the State University of New York at Binghamton who studies why women are paid less than men, said that most researchers have found that dropping out of the workforce for a time lowered women's future earning power by between a half percent to two percent of their salaries each year they stayed out of work. Women who dropped out received fewer promotions and advanced more slowly. Working part time exacted less of a cost, but it also slowed women's rates of promotion.[10]

The price paid depends on the kind of job. Relatively low-skilled jobs like housecleaning or jobs in which skills did not deteriorate over time, such as teaching, allowed workers to move in and out of the labor force without exacting much of a penalty. The highest costs, in terms of opportunity and advancement, were in managerial jobs.

Even though many women have told pollsters that they are happier working part time and feel less strain, several studies have also detected an emotional toll of part-time work. Elaine Wethington and Ronald Kessler found that working less than twenty hours a week had a negative impact on women's mental health, and five other studies of part-time work reported similar results. The researchers speculated that women who work part time may take on full responsibility for child care and household tasks because they have more time off from work and because they earn less money than their husbands. As a result, they could end up feeling more stress than full-time workers, who would delegate more of those tasks. In a different study, Pat Boyle followed fifty couples through the first year after their children were born; all the mothers had planned to return to work, but 40 percent did not return full time. Those mothers who were not working full time were less satisfied with their parenting, and their husbands were less satisfied with them.[11]

Statistics on career advancement or measures of stress do not tell the whole story. I know that such studies may not take into account the real rewards of such a decision: more time for mothers to spend with their children, to volunteer at school or in communities, to be with friends, and to have for themselves.

Nor is the news all bleak. Polachek said that in some cases, researchers had found a "rebound effect" when workers who left the labor force returned to jobs: The workers had a greater incentive to work harder because they knew they were going to stay. And one study that used a different way of evaluating the data found that part-time workers were not paid proportionately less.[12]

It is easy to overstate the danger of pulling back and ignore the new opportunities that can open for many women. Some have been spurred to start their own businesses or been led into different fields. When women know what the trade-offs are of treading a less conventional path, they can plan accordingly.

Several women I interviewed have found that part-time work has offered rewards without diminishing their commitment to a professional identity. When Lisa Evans was growing up in Florida in the 1960s, for example, girls did not set their sights on professional careers. Her mother had stayed home with her, gotten divorced, and quickly remarried. Few of Lisa's friends went to four-year colleges; they became legal secretaries, or if they were extremely gifted, nurses. Although Lisa excelled in school and loved mathematics and science, she did not dream of becoming a doctor; instead, she planned a career as a physical therapist. "Then my science teacher said, 'I think you're going to be bored with that after a while,'" Lisa stated.

So Lisa entered medical school and embarked on the grueling process of becoming a doctor, planning to specialize in the field of medical oncology, or cancer treatment. She married another doctor, Chuck Evans, an obstetrician.

Lisa got pregnant during her last year of residency, the final year of training before becoming a full-fledged specialist. She decided that medical oncology might be a difficult field to combine with motherhood because the hours on call were long and often unpredictable and her husband had to leave whenever a patient went into labor. So she switched to radiation oncology, which allows her to work regular hours, from about 7:30 A.M. to about 5:30 or 6:00 P.M. She is on call nights and weekends only every sixth week and knows in advance when that week will be.

Other than that concession, Lisa was determined to continue her career. "I'd spent eleven years training for that," she said. "There's no way I was not going to work. That never realistically entered my mind."

Lisa's affection for her children was obvious when I visited her in her home, but she was refreshingly unsentimental about mother-hood. "Chuck and I look at each other on Sunday night and say, 'Thank God we're going to work so we can rest,'" she said. "Being at home constantly is more difficult than going to work."

Yet Lisa did not hesitate to accept an offer of a four-day week when she was pregnant with her second child. Part-time work is traditionally extremely difficult to negotiate for doctors, particu-larly doctors on the staffs of both hospitals and medical schools, as Lisa is. In Lisa's case, a colleague of hers at Bowman Gray Medical College had been pushing for six years to create a part-time option.

"It made a huge difference," Lisa said. "You don't want to spend your weekends doing all the errands you have to do to main-tain your life. I know their teachers, know kids in their class. If field trips are on a Friday, I can do them and the teacher knows that. It allows you to be part of their world. And it allows you time on your own. On the weekends when Chuck's around, it's family time."

Lisa did not have to abandon her professional self, but she had more time for her personal life. She did not argue that her children were better off because she worked fewer hours; she felt her life was enriched and less stressful. Because she and her husband are both doctors, they can afford to keep their baby-sitter five days a week, even though Lisa works four days. Lisa could participate in her children's world, but she also took some time on Fridays for herself, to run errands, get a haircut, or spend a few hours relaxing.

Lisa Evans has been able to work part time and avoid some of the pitfalls because of her relative affluence, higher education, pro-fessional credentials, and years of work forging a good reputation and business connections that make her a desirable employee who can to some extent write her own ticket. Unfortunately, such women are often the exceptions. Mothers without those levels of skill or education can find that part-time work or sequencing keeps them in dead-end, low-paying jobs.

To make part-time work a really attractive option for a broader range of women, it is important to examine the potential pitfalls. It is true, as Rhona Mahony noted, that part-time workers may always be somewhat less valuable to employers than full-time ones, so there may be less incentive to offer them benefits that many mothers cannot afford to give up, such as health care. The dangers of the mommy track remain. Many employers could nonetheless rethink work so that a part-time path is not seen as a ghetto for the unambitious or a pink-collar trap.

In her book *Composing a Life,* the anthropologist Mary Catherine Bateson profiled several women whose lives did not follow the straight lines of men's. Her image that women compose a life, rather than merely follow a fixed track, holds great appeal (and no little poignancy, given that Bateson is the daughter of Margaret Mead, who, by Bateson's account, often slighted her personal responsibilities). The women Bateson wrote about found, as have many I know, that improvisation offers its own joys and the possibilities of unexpected discoveries.

One of my best friends has moved in and out of paid work as a lawyer; her most recent decision to slow down before both her children enter school resulted in several of her clients asking to stay with her. Now she is happily presiding over a part-time private practice, an end she never foresaw when she decided to leave a demanding and rewarding job. Another friend, a television producer, decided that her priority was to spend every summer with her children at an arts community. That means that each fall she must embark on a search for a new job. Starting fresh each year has meant that she has worked in some jobs that she merely endured, but others that pointed her down new paths.

Improvisation works only if it is undertaken willingly and with brio; if it is reluctant or forced or falsely offered as a panacea, the notes will not sing. Mothers must not be shamed or enticed into picking part-time work because they think it is the only way to fulfill their responsibilities toward their children, and they must be made aware of the potential costs as well as the rewards.

TIME

Most mothers, and many fathers, clearly want to spend more time with their children. Of all the costs of working, the most profoundly mourned and anguished over is the lack of family time. Many working parents, mothers and fathers, feel they do not spend enough time with their children; they confess their guilt in polls and interviews.

Their heartache reflects the sad reality that work swallows up too many hours for too many parents. Many parents believe that they must put in longer hours to save their jobs. With service jobs one of the fastest-growing sectors of the economy, more people must work at nights or on weekends, and about one-sixth of American parents of children under age six work split shifts, which can offer each parent time with children but less time together as a family.[13]

Popular writers, panels of experts, national commissions, and assemblages of scholars speak as one: The American family is starved for time, and children are the losers. Arlie Hochschild describes working households as a manic assembly line, with children run through their paces at the caprice of adults who do not even have time for a game of catch with them.

The Carnegie Commission, in a widely circulated report, noted that employed mothers spend less time with their children than do mothers who stay at home, but said nothing about the time that fathers spend with their children. William Mattox, of the Family Research Council, struck a typical chord: "Couples who work a combined 80-hour week find themselves too pooped to parent. It's time to quit pretending the two-career model is good for children."[14]

Yet we actually know little about how much time parents spend with their children now compared to the past or even how much time children really need with their parents to thrive. The debate about time is often completely specious, with statistics that capture the public imagination but often have little basis in reality.

One of the most widely quoted statistics is that in 1985, parents spent 40 percent less time with their children than parents did in 1965. The figure has been cited more than fifty times in newspaper articles: Lester Thurow used it in an opinion piece bewailing the rise of the two-income family. Elizabeth Fox-Genovese cited it in her book *Feminism Is Not the Story of My Life,* and David Gelertner quoted it in an article in *Commentary.* It's a dramatic figure, but on closer examination, it turns out to be wrong.[15]

In fact, John Robinson, the man who conducted one of the few examinations of how Americans spent time over the past three decades, the man whose study is cited as the source of that 40 percent figure, never used it. "It's one of those numbers like you have more chance of being hit by an asteroid than getting married," Robinson told me, as he explained how he had grown increasingly baffled and frustrated to see the 40 percent decline quoted and attributed to him in article after article.

Robinson, a professor of sociology at the University of Maryland, has been studying the time-use diaries kept by a nationally representative sample of Americans in 1965, 1975, and 1985. A time-use diary, in which people jot down the actual number of hours they spent on activities on a given day, is considered far more accurate than survey questions, which ask people after the fact how they spent their time.

The 40 percent figure was first minted by Mattox. When I called Mattox to ask him how he had derived the figure, he told me readily. Robinson published his 1965 and 1975 results in a book, *How Americans Use Time.* Some results from his 1985 study also appeared in an article in *American Demographics* magazine. In the book, Robinson reported that the total contact time between parents and children was about thirty hours a week per parent in 1965. A chart in *American Demographics* noted that the average contact time in 1985 was seventeen hours. Mattox did a quick calculation and came up with 40 percent.

But Mattox compared two numbers that Robinson says are not directly comparable. The thirty hours a week were hours spent per parent; the seventeen hours a week recorded the number of hours that all women spent caring for children, whether the women were parents or not. Obviously, if fewer people in the 1985 sample than in the 1965 sample were parents, that would bring down the average number of hours spent with children, and it did.

That error was compounded by other errors in the *American*

Demographics article: The chart was mislabeled as parents, and Robinson had made some errors and omissions.

Some months after I spoke with Mattox in spring 1996, a report questioning the 40 percent figure appeared in *U.S. News & World Report,* and Mattox has now stopped using it, citing an error by Robinson.[16]

Robinson's research paints a strikingly different picture of the time parents spend with children. Contrary to popular perceptions, Robinson found that since 1965, mothers have spent about the same number of hours a week directly caring for their children—feeding them, playing with them, talking to them, and dressing them. He has not, however, measured the number of hours that mothers spend caring for children while they are doing something else, such as housework. Mattox rightly argues that such time is also important, but Robinson has been unable to rerun his computer tape to produce the totals.[17]

Robinson's picture is therefore incomplete. Even though the number of hours spent on direct child care may be the same, because so many more mothers work now than did in the past, they must be spending fewer hours with children overall than they used to. But Robinson and his research collaborators suggest some reasons why the time mothers spend on child care does not seem to have dropped as much as one might expect. Working mothers appear to spend more hours with their children than employed mothers did in 1965 and spend less time on housework than they did thirty years ago. Since families were larger in 1965 than they are today, now mothers spend considerably more time with each child. Between the 1920s, when most mothers stayed home, and 1981, the amount of time spent per child nearly doubled. Time-use surveys also suggest that working mothers go out of their way to spend time with their children even at the expense of sleep and leisure time.[18]

Defenders of working mothers also point to other studies, notably those by Cornell University researchers, which have indicated that working mothers and at-home mothers spend roughly the same number of hours in "direct" interaction with their children—that is, reading to them or playing with them—because at-home mothers have other chores. The champions of at-home motherhood tend to down-play the undeniable fact that these mothers spend hours cooking, cleaning, washing, watching television, making telephone calls, and performing other activities with their children as observers.

While those who bemoan declining family time may be guilty of exaggeration, those who minimize the problem are equally culpable. I do not think that working parents can rest easy because they appear to spend about the same number of hours in direct interaction with children. Any parent knows that sometimes just hanging around with children produces memorable moments. There is much children can learn by watching their parents perform some of the household chores or even helping them do so. The presence of parents is reassuring, even if children simply play around them and never even ask them a question. Being there spells family, haven, security.

As the writer Barbara Ehrenreich, a mother of two, once told me, "I always thought the values got transmitted in the low-quality time, while I was doing housework while talking to them. You give them a rag, you're both doing something. That's where you teach them how to lead a good life, how to clean a sink."

I would never dream of arguing that you can raise children without spending many hours with them. Children need time, mothers need time, and families need time. Quality time is a bankrupt notion. It has been justly ridiculed because every parent knows that it is profoundly false.

Of course, it's absurd to cram a child into a factory model of time, chopped into fifteen-minute segments for this or that activity. Doing so doesn't respect children's different sense of time, their mercurial natures, and the rhythms of their days. We need to demand that employers think more creatively about how to give employees more time at home. We seldom ask why fathers are not compensating for the missing hours with mothers, why making time for family is not a responsibility of both parents.

As important as time clearly is, we know little about just how much time children need, how much work eats into time with children, and the real impact on children of too little time. One of the few studies to address this topic, by Steven L. Nock and Paul W. Kingston,[19] could not unearth any direct evidence that less time hurt children. Nor could the NICHD study, which found that the number of hours children spend in day care did not affect their intellectual ability or, in most cases, their attachment to their parents.

Many working parents, I among them, are desperate to know just how much time children should have with their parents to thrive. I asked many experts, and gradually I realized the question was impossible to answer. There is probably a threshold below which children may suffer, but no one can name a set number of hours because there are too many variables. How much time do children need when they are troubled and shaky, and how much when they are sailing along? How much time do families need when parents are under stress or when they are more relaxed? How much time do which children need at which ages?

In some ways, explained Dr. Donald Cohen of the Yale Child Study Center, how much time children need is the wrong question. "It's how much time does the mother need to feel she is with her child comfortably," he said. "Does she feel she's the presence in the child's life, and the child perceives her as if she's always there? I use the mom's feeling about this as much as I use the baby's behavior. The mom is the barometer." (Or, of course, the father; he and I were talking specifically about mothers.)

The answers vary widely, from working mother to working mother—and working father. For Kathy Klema, a New York City investment banker who works in a profession legendary for its punishing workdays and nights, bath and bedtime are the crucial hours. She has told her employers that she is committed to getting home in time for these rituals, and her husband, David Resnick, also an investment banker, made a similar commitment.

"My mom was home by 7; my goal is to get home by 7:30," said Kathy, whose mother worked throughout her childhood as a mathematician and whose father is a scientist. "My feeling is, if you miss bedtime, you blow it."

Reina Sanchez has raised seven children while working long hours in a New York City garment factory. She and her husband came to America from the Dominican Republic, and she boasts proudly that four of her children are students (three of them in college) and three are married. She must leave her home well before her children do to arrive at her sewing machine by 7 A.M. For her, the precious hours are after she leaves the factory at 4 P.M. and arrives home to talk to her children about their days. Her husband is also usually home at night with the family.

"I work because I have to, but I dedicate all my spare time to the children to raise them properly," Reina said. "I speak with all the children about what they've done. I answer their questions honestly, no matter how embarrassing the questions are. You have to make them see that you trust them and they can trust you, too."

For one friend of mine with responsibilities that often keep her at the office until 8:00 or 9:00 P.M., it's enough to come home at the end of the day and sit on her children's beds, half dozing herself as she and her daughters review each other's days until her daughters drift off to sleep. Her husband often beats her home and usually has dinner with the children before she arrives. But her half hour at her daughters' bedtime gives her a sense of intimacy and assurance that is evident every time I have seen her with her children.

I discovered that I have my own threshold of time spent with my children. Enough time, and I feel relaxed, confident, and in tune. If I shave off even half an hour, I am shaken and bereft. When I returned to my newspaper job after a year and a half away writing the first draft of this book, I immediately lost an hour each night with my children. It felt like three. I spent months struggling not to watch the clock at work, feeling my stomach tighten each minute I worked longer than the goal I'd set for leaving. When I decided to take on a more demanding, but more rewarding, job, I decided to try a rotation. I would work late some nights in return for leaving early on others. The extra time on the early nights helped tide me over the late ones, allowing me to feel that I still had enough time to read my children the way I needed to, to sense their moods and feel comfortable and relaxed with them. I continue to watch them and myself to see if that conclusion holds.

Am I, and these other mothers, spending enough time at home?

Are the fathers? Will some of their children grow up feeling they wanted more time with their parents? In some cases, the answer may be yes. The real test of whether the children got enough time will come when they are adults. I have talked to children of working mothers who yearned for more time with them. Before we condemn mothers, we need to assess how profound or debilitating those regrets proved to be. Have children grown up to be moral people, able to hold responsible jobs and form enduring relationships? Or do they feel a pervasive sense of loneliness and abandonment? These are the better ways to judge whether children's needs were met, not just how many hours parents were at home.

Just as an hour of quality time a day does not a real relationship make, more time does not automatically mean better time. Sometimes the time you set aside for special moments with children—whether you're working or staying at home—turns out to be the very time your child decides to act abominably or to clam up altogether. Hours spent with a mother who is bored, resentful, or even depressed, a mother who is at home because someone has told her that being there is better for her children, regardless of how she feels, are unlikely to yield precious childhood moments, either.

I found Hochschild's factory analogy specious and exaggerated. There are plenty of moments when working parents feel that way, but there are also occasions when hours alone are an inaccurate measure of what happens between parents and children. I can be home for hours on a weekend, with the children playing in another room, and I can feel as if we were not together at all. I can come home from work and have only a few hours together and yet feel as if the time stretches out forever, because I heard a confidence, or played a game, or had a long talk. Children and parents need both kinds of time—intense, focused exchanges and lazy, low-key time in which nothing special appears to happen. Tallying the number of hours spent at home and battering parents with it helps neither parents nor children, because it does not answer the most important question: whether children feel their parents are available to them, whether they feel valued and secure.

Mothers in the Dock

Women in courtrooms across America are hearing judgments on their motherhood. As Deborah Eappen and countless other working mothers have discovered, those judgments are often harsh, reflexive, and absolute. "I think she's guilty of manslaughter," a radio caller said of Eappen, who dared to hire someone else to look after her child.[1]

"Bad Mom, Good Prosecutor," a *Newsday* headline blared when Marcia Clark's husband filed for custody, charging that she never saw their two young sons because she was immersed in the O. J. Simpson trial.[2]

Sharon Prost, counsel to Senator Orrin Hatch, lost custody of her two sons as a judge berated her for being "more devoted to and absorbed by her work and her career than anything else in her life, including her health, her children and her family."

Custody cases like Clark's and Prost's are the ones that bring most mothers into a courtroom. In effect, they are public examinations of a mother's fitness, because judges are asked to decide whether the mother or father is the better parent. A mother's triumphs and failures are paraded before the courtroom, just as Deborah Eappen's were.

Everyone, from judges to Court TV watchers, has an opinion on what makes a good mother—and often they believe that working mothers, by definition, do not qualify. That was the real fascination with the nanny trial, which quickly became the trial of Deborah Eappen: Just what, exactly, is a good mother in this day and age?

Do good mothers work? Can good mothers choose to work even if they can afford to stay home? Can they hire au pairs if they want someone to be part of the family, or are they choosing the cheap alternative to more experienced, more expensive nannies and putting their children at risk? Is any day care safe? The nanny trial and countless other less publicized custody cases are public and painful attempts to search for answers.

THE NANNY-MURDER TRIAL

As the sorry tale of Matthew Eappen's death unfolded in a Cambridge courtroom, his mother's private decisions became public grist for a massive, extended, and vituperative debate on working motherhood. While the trial became a flashpoint for a host of legal and moral issues, it exposed the rigidity and hostility that mar any public discussion of working motherhood. The trial had everything—the theatrical Barry Scheck of O. J. Simpson fame, calling on his usual array of doubt-casting medical experts; high-stakes legal maneuvers such as the defense gambit of ruling out any lesser charge like manslaughter; the jury's conviction on the grounds of second-degree murder; the rare, dramatic spectacle of a judge reducing the verdict to manslaughter and freeing the young au pair.

The result was that millions were glued to the trial on television and millions more heard about it. Public sympathy—at least the loudest and most virulent strain of it—appeared to swing to Louise Woodward, the soft-spoken, sweet-faced English rose exploited by the selfish career woman. A mother had lost her child, but the mother became the object of scorn and derision, the au pair the object of pity and compassion. Of 26,000 calls to the MSNBC cable network, about 75 percent ran in favor of Woodward's innocence.

The *New York Post* reported that two out of three New Yorkers polled believed the parents guilty to some extent in their son's death, and 77 percent wanted the jury's guilty verdict thrown out.[3]

The facts of the trial were almost lost in the debate about it. Deborah Eappen, an ophthalmologist, and Sunil Eappen, an anesthesiologist, hired Louise Woodward in November 1996 to care for their two small sons. Deborah Eappen worked three days a week and often returned home for lunch. The Eappens' dissatisfaction—and Woodward's—mounted. Woodward was a teenager who liked to party; she resisted a curfew and was out so late that several times she had trouble getting up early enough to watch the children. Sunil Eappen returned early one day and found Woodward in the basement doing laundry, out of earshot of both children. Woodward spent long stretches on the telephone and on the computer e-mailing friends when she was supposed to be watching the children.

In late January of 1997, the Eappens told Louise she had to abide by new rules that included a midnight curfew and restrictions on her e-mail and phone calls when she was on duty. A few days later, Woodward called Deborah Eappen to tell her something was wrong with Matthew. Matthew died five days later, without recovering consciousness. Louise Woodward, who told police she "may have been a little rough with him," was charged with his murder.

The prosecutors charged that Woodward had shaken the baby and slammed his head against a hard object in frustration. A parade of medical experts called by Barry Scheck suggested that Matthew did not have some classic signs of shaken-baby syndrome and that the injury to his head was older.

Many legal experts believed that the defense's medical experts cast doubt on the prosecution's version of events, although the O. J. Simpson trial showed how it is possible to cloud a reasonable conclusion by exploiting the fact that there are often several possible interpretations of medical symptoms. Most people also believed that the charge of intentional murder, with its life sentence, was too harsh and that a more appropriate charge would have been manslaughter. That, in the end, was what the judge concluded when he took the extraordinary step of changing the jury's verdict. Yet if a mother had killed her own child—even a young mother, isolated and frustrated—no such understanding would have been proffered.

Whatever the truth about Matthew Eappen's death and whether or not Louise Woodward was responsible, the rush to judgment on Deborah Eappen was swift and inexorable. In a grueling four-hour cross-examination of her during the trial, defense attorney Andrew Good implied that her job had made her an inattentive mother.

Good harped on how Eappen had not called to check on the children all day, until Woodward paged her in a panic. "Is it true, ma'am, that you told the social worker that the reason you didn't call during the day was because you were too busy to call?" he asked Eappen. In fact, Eappen told him, she thought of calling, but was concerned that Woodward would think she was checking to see if Woodward was following the new rules.

In another exchange, Good accused Eappen of being a perfectionist who attends to detail yet did not notice her son had a fractured wrist. He tried to cast her as overwhelmed by the stress of working motherhood. "Is it fair to say your life was busy?" he asked Eappen.

"Busy," she said.

"Full?"

"In a good way."

"And would you say, ma'am, that your life was somewhat stressful in dealing with all of that?"

"It's a balancing act."

The defense had to tread warily, unwilling to appear to attack Eappen openly for fear of alienating the jury. No such constraints tamed the ferocity of the public debate, both for and against Deborah Eappen.

Testimony during the trial revealed Eappen to be a conscientious and involved mother. She asked au pairs to review a tape about discipline techniques. She taught them CPR. She checked references and interviewed several au pairs before hiring Woodward. She knew small details of her children's lives.

Nonetheless, the public could and did criticize virtually every move Eappen made. She should have spent more money on a better-trained nanny who would have seen the children as her charges, not as whiny brats who stood between her and American big-city nightlife. She should not have hired anyone else to take care of her children. She should have been more compassionate to a young English girl. She should have fired her at the first signs of trouble.

"If the mother can afford to send to England for a nanny, she should have stayed at home with her own child," read one online missive on Nation Talk.

"Louise was cheap (inexpensive) help for a cheapskate upper-class couple of Medical EGOS (as doctors are often known for)," another correspondent from Boston wrote on Thamesvalley.com's chat room. "THEY made the decision to delegate responsibility of TWO small children to a stranger (I don't care if Mary Poppins had vouched for her) and now they're 'victims.'"

Deborah Eappen had her defenders, too.

"Give into the ultraconservative religious right if you choose and condemn the woman to hell because she worked outside her home," ran one comment on Yahoo!'s Boston message board. "Personally, I don't find that child abuse nor a capital crime."

"As an at-home mom who has worked in the past, I am in disbelief that the attitude has been that because the parents worked they are being blamed for the death of their son," one respondent wrote to CourtTV.com's message board. "I can't believe that the people making these stupid remarks have never had a baby-sitter before."

It is possible to second-guess the Eappens, as it would be virtually any family whose inner workings are exposed to the light of day. Should they have noticed Matthew's fractured wrist? Should they have fired Woodward earlier? Deborah Eappen said after the trial that she wished she had, but she is not the only working mother who has hesitated before uneasiness with child care jelled into a conviction that a change was necessary. Should they have used an au pair at all?

There are legitimate questions to be raised about how well-trained au pairs are to care for young children, how many hours they should work, and whether they represent child care on the cheap. Au pairs were originally thought of as mother's helpers, not as full-time caregivers. The death of Matthew Eappen, though, does not make a good blanket case against using au pairs. In theory, the Eappens' situation should have been an excellent one for an au pair. The mother worked only three days a week and often returned for lunch, so she was not gone for the entire forty-five hours a week Woodward was supposed to work. With two previous au pairs, the Eappens had happy experiences, as have many other American families.

Attempts to move the discussion about the trial onto a more high-minded plane—the shortcomings of au pairs, the shortage of child care, the indifference toward child abuse, the British versus American legal system, the sanctity of jury verdicts—all pale before the passion that really engulfed the country: Was this a good mother or not?

"I just feel, how did Louise become the hero and I become the villain?" Deborah Eappen said in an interview with *Time* magazine that appeared in the November 11, 1997, issue. "I don't think anyone knew the Deborah Eappen they were talking about. . . . People are projecting their own guilt and fears onto me."

THE BATTLE FOR CUSTODY

Deborah Eappen's public trial was a landmark one, but it revolved around a relatively rare occurrence: the death of a child while away from his mother. Far more common in an era of divorce are wrenching battles about custody, and it is in custody suits that working mothers often end up in the dock. Custody cases raise many of the same issues aired in the nanny trial, because working mothers never know whether they will encounter a judge who, like much of the public, still believes that working harms a mother's ability to take care of her children. Like the nanny trial, several widely publicized custody cases have alarmed working mothers, who fear they are vulnerable whenever they walk into a courtroom.

It is important to remember that most mothers still get custody of children. Most divorce cases are still uncontested, and so the cases that surface in the news remain the exception. Yet reviews of custody cases have shown that when fathers fight for custody, they often win.

While most publicity has centered on mothers in custody battles who were professionals, like Sharon Prost, or the aspiring Michigan student who lost custody of her daughter because she planned to put her in day care, the suspicion that mothers who work are less devoted persists whether they are committed career women or reluctant shop clerks. Indeed, as Marguerite Gollahon and Mary Ann Holmes found, working-class women are often penalized because the only jobs they can get require night and weekend shifts.

Marguerite lost custody of her child not only because she worked, but because she could not afford a lawyer on the five dollars an hour she earned at the Hungry Harvey convenience store. No one knows how many cases like hers there are, because many never even get to court and most are never appealed, so they are not included in most legal databases.

In 1984, Marguerite married Charles Gollahon, who had a good job paying eighteen dollars an hour at a can factory. She left her job at a sewing factory when their son, Tyler, was born in March 1985. For seven years, she stayed at home raising Tyler while her husband worked. When they divorced in October 1992, she got custody of Tyler and a modest child-support payment.

To stretch that income, she worked two days a week on the second shift, from 4 P.M. to midnight, at the Hungry Harvey store in a small Georgia town on the border of Alabama. When she worked, she left Tyler with her husband's parents. Her former husband worked full-time on the third shift, from 11 P.M. to 7 A.M. When Tyler was visiting his father, he, too, left Tyler with his parents when he worked.

About a year after the divorce, Marguerite began dating someone new. She believes that is why her former husband filed for custody. "I couldn't afford a lawyer," she said. "My husband had a lawyer. He made it sound like I didn't have any family. My parents are dead. I didn't go to work until he filed for divorce. I was only working part time because Tyler was sick a lot. We were real, real close."

Marguerite moved through the short trial in a daze. She testified, "I was just terrified. There were so many things I could have brought up. Tyler has allergy problems real bad. He's allergic to dogs and cats. They have three dogs and three cats. They smoke around him. I see now I could have stood up. I just didn't."

She also saw the report of a worker from the local department of children and family services, who had visited Tyler at school and at home. The report concluded that there was no reason to make any change in Tyler's custody. Two weeks after the trial, Judge Arthur W. Fudger's decision arrived in the mail. Tyler's "best interests" required changing custody to his father, he wrote, because his mother is "now working nights in a convenience store" and his father's parents had been keeping Tyler "a majority of the time in the past."

Marguerite blamed herself for allowing Tyler to visit his grandparents whenever they called for him. "Anytime they called, I would let them have him. A friend of mine said, 'Don't leave him there too much.' I said, 'I don't want to be too ugly.'" She said she never believed she would lose custody. "It was really a big shock. I didn't abuse him. Nothing was so bad about me."

When we spoke in 1995, Marguerite was working full time at the Hungry Harvey, on three days, off for two, then on for three days again. She saw Tyler on her days off and on alternate weekends. She did not harp on her loss. She did not tear up when she mentioned Tyler, preferring to talk instead about how they remain very close. She is a soft-spoken woman, but flashes of bitterness occasionally punctuated her gentle conversation. "He's not raising our son," she said of her ex-husband. "His parents are raising our son."

Nonetheless, Marguerite did not plan to appeal. She could not afford to do so in any case, but she knew it would upset her son. "I promised him I wouldn't fuss any more," she said. "I think when he gets old enough he will come back." Tyler's voice remained on her answering machine.

*   *   *

When Mary Ann Holmes got married four days after her high school graduation, she had already mapped out her life's work: raising children and making a home for her husband. Eleven months after the wedding, her twin daughters were born. But when the marriage fell apart three years later, Mary Ann walked out of court with custody of her two-year-old daughters, a onetime $750 alimony payment, and $225 a month in child support. There was no house for her because she and her husband had been living with his grandfather.

"When I left, I had no place to go but my family," she said. "I was forced to move in [to her sister's] with the girls and look for a job."

For the first time in her life, Mary Ann had to work. There weren't many choices in Westville, the small rural Florida town where she lived, and she didn't have any special qualifications, either. So she found a job as a waitress at a Pizza Hut, working nights.

"Nights is when you make your tips," she said. "You don't make nothing on lunch buffets." Soon she was promoted to shift supervisor, first at Pizza Hut and later at Kentucky Fried Chicken. Her promotions allowed her to work days and every other weekend, except for one night shift a week, from 3 P.M. until 11 P.M. She remarried and had a son.

Even so, there wasn't much money for extras. Her daughters wanted to be cheerleaders, but she couldn't afford the $100 for each of them; she said their father did not offer to pay half. In 1992, she went to court to try to win an increase in the $225 monthly child support payment, which had not risen in seven years. She failed.

Meanwhile, the girls' father beguiled them with tales of the treats in store if they came to live with him and his new wife. She said he promised them dancing, karate, and band lessons and excursions to Disney World. In October 1993, eight years after their divorce, he went to court to ask for custody of the girls, charging that because Mary Ann had an irregular work schedule, she was "unable to spend quality time with the children, unable to establish an appropriate schedule and unable to permit the children to participate in school activities." By contrast, he told the court, he and his new wife worked more conventional hours, from 7:00 A.M. to 3:30 P.M.

"He had been telling the girls for a long time that he'd get custody of them," Mary Ann said, her voice rising at the memory. "He would tell them, 'We'll take you to Disney World,' he would give them the finer things that I couldn't give them. Two hundred twenty-five dollars child support for both of them for ten years—that's why he could give them the finer stuff. He was not paying no money. That's why I had to work odd hours."

Mary Ann had only about $200 to pay a lawyer to fight the custody challenge and more troubles at home. Soon after her first husband filed for custody, she filed for divorce and for an injunction to keep her husband out of their house.

In court, she was in for a shock: The judge gave custody of the girls to their father. The girls would be better off with him, the judge ruled, because the father's work schedule was more stable, while their mother had to work "odd hours and on weekends." He also mentioned the rural location of Mary Ann's town, which prevented the girls from participating in extracurricular activities, and the girls' testimony that they wanted to live with their father. The girls went off to their father and a life of karate, dancing, and band lessons. Mary Ann, shaken and furious, went to find a better lawyer.

Mary Ann's story had a more or less happy ending, although, as in all such cases, everyone suffered. Her sister decided to open a clothing business and hired Mary Ann to work from 9 A.M. to 5 P.M. at the store. Mary Ann is now off on weekends—"Every weekend," she said, singing out the words.

Her sister gave her money to hire a new lawyer, Timothy H. Wells, who argued her case before the Florida District Court of Appeals. The appeals court reversed the decision, writing that few other jobs would be available to Holmes in the rural area where she lived and that the girls testified that they wanted to live with their father primarily because he had more money. In stinging terms, the judge castigated her ex-husband for his meager child support payments: "Moreover, the evidence strongly suggests that, were the former husband paying a sum remotely approaching that which the child support guidelines reflect should be his child support obligation, it would not be necessary for the former wife to continue working irregular hours. It would be anomalous indeed to penalize the former wife because she is compelled to work such hours to support herself and the two girls."

Sadly, as in so many custody battles, the children remain victims. They lived with their father for about nine months, and when Mary Ann and I first spoke in 1995, they were back, but none too happy about it. She took them out of karate, band, and dancing lessons, partly because she could not afford to pay for them and partly because their grades had dropped and she told them they had to concentrate on their schoolwork.

"It has messed them up," Mary Ann said. "I took one of them to a psychiatrist because she's just hateful. She has no respect for me or any of my kinfolk. She keeps saying, 'I'm going to do this because I want to go back to my daddy, because he said if I aggravate you enough, you'll let me go back.'"

When Mary Ann and I talked again almost a year later, she had won an increase in her child support, to $455 a month. The conflict with her daughters continued. Their grades had dropped, and their father had filed another request for emergency custody. The judge refused, and the girls ended up in court for hitting their mother. The judge ordered their father to attend counseling with Mary Ann and the girls.

I WIN, YOU LOSE

For every case like Holmes's or Gollahon's that reveals a bias against working mothers, fathers' rights groups brandish their own examples of discrimination. The debate is littered with specious statistics, claims, and counterclaims. Women's legal advocates point to statistics assembled by gender-equity task forces documenting discrimination against mothers; fathers' rights groups condemn the task forces as feminist rigged and their statistics as phony. Fathers' rights groups point out that the majority of custody decisions favor women; women's groups counter that fathers often prevail when they challenge mothers for custody.

There is no way to prove beyond doubt who suffers more; no one keeps track of the custody disputes that reach trial courts throughout the country. The only cases that are systematically recorded are those that are appealed; counting them is misleading because they provide only part of the picture.

Some of the few clues available come from studies of trial and appellate court cases, as well as surveys of judges and attorneys, conducted in dozens of states by task forces set up to study gender bias. These studies suggest that traditional attitudes linger among many judges. And, in an irony that escapes the advocates of fathers' rights, those attitudes hurt both working mothers and fathers.

Judges' beliefs are crucial because in divorce courts, parents usually offer completely different versions of reality, dueling psychological experts vie for the parent paying their fee, and custody guidelines are imperfect at best. Judges are given tremendous discretion to decide which side to believe, which expert's opinion to endorse, and how to interpret custody guidelines. Lawyers and custody experts say that it is often judges' individual biases that decide who gets custody: how the judges were brought up, how they raised their children, and what their wives or husbands do.

A 1989 task force in Massachusetts found that half the judges who were surveyed agreed with the statement "Mothers should be home when their school-age children get home from school." Forty-six percent agreed that "A preschool child is likely to suffer if his/her mother works." In Connecticut, one-fifth of the judges who were surveyed said they did not believe that mothers who worked full time developed as warm relationships with their children as did those who stayed at home. One-third of the Vermont judges who were surveyed said that mothers were sometimes deprived of custody because they work.[4]

Judges in Connecticut, Massachusetts, Nevada, and New York State sometimes or often gave custody to the father if the mother was working and the stepmother was staying at home, task forces in those states reported. And in Georgia, Illinois, Louisiana, Maryland, Massachusetts, Minnesota, and Vermont, task forces found evidence of a double standard: Fathers who took any part in child rearing were rewarded, while mothers who did less than traditional mothers tended to do were penalized.[5]

These beliefs can sway custody decisions. Judges whose mothers greeted them at the door on their return from school may look askance at mothers who don't do the same thing. Judges who cut their hours to part time when their children were young may question the devotion of mothers who didn't make the same choice.

It was a judge's belief that a child was better off being taken care of by relatives than living with a mother who used day care that led him to deny custody to Jennifer Ireland, a Michigan student. Instead, he awarded custody to the child's father, whose parents would care for the child. That judge, like several others with such convictions, seemed to see working mothers as second-rate mothers and as interchangeable with other women. Since a working mother is not really *there,* she can easily be substituted for by a grandmother who is there—even if the father is not there, either. The Ireland decision was reversed on appeal.

Yet several experts who follow court cases involving working mothers, including Nancy Erickson, a former staff attorney for the Center on Women and Family Law; Lynn Hecht Schafran, director of the National Judicial Education Project of the NOW Legal Defense Fund; and Carol Bruch, of the University of California at Davis, have seen case after case in which working mothers lost custody to working fathers whose parents or new wives would be the ones at home caring for the children.

When the state task forces examined actual cases, they found that while most mothers win custody of their children, when fathers fight for custody, they have a good chance of winning. For example, of the fifty-five contested custody cases heard between 1983 and 1987 in Orange County, North Carolina, 62 percent of the fathers won custody and 22 percent shared custody; mothers won sole custody in 16 percent of the cases.[6]

In Middlesex County, Massachusetts, fathers filed for custody in fifty-seven of seven hundred cases between 1978 and 1984; two-thirds of the time, the fathers won primary physical custody (when the child lives most of the time with the parent). In 42 percent of those cases, the fathers won sole primary and legal custody; that is, they had the right to make all decisions, such as education or religious training, affecting the child. In 25 percent of the cases, they had joint legal custody; the child lived with them, but they had to consult with the mothers on such decisions.[7]

Jeff Atkinson, a custody expert and former chairman of the American Bar Association's custody committee, examined every custody case in the nation's appellate courts from 1982 to 1983; he found that fathers won custody 51 percent of the time and mothers, 49 percent.

As Atkinson and others point out, none of these statistics alone proves bias; fathers who fight for custody often have stronger cases to begin with, and such cases are more likely to end up in appeals courts. But what meager statistics exist, together with the surveys on attitudes and individual cases, suggest that mothers who do not fit the traditional mold are at a greater risk of losing custody.

The same judges who believe that the good mother stays at home, though, are also most likely to award the traditional mother custody over a father. Just as many judges—and many in society as a whole—believe that children suffer if their mothers work, many judges still harbor the belief that women are better suited to nurture children, particularly young children.

In a 1994 review of custody practice, Atkinson found seven southern states in which case law or statutes indicated some preference for mothers, either through tiebreakers that award custody to mothers if all other factors are equal or allowing judges to take into account a child's age or sex as a factor in deciding custody.[8]

The same state gender-equity task forces that saw patterns of bias against mothers found bias against fathers, too. In Colorado, Florida, Georgia, Illinois, Louisiana, Maryland, Minnesota, New York, Washington, D.C., Washington State, and Wisconsin, the task forces found vestiges of traditional attitudes favoring mothers. In several states, attorneys said they often dissuaded fathers from fighting for custody because they believed they would not win. In New York, attorneys told the panel that some judges were reluctant to allow fathers overnight visitation if children were very young; in Washington State, more than half the attorneys and judges believed that when other conditions were the same, fathers were less likely to win custody of young children.[9]

GUIDELINES: PAST AND PRESENT

The debate over who suffers more in the courts may be spurious at times, but it reflects the turmoil over how to decide custody now that courts have officially abandoned the presumptions that once automatically favored fathers or mothers. Custody cases are notoriously difficult. With traditional roles in flux, with the advent of the working mother and the involved father, judges are often forced to make Solomonic decisions, often between two loving parents, leaving heartache and bitterness in their wake. The truth is that children usually need both parents because each parent tends to compensate for the other's flaws and blind spots. Yet judges must choose one. For most of history, that person was invariably the father. Fathers, not mothers, were assumed to be better suited to educate and guide children. Then, during the Victorian cult of true womanhood, women were revered as natural mothers and regarded as the natural guardians of children, particularly during their "tender years." The tender-years doctrine ruled from the mid-nineteenth century until about 1970. In similar language to that used today to argue that women are biologically suited to nurture, a Florida court ruled in 1939 that "Nature has prepared a mother to bear and rear her young . . . and give them many attentions for which a father is not equipped."[10]

Now that judges are no longer supposed to cast either the mother or the father as the natural parent, they rely on custody guidelines outlined in legislative statutes and court precedents. Although these guidelines vary from state to state, they typically instruct judges to examine which parent does most of the day-to-day caring for the children, the amount of time each parent spends at home, the stability of the child care arrangements, parents' relative financial resources, how much help is available from relatives, and which parent is more cooperative in allowing children to see the other parent.

But all too often, these guidelines are treated as rigid rules, enforced without much attention to the psychological reality that may be the most important, but least quantifiable, criterion: the quality of the relationship between the parent and child.

Many experts believe that custody should go to the parent who has been most intimately involved with the child, the one a child runs to after skinning a knee. They use terms like the "psychological parent," defined as the person who meets the child's day-to-day needs for "physical care, nourishment, comfort, attention and stimulation," or the "primary caretaker," the one who actually takes charge of children's daily physical and emotional needs.[11]

Trials often feature dueling psychological experts, testifying in succession that the mother or the father is really the psychological parent. Judges often view these experts as hired guns, and lawyers for both mothers and fathers worry about the accuracy of evaluations that are frequently based on one or two sessions at a time when parents are under severe stress. Many judges and attorneys are deeply suspicious of psychological testimony that is, at heart, subjective and unverifiable according to standard rules of evidence.

The former chief justice of West Virginia's Supreme Court, Richard Neely, deliberately tried to design guidelines that would prevent the need for psychiatric testimony in a landmark 1981 case, *Garska v. McCoy*. He outlined ten tasks that would prove who was the primary caretaker, on the theory that the person who performs these chores is usually the person closest to the child. The list includes preparing and planning meals, bathing and dressing children, buying clothes, being responsible for medical care and trips to the doctor, arranging children's social lives after school, finding baby-sitting or day care, putting children to bed and attending them if they wake at night, disciplining, and teaching social and academic skills.[12]

These criteria are helpful, and many women's advocates

applaud the primary-caretaker standard because women are still the ones who usually take charge of most of these chores. Yet simply counting up tasks does not address the amorphous but decisive psychological issue: Who is the child's emotional center? For example, one 1992 case in West Virginia turned on canceled checks, as if who paid for groceries, clothes, and doctors' fees actually proved anything about the quality of the relationship between the parent and child.[13]

SHARON PROST AND THE HEARTLESS CAREER WOMAN

The fate of Sharon Prost, the counsel to Orrin Hatch who lost custody of her two sons, shows how difficult and arbitrary decisions about the primary caretaker can be and how judges' attitudes can play a crucial role. The judge's decision in Prost's case also shows how harsh the judgment can be on mothers that the society deems unnatural. Prost was unapologetically driven—a word that still types women as shrill, obsessive, and hard. In certain ways, indeed, she was more successful than her husband, who struggled with a nearly two-year spell of unemployment. In her losing fight for custody, her accomplishments were held against her—deducted from her quota of mother love, as if more of one automatically meant less of the other.

Prost was a woman on the fast track. Like many mothers with demanding jobs, she had to shoehorn her work and her family together. She got up at 5:30 A.M. with her youngest son and played with him and his older brother until she left for work at 8 A.M. Sometimes when she worked late, she would drive home to put the children to bed and then head back to the office.

Her former husband, Kenneth Greene, had once appeared to be on the same trajectory, working virtually seven days a week as a union official. At the time of their divorce, he had a less demanding job as an assistant executive director of the American Federation of Television and Radio Artists. It was easier for him to get home early. Like more and more fathers today, he took time to visit his son's kindergarten class. He liked to put his older son to bed. He cooked dinner more often.

Many witnesses, including her older son's kindergarten teacher and Joseph Noshpitz, the psychological expert who was chosen by both sides to do a custody evaluation, talked of Prost as an attentive, concerned mother who was deeply involved with her children, despite her admittedly demanding job.

Judge Harriett Taylor dismissed that testimony and issued a decision full of stinging lines about Prost's obsessiveness and devotion to her career above family. Prost, she said, had earned her graduate degrees at night school while working (though she did so before she married or had children). Prost had begun a new job soon after a serious accident. She had worked throughout her trying pregnancy and returned to work a week after her second son was born (although Prost said she worked to finish up one case and then did not return to work regularly for some time). In her opinion, the judge wrote as if Prost deliberately chose her career over motherhood, rather than tried to break the mold and do both at the same time: "Her career choice of demanding jobs that require her to work late nights and many weekends necessarily cuts into the time available for her family. Plaintiff's involvement in the children's lives takes place *around* her long work day and, even then, her devotion to her job and/or her personal pursuits often takes precedence over her family."

It was as if Prost's undeniable ambition simply disqualified her as maternal; there is no acknowledgment in the opinion that Prost could bring this same level of intensity and commitment to motherhood.

Noshpitz, the psychiatrist, who testified in court that Prost should be awarded custody, wrote after he read the judge's opinion that what she saw as plain to any objective observer was not plain to him. "The care, nurturance and rearing of her children are among mother's most vital goals, and emerged for me as at least on a par with if not well in advance of any other goals in her life," he wrote in a letter to Prost's lawyer. "In this, it seems to me, she is not different from many women who are at once ambitious activists doing the world's work and caring and devoted parents who love their families intensely."

In contrast, Judge Taylor was unfailingly generous to Prost's ex-husband Greene. She believed his version of events, not Prost's. She concluded that from the time that Prost took her job with Hatch, Greene "has been the more nurturing parent of the children, assuming the greater portion of the parental obligations and handling the daily details necessary to provide for the children's physical and emotional well-being and development. Moreover, because family is of prime importance to defendant, he has been very involved in the children's activities and has made them a priority in his life."

Certainly, Greene appeared to be an involved and caring father, but Taylor extended no such credit to Prost. She praised Greene for attending a parent interview, going on a class field trip, reading the children in the class occasional stories, and giving some presentations to the class. She did not cite the same kindergarten teacher's testimony that Prost dropped off her son at kindergarten three or four times a week and was so involved that she was a "surrogate room mom."

Judge Taylor gave credit to Greene for eating dinner with the children, but none to Prost for rising early to play with them before she went to work. What others saw as Prost's devotion for driving home to say good night to her children and then returning to work, the judge condemned as workaholism.

At least one conclusion the judge made was based on a clear error: She noted that she found it "quite telling" that Prost testified that she got home by 5 P.M. on days when the Senate was in recess, which she assumed to mean holidays ("Plaintiff's work took priority over virtually all else—even on holidays"). In fact, the Senate is not in session about half the year.

To point out the double standards that permeate the language of the opinion is not to say that the judge necessarily made the wrong decision about custody. The judge's opinion is unusually long for a custody case, copiously documented, and closely argued. Her thoroughness impressed many custody experts I consulted and evidently convinced an appeals court, which dismissed Prost's complaints of gender bias and rejected her appeal in January 1995.[14]

The judge believed that Prost would be more likely to limit Greene's access to the children than if he had custody, an accepted criterion for deciding custody cases in many states. It is possible that the judge preferred what she saw as Greene's mellower, more relaxed style of parenting. There was a credible case that Greene's more flexible job would allow him to be home earlier and physically present more often.[15]

The judge also cited some undeniably damning evidence against Prost (though, as in all divorce cases, these were highly partisan accounts from witnesses testifying for Greene): incidents of arguably rigid discipline, such as throwing out a toy if a child failed to put it away; a witness's account of Prost working throughout her son's fourth birthday party; and the au pair's account of Prost at home, eating "dinner alone and very late at night—often, while sitting on the kitchen floor, with her plate on the floor, talking on the telephone or writing while she was eating."

Whatever the merits of the custody decision, however, what stands out in the opinion is the harshness of the language. The judge's many acid comments lashed Prost for trying the juggling act of countless other working mothers. Other mothers don't have the bad luck to have their marriages collapse and their mothering subjected to such withering public scrutiny.

MARCIA CLARK AND THE MORALITY PLAY

That, too, was the misfortune to befall Marcia Clark, whose individual custody battle was transformed into something far larger: a nationwide morality play on working mothers and children. It was Clark's case that brought the full glare of the spotlight onto working mothers' tribulations in the courts.

Clark filed for divorce from her husband of fourteen years on June 9, 1994, three days before Nicole Brown Simpson and Ronald Goldman were killed. In December, she filed for an increase in child support, arguing that the long hours and intense publicity of the trial had forced her to spend more money on baby-sitters, personal grooming, and new clothes (five new suits for $1,500). She told the court she had been working six- or seven-day weeks for sixteen hours a day. As a result, she needed baby-sitters to pick up her children from school, spend time with them at night, and cover for her on weekends when she worked.

Gordon Clark's court papers show a man devastated and bitter at his wife's insistence on a divorce. Gordon accused Marcia of infidelity, deceit, and neglect of their children. He said that his former wife worked an intense schedule at least half the year, whenever she was in a trial. "While I commend petitioner's brilliance, her legal ability and her tremendous competence as an attorney, I do not want our children to continue to suffer because she is never home, and never has any time to spend with them." Gordon charged that Marcia saw her two sons, then three and five years old, at most one hour a day.

The Clarks' custody battle, like everything else even remotely connected with the O. J. Simpson case, drew wide coverage that helped chart the national confusion and anguish over the issue. Much of the coverage strove to be sympathetic. Articles featured accounts of working women's struggle to balance career and family, with stories of successful lawyers and their children. Many commentators pointed out the bad-faith timing of the episode: Gordon Clark didn't file for custody until Marcia Clark asked him for more child support, and he did so in the middle of the most extraordinary, most demanding case of her career.

The case raised troubling questions, too. Many women could not justify an argument that Marcia Clark should be the primary caretaker of her children when she had to work, by her own admission, six- to seven-day weeks, sixteen hours a day, and Gordon Clark, a computer engineer, arrived home every night by 6:15 P.M.

More telling, though, was the criticism she received for failing to trim her sails to accommodate her children—criticism virtually never made of men. Clark had tried a supervisory job with better hours and the same pay, but she didn't like it. Her ambition smacked to many of hubris. "We can't always be great all the time at all the things we have to do," chided Judy Markey, a columnist for the *Chicago Sun-Time*s. Other commentators noted the double standard, pointing out that Johnnie Cochran not only spent little time with his children, but was being sued during the trial for unpaid child support for a child he had fathered with his mistress.

The same theme ran through much of the coverage: You can't have it all. That was the tidy moral message of most of the pieces, and it came in the "kicker," the last quote of the story, one often chosen to leave an impression on the reader or sum up an article. The kicker in the *Washington Post* story was Rita Bank, a Washington divorce lawyer, who told the reporter that she had worked full time throughout her children's lives and that they had turned out fine. Then, in a reflexive mea culpa, she contradicted the value of her experience and said, "But maybe we can't have it all. Maybe there are some irreconcilable problems with working long hours."[16]

A BETTER STANDARD?

That's the conventional wisdom of our day—and to some extent at least, it is true. The cases of Clark and Prost touch on a universal dilemma for working mothers and fathers. Few would want fathers who worked all the time to get custody, either. Eleanor B. Alter, a prominent divorce lawyer in New York, said that she counsels mothers and fathers to cut back their hours if they want to win custody because judges must choose between two alternatives, and the parent who works fewer hours often looks like the better choice. "Often it's one investment banker against the other," Alter said. "It's not just that women cut back on their careers. I've told men to cut back, too. Maybe his wife is awful, but she's at home."

Even those who believe most passionately that working mothers face bias in the courts say they do not deny the importance of time, but they believe that mothers with demanding careers or who work odd hours are often judged more harshly than fathers. "I don't think it should come across as the women's movement saying that women should get to have ninety-hour-a-week careers and their children regardless of what's going on with their children," said Nancy D. Polikoff, a law professor at American University who was one of the first to call attention to the tribulations of mothers in the courts. "Judge mothers and fathers by the same standard. That requires an in-depth look at what is really going on in the parenting of the children. If the baby-sitter takes the kid to the shoe store, it shouldn't count against the mother if she's the one who noticed they needed new shoes."

By fixating on whether mothers or fathers lose more custody cases, we fail to recognize that when judges hold traditional views, that means mothers and fathers both lose. The public wrangling distracts us from the more important question of how to hammer out more subtle, sensitive, and just ways to decide who gets custody of children.

The guidelines judges rely on to help them decide where to place children can be arbitrary and incomplete measures of the tie between parent and children. Often, the legal process ends up reducing intangible qualities like emotional bonds to standard sets of rules and precedents. Lawyers and witnesses tot up each breakfast prepared and each dinner missed, compare how often Mommy took the child to the doctor with the times Daddy visited kindergarten. Judges are too often reduced to travesties like counting hours of daylight that mothers are there—a standard that any parent knows does not reveal much about the crucial emotional exchange between parent and child, about whether those hours together prove to be an ordeal or a delight.

That emotional exchange is the real criterion for judging a child's relationship to a parent—whether a working mother, a mother at home, or a father.

In the case of Sharon Prost, a court-appointed psychiatrist testified that he believed that Prost's children saw her as the primary caretaker and as their emotional center, regardless of her grueling work schedule. It is interesting that a psychiatrist could make such a judgment about a woman who worked so long and hard. Children know when a mother is dedicated to them.

Describing Prost and women like her, the psychiatrist wrote,

"One of the basic leitmotifs that echoes through their lives is a deep love for and commitment to their children. I feel that this was so with Ms. Prost, and what is more to the point, I feel that the children experienced it that way as well."

That is the crucial point overlooked in this and countless other custody battles, as well as the nanny trial and the broader debate over working mothers it reflected. How do children experience their mothers? What internal picture have they painted of her? A mother can be around all the time and her children can experience her as intrusive, destructive, oppressive, or completely disengaged. Children can experience a mother as devoted and attentive even when she is not physically present.

In custody cases, the problem is how to weigh such subtleties using case law that emphasizes concrete, measurable actions. Many judges are suspicious of psychological testimony and understandably skeptical of experts for hire.

Polikoff shares the concern of judges who dislike dueling experts, but she also believes that there may be other ways to broaden the custody guidelines to try to gain a more sensitive assessment of which parent is more intimately connected to a child. "I do think there is something about being tuned in to the child's needs that is not encompassed by the [West Virginia] test," she said. "I think it would be possible to develop a series of questions that would get to quite a bit of it. What size shoe does the kid wear? Who is the best friend? What does the child need to go to sleep at night? If the child is in high school and able to pick electives for classes, what electives is the child choosing? The kind of things that you would think somebody would talk about if they were talking to the child. At different ages, different questions would be appropriate."

Such measures are still imperfect because they could easily degenerate into a quiz of discrete bits of knowledge about a child, rather than a measure of parental connection or sensitivity. Indeed, no set of criteria can entirely decide custody cases; no guidelines can substitute for good judges' perceptiveness about character and credibility. Because most cases come down to gut feelings in the end, it is particularly crucial that judges not be swayed by old biases about the good mother.

The nanny trial showed that these biases continue to resonate inside and outside of the courtroom, contaminating the way we judge mothers and provoking ugly attacks. The viciousness of the resulting debate prevents a more sophisticated, more probing public exploration of what parents owe their children and how they can best meet their needs.

Courting the Soccer Mom, Hounding the Other Moms

In 1996, mothers finally seemed to have arrived in politics. Mothers, we were told, would determine the course of the election—and their needs would finally emerge from the policy netherworld.

Politicians courted the elusive soccer mom. In pursuit of women, consultants pushed stoic Bob Dole to proclaim his pain and showed Bill Clinton how to gussy up his policy tidbits on V-chips and school uniforms as substitutes for more expensive measures. Republicans showcased Susan Molinari, a Newt Gingrich acolyte who is now a television talk show host, parading her newborn baby before the cameras to prove her bona fides as a compassionate working mother for the masses.

What a contrast to 1992, when an entire campaign seemed to proclaim the public's ambivalence about working mothers. That summer at the Republican convention in Houston, a parade of true believers extolled traditional motherhood. Marilyn Quayle cast herself as the good witch to Hillary Clinton's bad witch, as an accomplished woman who had happily subordinated her ambition for the sake of her children and husband. Struggling to find and please the public pulse, Hillary Clinton lurched from a proud embrace of working motherhood to a hasty retreat as a cookie baker.

Yet in many ways, 1996 was a hollow victory. Politicians may have begged for mothers' votes, but in so doing, they pandered and condescended to them without enacting policies that would really help them. Pollsters spun theories about how to win over women, each more insulting than the last. The gender gap conferred political respectability on popular culture's embrace of the differences between men and women. Our political discourse has not traveled far from Marilyn Quayle's taunt in Houston that liberals were "disappointed that most women do not wish to be liberated from their essential natures as women."

That theme has resonated throughout political debates like the vibrating tines of a tuning fork. The notes were first struck by the religious right, who claimed a biblical rationale for keeping women at home. The melody has been taken up, if rearranged, in more surprising quarters—by conservative and mainstream academics who call for a new emphasis on family that harkens back to traditional divisions of labor between mothers and fathers and among feminists who celebrate women's "maternal thinking."

This obsession with biology as destiny has produced a public discourse that sentimentalizes motherhood and narrows women's acceptable choices. Contemporary echoes abound of the Victorian cult of domesticity, along with the Victorian stigmatizing of women who are classed as unnatural mothers, whether they are working, unmarried, or on welfare.

It is tempting to dismiss the remarks of the political right—and even of some in the center—as mere ravings from peripheral groups. Competing messages permeate our culture and have mainstream support. Neither Bill Clinton nor Bob Dole tried to relegate women to the home. Hillary Clinton remains a polarizing figure, but few dispute how well she has brought up her daughter.

Yet there are reasons to worry, in the realm of both public debate and policy. The conviction that mothers belong at home and that working mothers are imperiling civil society by producing damaged children infuses much of the conservative intelligentsia at a time when conservative ideas are helping to shape the public agenda. Clinton won reelection only after swinging sharply to the right and recasting some of the family values issues. Many mainstream academics who identify themselves as centrist Democrats and are close to the Clinton administration share the conservative unease with the influx of mothers into the workforce. Many of these assumptions about the natural and unnatural spheres of women have begun to shape policy, from tax law to welfare reform.

THE NATURAL MOTHER: THE RELIGIOUS RIGHT

The standard-bearers of natural motherhood are the newly prominent and influential forces of the religious right, who share the belief that the family is the last redoubt in a society under siege from the forces of secular humanism. They argue that the family can be preserved only when men and women cleave to the traditional roles that God and nature assigned them, with mothers at home personally overseeing their children's moral development.

Leading the charge are James C. Dobson Jr. and Gary L. Bauer, who were little known outside their devoted flocks until the 1996 campaign. Dobson, a former associate professor of pediatrics at the University of Southern California School of Medicine, is a psychologist with a genial, folksy air who hosts a daily thirty-minute radio program that is the second most widely syndicated in the United States, after Paul Harvey's. He dispenses his blend of child-rearing advice, religious evangelism, and exhortations to conservative political activism to millions of families through his best-selling books and videos, more than a dozen magazines, radio shows, and appearances on cable television. More than 200,000 families make pilgrimages each year to the Colorado Springs headquarters of the group Dobson heads, Focus on the Family.

Bauer has emerged as a ubiquitous commentator and conservative power broker. Much of his power derives from his association with Dobson, who originally recruited him to run Focus on the Family's Washington office. Now the Family Research Council Bauer leads is a separate, if like-minded, think tank, with Dobson on its board. Other "pro-family" warriors include Beverly LaHaye, of Concerned Women for America; Phyllis Schlafly, of Eagle

Forum; and Allan Carlson, the head of the Rockford Institute, a conservative think tank based in Rockford, Illinois.

Dobson and Bauer, in particular, have increasing political clout and know how to use it in ways that skirt close to the line they are not supposed to cross as heads of tax-exempt organizations. Although they are careful not to endorse anyone explicitly, they make no secret of their hatred of Clinton and Democratic policies and were crucial players in the 1996 presidential race. Republican candidates in the primary courted them. Dole asked Bauer's help with his widely reported attack on Hollywood's family values.

Policies championed by the religious right found their way into the campaign. Dole proposed family tax cuts using language virtually identical to Dobson's and Bauer's, arguing that they could help women afford to stay home. Bauer and other religious conservatives won the fight to keep the antiabortion plank in the Republican Party platform, despite moves by Dole to soften it.

Although there is much about the religious right that repels me, I think they have been correct in seizing on most politicians' failure to understand the depth of Americans' concern about the violence, sex, and amorality that seem to permeate American culture. I believe we could even share some common ground, particularly in efforts to appeal for a more civil, less violent, and less sexualized popular culture and more flexible work policies that would allow mothers more time with their families.

Yet religious conservatives' absolutism on what makes the right kind of family leaves no room for many Americans, working mothers among them. The religious right cast themselves as the defenders of stay-at-home motherhood in the face of indifference from mainstream politicians, hostility from a liberal press, and what they see as a radical feminist conspiracy to blur the differences between men and women. If biology does not dictate women's destinies, if men can bring up children as well as can women, then there is less of a rationale for women to stay at home, and that puts the family at risk.

Dobson gave his readers a guided tour of the horrors of this conspiracy in discussing the United Nations Fourth World Conference on Women, held in Beijing in September 1995. Calling the conference "Satan's trump card," Dobson recoiled at the thought that society, rather than biology, creates expectations about what being male or female means. If so, he wrote in an August 1995 mailing, then radicals can "dissolve the traditional roles of mothers and fathers" and then "all household responsibilities will be divided 50/50 by government decree." This state of affairs violates God's decree as expressed in Genesis 1:27 ("So God created man in his own image; in the image of God he created him; male and female he created them").

Religious-right groups share a visceral horror of androgyny. In its newsletter, the Rockford Institute warned that deviating from the natural spheres of men and women would create pathological androgynous children: "Psychological tests confirm what Hitchcock told us through Norman Bates: low masculinity and high femininity scores are common among male psychopaths." A companion article about the United Nations conference was entitled "Valkyries Ride Again."[1]

This message plays well to many women who were offended by what Marilyn Quayle rightly perceived in Houston as the Achilles' heel of the feminist movement: the perception that by embracing opportunities for women outside the home, feminism puts down the choice to stay at home.

Since Dobson and other religious-right leaders believe that most mothers yearn to be at home anyway, they concentrate their energy on helping mothers get there. For those mothers who believe they cannot afford to stay home, Focus on the Family's March 1996 magazine offered its version of voluntary simplicity, an article on "Women Leaving the Workplace," a book full of practical tips to help mothers trim their budgets.

"While many in the Christian community sanction the concept that mothers *should* be at home, we haven't done a very good job of teaching young families how to accomplish that without destroying their finances—and sometimes their marriages," wrote the book's author, Larry Burkett. Although his advice about financial planning may help many women who want to be at home, the premise that all women should be at home poisons the atmosphere for those women who have found work rewarding.

Cheryl Moorefield, the Winston-Salem nurse, is one such woman. She belongs to Focus on the Family, one of many members in two-earner families. Cheryl faithfully attends church and has enrolled her children in church youth groups to help arm them against temptation. She asks her children to watch the videos Focus on the Family produces specifically for teenagers that stress traditional values, abstinence, and moral precepts. Cheryl loves her work and is proud of her accomplishments. "I was raised to be a housewife," she said. "But that's just not what I am. Everyone has gifts and talents. We need to find ways we can use them."

Her confidence is sometimes shaken, though, when listening to Focus broadcasts. The day we spoke, on a Sunday after church, she had just heard Burkett on the radio and wondered if she shouldn't have tried harder to stay at home. "I do kind of feel guilty a little bit listening," she said.

Because there are many Cheryl Moorefields among their members, both Dobson and Bauer are careful to add disclaimers to their writings stating that they are not trying to dictate to anyone and that the decision to work outside the home is one that can be made only by women and their husbands. Dobson, however, makes no secret of his views. "I'm going to venture boldly into this arena and say what I believe with all my heart," he wrote in one advice column. "A mother's care is the preferred choice. I don't say that to make anyone feel guilty; it's just a fact."[3]

A mother who put her children in day care centers risks having her daughters taught to become unnatural women. Dobson wrote his flock about a letter he received from a day care worker named Kendall, who doesn't approve of working mothers—a common attitude among day care workers, many researchers have found. "Our little girls are growing up playing office, banker and travel agent while they take their baby dolls to a day care center or sitter," Kendall wrote.[4]

The center is a veritable androgynist hell: "These little girls don't play house," Kendall told Dobson. "They never cook a meal; they microwave everything. I never see them nurturing their dolls. They just put them in a crib and have their friends take care of them. These little girls all want to be like boys. They're very competitive, but they're not at all nurturing."

The stay-at-home mother has not just made the preferred choice in the eyes of religious conservatives; she has made the right, the moral, choice. Her reward is the kind of unapologetic sentimentality lavished on the Victorian mother.

Mothers and fathers are at last heeding "the whimpers of precious little children," Bauer wrote in *Our Journey Home,* his call for a return to bedrock values.[5] In the conclusion to this book, Bauer pulled out all the stops in a perhaps unconscious echo of Victorian literature, with its stock characters of sick or dead children. He described his despair when his daughter fell seriously ill and how he helped feed her with a dropper until she recovered. Armed with these evocative images of parental devotion, he summed up the kind of family he sees as the "cornerstone" of American life: "Being a good father, a sacrificing mother, a dedicated son, a loyal daughter."[6]

MAINSTREAM CONSERVATIVES

This faith in natural motherhood is not confined to the religious right. What makes these themes so powerful is precisely how widely they are accepted and how many ideologically disparate groups propound them.

Many conservative groups often sound little different from the religious right on the topic of feminism and working motherhood. They are just more likely to invoke pseudo–social science than biblical certainty, and their views are even more dangerous because they lack the taint of extremism and religious zealotry. Irving Kristol, an intellectual lodestar of neoconservatism, has made common cause for several years with some of the religious right's agenda. In a March 6, 1996, article in the *Wall Street Journal,* he discussed the biological roots of differences between men and women and suggested that more and more women are discovering that "raising children is more important to them, and more gratifying, than coping with disagreeable colleagues and clients."

The pages of *Commentary,* the neoconservative magazine published by the American Jewish Committee, are filled with tirades against working mothers, attacks on feminism, and defenses of traditional sex roles. "For women, the shift away from the primacy of the homemaker's role was as radical a shift as there could be, and it set the stage for all the feminist radicalism that was to follow," wrote Carol Iannone in a June 1995 article charging that feminism's real goal was "to make the full-time homemaker role seem fit only for subhumans and to force women into 'careers.' "[7]

The idea that motherhood is women's real calling is also championed by the Independent Women's Forum, a group of professional women. From its beginnings as an informal organization of conservative women who supported Clarence Thomas's Supreme Court nomination in 1991, the Independent Women's Forum has emerged as a highly visible, politically well-connected counterpoint to feminism. Its members include Lynne Cheney, the former chief of the National Endowment for the Humanities, and Laura Ingraham, a former law clerk for Thomas who appeared on the cover of the *New York Times* magazine as a member of the new conservative elite and emerged after the birth of her child as an advocate for the new traditionalist mother.

Danielle Crittendon, who edits the group's publication, seems to be making a career out of proclaiming herself a proud mother at home. In one article admonishing feminists who press for equal pay, she argued that women's pay is lower than men's because women voluntarily take themselves off a career track when they become mothers. This "is an issue to take up with nature, not Congress," she wrote. Even mothers with good child care are "collapsing under the mental strain of walking out the door every morning (a strain, by the way, which their husbands, thanks to *their* genetic wiring, blissfully do not suffer)."[8]

What keeps mothers from heeding the call of nature? A frenzied materialism that pushes mothers to take jobs to afford VCRs, fancy sneakers, and trips to Disney World for their children, if we are to believe the conservative editorialists of *Commentary* and the *Wall Street Journal* or even articles in the mainstream *U.S. News & World Report*. These writers have clearly not spent any time talking to real people. There is no mother in the country who is working solely to afford Nikes or fancy vacations. The median income of an American worker is $28,300 a year—an amount that does not go far anymore.[9] The scarcity of jobs paying decent wages, the need for health insurance, the ability to afford a house in a good school district to equip children to thrive in an increasingly education- and technology-driven world, the cost of computers or private lessons to help children achieve, and the need to save for college—these are the real reasons that most mothers and fathers are working.

An article in *U.S. News & World Report* in the spring of 1997 branded the idea that most women are working because they must one of the "lies parents tell themselves about why they work." The defense of financial need applies only to women in low-paying jobs, the authors wrote, not to middle- or upper-middle-class women. Housing and college costs have risen, but not enough to account for the massive flood of mothers into the workforce, the authors argued. Many families today could survive on one income, but that would entail considerable financial sacrifice. To cite just one example, it may be true that most students attend public colleges, but many of the upper-middle-class families that *U.S. News & World Report* lambastes in the article want to be able to send their children to more expensive private universities.[10]

Some women, indeed, have a secret vice—they find work rewarding or enjoy the independence their own income provides them. Such reasons are socially unacceptable, though, which may be one reason that some relatively privileged women try to hide behind the rationale of economic need. These women are pilloried because they dare to believe that women, as much as men, have a right to power and autonomy.

NEW FAMILISTS

On the state of the American family, conservatives find some measure of common ground with another group of scholars and policy analysts who are trying to forge a new social consensus about parents' responsibilities to their children. This group believes that families are foundering, in part, because parents are too busy working to tend their children. Like conservatives, they blame cultural attitudes, not economic forces, for this decline.

These scholars range widely in their political affiliations and have not declared themselves part of any formal group, though they generally subscribe to a set of ideals the writer Barbara Dafoe Whitehead dubbed "new familism." They include William Galston, a former domestic policy adviser to Clinton; Jean Bethke Elshtain, a professor at the University of Chicago Divinity School; David Popenoe, a Rutgers University sociologist; David Blankenhorn, president of the Institute for American Values, a New York think tank; Sylvia Ann Hewlett, the economist and author; and Whitehead, who wrote "Dan Quayle Was Right," an influential 1993 article in the *Atlantic* bemoaning the rise of single-parent families.

Several of these new familists are also members of the communitarian movement founded by Amitai Etzioni, a sociologist at Georgetown University. The movement is not a conventional political party, but an attempt to forge a new public political philosophy, one that pushes Americans toward an acknowledgment of responsibilities and away from a preoccupation with individual rights. Communitarians issue position papers and policy recommendations, much like the Heritage Foundation. Clinton has also echoed communitarian values in several of his State of the Union speeches and in the way he framed his proposals on welfare reform as demanding responsibility from the beneficiaries of governmental largesse.

New familists may be loosely organized, but they have already helped recast the framework of public debate on family issues. While they differ on specific policies, they believe the answer to family decay is to impose new social norms in place of what they see as a destructive refusal to make moral judgments on individual behavior.

Popenoe's solutions are the most extreme. In an essay, Popenoe outlined a new cultural norm: Women should stay at home full time for three years with each child and then work only part time through their children's early teenage years. He gave a small nod to fair play: After a child is three, the father could work part time and the mother full time."

What justifies this blithe condemnation of women to second-class career status? Women are natural parents, and men aren't. Based on the scientific finding that men tend to be better at spatial relations, Popenoe's conclusion was worthy of the Victorian medical quacks who declared that if women pursued higher education, their uteruses would wither. "While male superiority rests with 'things and theorems,' female superiority rests with personal relationships," he wrote.

Popenoe added the spurious reasoning of sociobiology: To maximize his genetic survival, the male needs to inseminate widely; his natural promiscuity makes him an unnatural parent. By contrast, females' best chance of genetic survival is nurturing the children they bear. The hormonal changes of childbirth and breast-feeding predispose women to love their children. Even though Popenoe admitted that the attachment theory research is not conclusive, he stated without qualification that mother-reared children are superior. Popenoe's ideas are merely the warmed-over conclusions of Talcott Parsons, the sociologist whose thesis that men were "instrumentalist" and women "expressive" helped define the 1950s cult of domesticity.

Few of the other new familists would go that far. Many believe that dictating one course for women is unnecessary; most women will want to stay home because of their natural ties to children. Whitehead argued that particularly among the baby-boom generation, especially the trend-setting privileged tier who can afford to make such choices, more parents are breaking with the narcissism of the past and are pulling back from careers to have more time with their families. Anecdotes abound of such cases, though there is little demographic evidence to confirm them.

Whitehead quoted a newspaper account of an attorney who left a full-time job for less demanding but engrossing legal work for the poor while her husband left his partnership in a law firm for a judgeship offering him more flexible hours. "The woman makes the larger concession," Whitehead wrote, "but it is one she actively elects and clearly sees as temporary."¹²

Most new familists try to phrase policy proposals in gender-neutral language, suggesting that their concerns apply to mothers and fathers. They deflect charges of sexism by saying that both parents should give up something in their work lives when they choose to have children. Galston has lived by his principles; he resigned his White House job in 1995 to spend more time with his son.

In practice, though, the person who makes a sacrifice is the woman. It is true that more women than men seem drawn to leave or cut back on their jobs to spend more time with their children. Yet that choice has an important element of coercion in it, a coercion fueled by social scientists who simplistically assert that it is better for children to have a parent at home or, at the least, one parent who drastically reduces her work hours. It is a choice shaped by policy decisions and corporate structures that make it difficult to balance work and family. It is a choice reinforced by economic inequalities that make it easier to forgo the mother's salary than the father's. That's not much of a choice.

The new familists raise important questions about responsibility, the dire straits of many American families, and the need to weigh the consequences of individual rights on society as a whole. Yet much of the communitarians' emphasis on moral character and personal responsibility, admirable as it is, leads them to downplay broader social and economic injustices. I find their vision of motherhood too narrow, too swayed by biological determinism. In pitting mothers' needs against children's needs, they fail to imagine new ways to accommodate both.

THE NATURAL MOTHER: FEMINISTS

Many feminists have been just as guilty as the religious right, conservatives, or some new familists of assigning women special status as caregivers and relationship-tenders.[13] A torrent of feminist writings celebrates women's differences, rooted in women's ability to bear and rear children. These writings claim that women are more caring, more empathic, more pacifist, more intuitive.

Ecofeminists praise women as natural environmentalists,

equipped by nature to walk more gently on this earth. In such books as Riane Eisler's *The Chalice and the Blade* or Merlin Stone's *When God Was a Woman,* feminist historians have described ancient matriarchal societies, such as Crete, in which women were worshipped as goddesses, their contributions in gathering food were valued just as much as men's in hunting food, and their values of peace and relationships ruled. Sara Ruddick, in *Maternal Thinking,* suggests that women's experience of child rearing makes them more patient, more attentive to emotions, and more peace loving because women are naturally more protective of the children they raised. Carol Gilligan's *In a Different Voice* has become a cultural phenomenon; many women have recognized themselves in Gilligan's descriptions of women emphasizing compassion and relationships in their attempts to solve moral dilemmas, in contrast to men's reliance on abstract principles of justice. Gilligan contrasted Abraham, ready to sacrifice his son Isaac to prove his faith, with the mother who stood before Solomon, ready to deny that she was the mother and give up her child to another to spare his life.

As Carol Tavris pointed out in *The Mismeasure of Woman,* many of the much-vaunted differences between men and women are exaggerated or do not hold up under scientific examination. While Gilligan made an important contribution to psychology by exposing the bias that declared an ethic of caring to be an inferior level of moral reasoning, several reviews of all existing studies have rebutted her thesis that men and women reason differently. The studies found no average differences between men's and women's style of moral reasoning. They also found that men and women use both care-based reasoning and justice-based reasoning.

Although matriarchal civilizations certainly existed, respected feminist historians, such as Bonnie Anderson and Judith Zinsser, have disputed as speculation the idea that women's values shaped these societies. Women, who are touted as pacifists, have actually supported war just as vociferously as men, Elshtain has shown.

Moreover, in most studies that have found differences between men and women, Tavris noted, more men and women are alike than different; a picture of the statistical results shows a huge area in which the scores of most men and women fall in the same range and a small band in which they diverge. The male edge in mathematics and spatial relations, and the female superiority in verbal abilities, which Popenoe cited as evidence that women should be doing the caring and men the earning, are actually small differences and are narrowing. A review of more than 100 studies that assessed the mathematics ability of nearly 4 million students found small differences; men were ahead only in highest-level mathematics. Similarly, a review of 165 studies of verbal ability of 1.4 million people found no gender differences in verbal skills.

Nor are women innately more capable of caring or empathy than men. One study showed that men who brought up children or cared for sick relatives were just as attuned, sympathetic, and reassuring as women; in several reviews of psychological studies, men demonstrated as much empathy as women. Men also showed just as much desire to be attached to someone as women; in fact, several studies have found that married men and women enjoy better psychological and physical health than unmarried ones.[14]

Why, then, does virtually everyone, from across the ideological spectrum, harp on differences between men and women? Largely because most people intuitively believe in such differences; the differences fit their experiences. Of course, some differences between men and women are real. The biological experience of pregnancy and childbirth often leads women to feel a greater attachment to infants, and more women take on the nurturing role. Men and women frequently communicate in different ways, using different styles. Women are often more aware of others' emotions.

Tavris suggested that most differences stem not from biology, but from the gap between men and women in power and status. Women, who are often less powerful, often need to persuade, rather than dictate and to read other people's reactions and adjust to them. These styles are also typical of working-class people talking to their employers, prisoners talking to guards, and African Americans talking to whites, Tavris pointed out. Tavris cited studies that showed that women who adopt such a deferential style are more influential. In a famous study, Eleanor Maccoby found that girls were not more passive when they played with each other, only when they played with boys.[15]

A belief in sex differences not only feels right, but it justifies maintaining these imbalances of power. The result is the conviction that a life in which women tend children and men earn money is not only inevitable but also fair.

THE NATURAL MOTHER: THE GENDER GAP

These lessons about women's power and status were lost amid the swarm of stereotypes offered to explain one of the great forces of the 1996 election: the gender gap. During much of the campaign, more than 20 percentage points divided men's and women's choices; in the final vote, men and women were split by 11 points. Women, far more than men, liked Bill Clinton and disliked Dole and the Republican Congress.

Casting about for an explanation, pollsters alighted on the Mars-and-Venus gambit. Women are nicer than men, and Newt Gingrich just did not project nice. Mothers like big government more because mothers are more compassionate; they worry about the less fortunate who may suffer if politicians shred the safety net. Women seek protection from the government as a kind of surrogate husband. Women do not like conflict, so they were disgusted when the government ground to a halt during the budget standoff of 1995.[16]

At times it seemed as though politicians and pollsters could not spout the stereotypes fast enough. "Women tend to be more people-oriented," Governor Christine Todd Whitman of New Jersey said, explaining why Republicans had to recast their issues in people terms.[17] "Women want to hear that you as a candidate care about things that affect others and not just yourself," said Kellyanne Fitzpatrick, a Republican pollster.[18]

The scramble to woo women was often as hilarious as it was insulting. Polls showed that far more women than men were repulsed by Gingrich and the policies of the Contract With America: the House Republicans held a briefing entitled "Communicating with Women" in which pollsters taught Republicans how to "show the public more of their soul."[19]

The biggest political prize, the most sought-after woman, was the married suburban mother. Pollsters dubbed her the "soccer mom," who, just as a good mother should, defined her entire world in relation to her children. Playing right into the idea that mothers naturally abandon any other ambition, Kellyanne Fitzpatrick told the *New York Times:* "Soccer moms of the 1990s were the 'super-moms' of the 1980s. Many of them have kicked off their high heels and replaced them with Keds to watch their kids. If you are a soccer mom, the world according to you is seen through the needs of your children."[20]

Many women told pollsters and reporters that having children had changed the way they saw politics—change that may account for women's disproportionate concern with funding for education, for example. Yet many of the comforting truisms pollsters advanced to explain women's voting patterns missed the most obvious and compelling explanation: self-interest, not a maternal ethic of compassion for others.

Women, far more than men, believe they need government because they have a greater need for its benefits. They tend to care for elderly parents, so attempts to rein in Medicare and Medicaid spending frightened them. Women lead more economically precarious lives than men. According to statistics released during Clinton's presidential campaign, women account for 60 percent of Medicaid and 57 percent of Medicare beneficiaries; 60 percent of those benefiting from the increase in the minimum wage (which Republicans opposed) are women, and almost half the households who gained from Clinton's increases in the Earned Income Tax credit are headed by women.[21]

The 1996 campaign showed that far more than ever before, the worries of working mothers are reaching the major parties. Dole's and Clinton's political advisers all spoke of the need to target mothers who are struggling to balance the needs of work and family. The mainstream political debate about the working mother is as complicated as the competing cultural messages that swirl around her. Dole said his tax cut was aimed at the mother who works, and he defended that mother's right to choose her lot. Yet he also promoted the cut as allowing a mother to stay at home. Clinton's advisers believed that calling for school uniforms, more educational programming, and a V-chip to screen out television content appealed to working mothers who are worried about cultural influences on children because they are not at home to supervise their children during the day. The advisers made sure he told voters about the law he signed allowing parents to take leaves to care for children or aging relatives.

Working mothers may have gained public respect and a measure of political power absent from other campaigns in 1996. At the same time, the public discussion of the gender gap revealed an undercurrent of longing for the old-style natural mother and a broad endorsement of differences between men and women that is used in some quarters to argue that mothers belong at home.

THE UNNATURAL MOTHER:
HILLARY RODHAM CLINTON

Surely there is no better mirror of the passions that swirl around women's departure from their appointed spheres than the public furor that Hillary Rodham Clinton evokes. Denunciations of Hillary Clinton surpass even the savage caricatures of Nancy Reagan or the political storms over the influence of Rosalynn Carter.

It would be easy, but inaccurate, to paint her only as a maligned woman. Her public statements about commodities trading, the White House travel office, and the Whitewater affair have exposed her to questions about her veracity. Long before any of these scandals broke into full public view, though, Hillary Clinton came under sustained and extraordinarily personal attack.

Talk show hosts labeled her a lesbian and femiNazi. David Brock quoted White House guards complaining that she forced them to buy her "feminine napkins." She was mocked for dropping and adding Rodham from her name, for changing hairstyles, and for trying to channel Eleanor Roosevelt. She was vilified for attempting to redesign the post of First Lady for a wife who wanted to be more than a helpmeet. And she waded right into the divide between working and at-home mothers with her infamous remark about staying home and baking cookies.

Like many women today, though, Hillary Clinton was making up the rules as she went along. She reflects the vast changes and deep uncertainties that have swept through women's lives. By all accounts a brilliant and ambitious student, she relinquished a separate career when she fell in love with a more ambitious and skillful politician. Like many professional women of her generation, she kept her name when she married, but that decision alienated Arkansas voters, so she was forced to take her husband's name. In Arkansas, she was able to use her talents by taking on educational reform, but in Washington, her attempt to refashion health care spelled political disaster.

Hillary Clinton tried to reinvent herself by falling back on her credentials as a mother and children's rights advocate. Her best-selling book, *It Takes a Village,* portrayed her as a family-values mother, disapproving of both premarital sex and divorce while evoking the tightly bound communities of the past that monitored children. At the 1996 Democratic convention, the transformation to First Mother was complete; with her daughter, Chelsea, beaming down at her, she recited a list of her husband's accomplishments, all filtered through the prism of their devotion to their daughter.

Hillary Clinton has been so analyzed that she can be made to stand for virtually anything. In a psychosexual biographical sketch in the *New Republic,* Camille Paglia embarked on a frenzied search for symbols. She noted that Hillary Clinton has told how she was kissed against her will as a little girl and washed her face again and again, which, according to Paglia, shows how she resents male intrusion. Hillary remembers Bill talking about watermelons in Arkansas when she first met him; the watermelons signify the sexuality she cannot permit herself, Paglia charged.

"Hillary is pulled between the poles of cordial, yielding Gennifer Flowers and grim, lantern-jawed Susan Thomases,"

Paglia wrote. "One is the watermelon of lush, slippery fleshiness; the other is a stonily sealed, skull-like coconut . . . harsh, ungiving, withholding the milk of human kindness."[22] At the least, the passion evoked by Hillary Clinton indicates how profoundly uncomfortable our society remains with a First Lady who does not act the way traditional wives and mothers do.

THE BAD MOTHER: THE WELFARE MOTHER

If working mothers are unnatural for failing to stay home with their children, welfare mothers who stay home with their children instead of working are immoral. The welfare reform movement of the past few years has revealed a hypocrisy and class bias that debase our public discourse. All the crocodile tears shed over the rights of children to a mother at home are largely tears saved for the middle class.

We can extol the virtues of working motherhood when we talk about poor women, even as we bemoan the costs to society of forcing working-class or middle-class mothers to work. John Ensign, a Nevada Republican, said on the floor of the House of Representatives: "I grew up with a single mom. There were three of us at home. My father provided no child support when I was young. And I watched my mom get up every day and go to work. That is what we need in this country: to have children watching their parents go to work on a daily basis."[23] That's character building for poor children and soul destroying for middle-class children.

To be fair, from my own interviews with welfare recipients, I have come to believe that we must make welfare transitional. I am open to imposing limits on the number of years anyone can receive welfare and requiring mothers on welfare to work if ample money is provided for high-quality child care.

Politicians have made this case, though, by attacking welfare mothers' character and morality. Just like the Victorian condemnation of the undeserving poor, the modern-day demonizing of the welfare mother allows most Americans, who live in a segregated world that insulates them from even speaking to a poor mother, to see her as alien and to accept harsh cuts that were politically inconceivable not long ago. "The Party's Over," read the headline in the *New York Post,* describing a New York State plan to cut benefits to welfare recipients.[24]

Even members of Congress and the majority leader of the House of Representatives—who generally know better than to attack working mothers directly—feel free to describe welfare mothers as subhuman. During the debate on welfare reform in the House in March 1995, John L. Mica, a Florida Republican, held up a sign reading, "Don't Feed the Alligators." In his remarks, he elaborated: "We post these warnings because unnatural feeding and artificial care create dependency. When dependency sets in, these otherwise able alligators can no longer survive on their own."

A Wyoming Republican, Barbara Cubin, thought a better comparison was to wolves. "The Federal Government introduced wolves into the State of Wyoming and they put them in pens, and they brought elk and venison to them every day," she said. "This is what I call the wolf welfare program. The Federal Government provided everything that the wolves need for their existence. But guess what? They opened the gates and let the wolves out, and now the wolves won't go. Just like any animal in the species, any mammal, when you take away their freedom and their dignity and their ability, they can't provide for themselves."[25]

Wolves is an apt metaphor, for wolves are what will lurk at the door of these women and wolves are what we are consigning their children to. Yet there is no need to worry about their fate, because these are not mothers and children like us. Just ask Gingrich. Why did three killers murder Debra Evans, a Chicago mother on welfare, and cut her unborn child from her womb in 1995? "What's gone wrong is a welfare system which subsidizes people for doing nothing," he said. "We end up with the final culmination of a drug-addicted underclass with no sense of humanity, no sense of civilization and no sense of rules of life in which human beings respect each other."[26]

Even Gingrich didn't go as far as the editorial writers of the *Wall Street Journal,* who lumped Debra Evans together with

Awilda Lopez, who tortured her six-year-old daughter Elisa Izquierdo to death, and preached that welfare was to blame. "Consider the behavior of Debra Evans and Awilda Lopez," the editorial of November 29, 1995, scolded. They had children out of wedlock by different men, and their children were supported by welfare. Therefore, every welfare mother is so morally debased that she is capable of torturing her child to death.

As for Evans, the *Wall Street Journal* editorial never acknowledged that she was the victim. Just how representative of the "underclass" was her murder, apparently because her killers wanted a child? Didn't that killing get all the publicity just because it was so unusually gruesome? That's just as obscene as saying that the Menendez brothers' murder of their parents is symptomatic of a breakdown in values among Republican millionaires. A well-documented and sordid spate of murders among the wealthy didn't prompt Gingrich or the *Wall Street Journal* to condemn an amoral culture of capitalism that values money above integrity, which is just as much a caricature of capitalism as is their portrayal of welfare mothers.

Alongside the portraits of welfare degenerates place one of Dorothy Carmona, a twenty-eight-year-old who went on welfare, reluctantly, after her husband abandoned her when she was pregnant with their second child. About a year later, her husband was killed during a visit to the Dominican Republic, in what Dorothy suspects was a drug-related execution. As someone who had worked since she was fourteen, Dorothy hated welfare and sank into a depression. "What does a depressed person do? They lounge around, with no energy to do anything. I don't want to plop my child in front of the TV and let the TV be the parent. That's never been me."

Within a year, Dorothy found a job working in a nonprofit agency. When her mother died, she also took in the two foster children her mother had been tending. That swelled her family to two three-year-olds, a two-year-old, and a one-month-old infant. From Dorothy's living room in a Brooklyn housing project, she could hear gunshots and watch drug sales in the courtyard. Although she was too frightened to allow her children out to play, the scene fueled her resolve to work. Dorothy was up at 5:45 A.M. each weekday, dressing the children, feeding them breakfast, and dressing herself before work. At night she cooked dinner, bathed them, and put them to bed and started all over again.

I first met Dorothy in spring 1994 while researching an article on what happens to children when mothers move from welfare to work. I had been impressed by her zest and her commitment to her children. "Let me take time for these kids, individually, to make them feel special," she said. "I tell them, 'I have to work so you can get a better education.' I know my neighbor is selling drugs. If you don't want them around you, you have to work harder. At least you know you're achieving something. Your self-esteem goes up. You can set goals."

When we last spoke in spring 1996, Dorothy had switched jobs to a better-paying one as a payroll bookkeeper with Catholic Charities. A grandmother had claimed the infant she had taken in, but Dorothy had adopted the child's older sister. Dorothy was supporting her family on about $22,000 a year and was considering going to night school to get a college degree she knew would allow her to earn even more money.

She loved her work, which offered her health insurance and low-cost child care. After several weeks when she stayed late to help a new supervisor, she noticed that one of her daughters was unhappy and told her supervisor she needed to return to regular hours. When the stresses of single motherhood loomed, Dorothy sought solace from her church, which runs a children's program two nights a week. "I get to worship God upstairs by myself and soak it in. When I come home I'm released."

You won't find me—or Dorothy, for that matter—defending teenage motherhood, pretending that raising children alone without enough money to support them is the right choice, or denying that welfare as we know it has sent the wrong signals about responsibility and initiative. Nor would I claim that every welfare mother is as devoted to her children as Dorothy is. I have seen enough cases of child abuse and neglect to know that the combination of poverty, depression, the lack of models for good parenting, and the stresses of child rearing can be lethal and that children are the real victims.

Yet welfare mothers are reviled if they show the very maternal instincts they are so often criticized as lacking.

Listen to Gail Abney, a Brooklyn mother of three who, when I interviewed her in spring 1994, was off welfare and working as an administrative aide in a police station: "A child's most important year is the first year. You build a bond with that child. To force a mom to go back to work, it's kind of hard. A child at three months old is not sure who the parent is. Let me be there for the baby's first smile, first tooth."

That's what we tell mothers they are supposed to feel. Abney is just one example of how the propaganda about attachment has misfired. She's been convinced by the very arguments aimed at working-class and middle-class mothers.

The dozens of welfare caseworkers and welfare families I have interviewed over the years have convinced me that few women get stuck on welfare for one reason—and that the public debate about welfare ignores just how many different kinds of welfare recipients there are. Some women lost jobs, got divorced and did not receive child support, needed medical care, or grew up in neighborhoods and families where almost no one they knew had ever worked.

Usually there are emotional problems, too; the men in their lives abused or abandoned them, or they are suffering from depression. A recent study found that 42 percent of welfare mothers studied showed symptoms of clinical depression, twice the proportion of the general population.[27]

One Ohio teenager I met, Cassandra Clark, was so busy caring for two young daughters, a fourteen-year-old brother neglected by their mother, a young cousin whose mother died, and a jealous boyfriend just out of jail that she hardly blinked when her welfare checks were docked for a full year after she dropped out of school.

For several of the women I spoke with, it seemed as though their reluctance to leave their infants—and their problems finding child care they trusted—delayed their search for jobs. Sadly, some welfare mothers are living under the delusion that they're owed time with their children even though our society doesn't extend that privilege to working-poor or working-class women.

Theresa Covington, who had worked for years in New York City in the retail trade, got laid off and then got pregnant, and stayed at home with her child for two years. At the time, she was living with her husband; they later separated. Now Theresa is working again, supporting her five-year-old daughter by herself, earning about $25,000 a year as a merchandise assistant in the garment district, buying trims, buttons, and other accessories.

Theresa applied for welfare when her unemployment insurance and her savings ran out because she did not want to return to work when her daughter was too young. "I wanted to spend the first two years at home," she told me. "That's the way I was raised. My mother didn't work until we were in school."

Many of the working-class women I interviewed wanted that option, too—and many were enraged that they, who wanted to stay home with their children but couldn't afford to, were paying taxes that helped support welfare mothers. "My children suffer because of all these people that choose to stay on welfare forever," Jan Flint told me the first time I met her, over breakfast as she came off the night shift from the Welch's plant in Michigan. "I'm working my kids' life away to pay my bills. I want to see that change."

Yet Flint and Covington share the same devotion to their children and the same fears about how children will fare when mothers work. Our policies are failing them both. If working mothers get only three months' unpaid leave after childbirth, it's hard to justify giving more to welfare mothers; one obvious answer is a more generous paid family leave.

We can admit that welfare has helped breed in some women a mistaken sense of entitlement without treating welfare mothers as a lower life-form, immune from the same pain as other mothers and the same concern about their children. There is ample evidence that many mothers on welfare feel demeaned.

A vivid sense of humiliation still clouds Frances Jean, a Brooklyn mother, from her welfare days. Almost as soon as we started to talk, Jean hastened to assure me that she was no longer on welfare. It was a technical distinction; in winter 1995, her family was living on disability payments because her husband was in the hospital.

During our conversation, she spoke quietly, with an almost regal sense of composure. Yet her self-assured words, it was clear, hid a shaky sense of self. In one breath, she talked of continuing her education, and in the other of her pride in being a "full-time mother" who was teaching her children "all the things they should know." At times, she seemed to be trying to convince herself that she would get her degree and get a good job. At times, she seemed to be trying to convince a world she knew belittled her and her capabilities.

"I feel welfare should be there temporarily until you can get off your feet because society will put a mark on you," she said. "They don't know your ability. They *assume*."

WELFARE REFORM

The way we sentimentalize good stay-at-home mothers and demonize unnatural ones who work or go on welfare paves the way for policies that hurt both groups. The religious right's horror of illegitimacy and its demand for family tax cuts so mothers can stay at home made them powerful allies of the Gingrich budget-cutters. Indeed, the religious right, along with influential conservative thinkers such as Charles Murray, was a prime mover in the fight to impose a Victorian chasm between the deserving and the undeserving poor.

In the space of only a year, these groups helped reframe the debate on welfare reform. In 1994, when some members of Congress borrowed an idea from Murray and introduced a law banning federal welfare payments to unwed mothers, the proposal was dismissed as extreme and had no chance of passage. Just a year later, after the Republican victory in the Congressional midterm elections and a vigorous campaign joined by the religious right, such a law passed the House of Representatives. It failed to pass the Senate.

The welfare debate, though, had been permanently transformed, and the Republicans were setting the agenda. Clinton contributed to that changing public mood with his pledge in 1992 to "end welfare as we know it." He proposed setting limits on the number of years any family could receive welfare, but the bill he backed in 1994 would also have spent $10 billion to create jobs for those who could not find any in the private sector and pay for child care.

By 1996, facing a reelection campaign and leery of being mocked for breaking his promise, Clinton agreed to sign a bill drafted by Republicans that many of his own advisers and Cabinet members denounced as harsh and punitive. The bill marked a historic break from past decades of welfare policy. It ended the sixty-one-year-old guarantee of welfare payments, barred families from receiving welfare for more than five years, and required most adults to work after two years on welfare.

FAMILY TAX RELIEF

With the money saved from cutting benefits to bad welfare mothers, conservative groups argued politicians should give money instead to good mothers who want to assume their rightful place at home. James Dobson made the case well, in his homespun way. "Huge numbers of wives and mothers are forced into the workplace because of the wasteful policies of the tax-and-spend liberals in Congress and the White House," he wrote in his August 1994 newsletter.

In 1949, his mother could stay at home with her children, even though his father earned very little as a professor in a small Christian college. The reason? Just 4.5 percent of his father's paycheck was deducted for taxes. These days, Dobson wrote, an average family pays 37.6 percent of its income for taxes, an average payment of $10,060, which exceeds the annual cost of the average home mortgage. He urged his readers to call the congressional switchboard to ask for family tax relief.

The religious right has shaped the tenor of the debate on tax cuts. Now Republican leaders such as John Kasich, who heads the House budget committee, are linking tax cuts to family values and working mothers to cultural decline, proclaiming, "The single biggest problem we have in the country today [is that] you've got to have two people working, and this has had the most profound impact on our culture."[28]

The religious right has rallied around a per-child tax credit as the first step to reform the tax code to reward marriage, encourage large families, and help mothers stay home. Dobson and Bauer campaigned vigorously for the credit, and Bob Dole backed it in his presidential campaign in terms very similar to the rationale Dobson used. Bill Clinton has also included a $500 per child tax credit in several budget proposals.

Republicans and religious right leaders are also backing several other proposals giving tax breaks to one-breadwinner families and creating a "homemaker IRA," which would allow mothers at home to put aside money for retirement in Individual Retirement Accounts. These tax credits hold great political appeal, and religious conservatives raise the legitimate question of whether the tax structure discriminates against mothers at home. Tax breaks, however, cost money—the child tax credit alone is estimated to cost the Treasury billions of dollars—so they require cuts elsewhere.

Religious-right leaders have a prime candidate for cuts: benefits that help working mothers. Bauer and Beverly LaHaye of Concerned Women for America have campaigned to abolish federal tax deductions for child care expenses and a program that allows parents to allot up to $5,000 of their pretax income to pay for child care expenses. They argue that these measures, which are crucial for working mothers, penalize families who sacrifice income to keep mothers at home or split work shifts so that one of the parents always cares for the children.[29]

In fact, the religious right has opposed some proposals to ease the conflict between work and family, essentially on the grounds that in their world there wouldn't be one: Mothers would stay at home. They oppose corporate benefits for day care because they say that such benefits allocate corporate money for plans that traditional families with mothers at home would not use. Instead they back higher wages and fewer corporate benefits, so that employees can spend money directly on the benefits they want.

Bauer even opposed the Family and Medical Leave Act, which requires companies with more than fifty employees to offer twelve weeks of unpaid leave after the birth of a child or to care for a sick family member. His reasoning: The bill's "primary purpose was to strengthen a new mother's attachment not to her baby but to her career."[30] Clinton eventually signed that bill into law.

COMMON GROUND

For all that divides the players in a public debate gone awry, there is some important common ground. Nearly everyone, including the religious right, feminists, communitarians, new familists, child care researchers, and baby care experts like Leach and Brazelton, agrees that work should be reshaped to ease the burden on American families. All these groups want to see more part-time work available, preferably with benefits and without lasting career penalties. All would like to see more home-based work; more flexible work hours, particularly hours built around a child's school day; and more telecommuting. William Mattox, of the Family Research Council, offers the example of his own father, who put off his ambition to be a lawyer until after his children were grown, as evidence that men, too, can sequence their careers.

Although feminists may back flextime as a way of getting women into the workforce, Mattox said, "There are those of us who believe that mom and dad collectively are spending too much time at the central workplace. So flextime and home-based work now become a way station on the route not to full time employment, but to a more sane and balanced life."

That so many different and often hostile groups all champion a single set of ideas is a rare, welcome sign of hope amid the acrimony surrounding working and child rearing. With skill and strategic alliances, these combined forces may be able to mount enough public pressure to see more of these ideas realized on a broader scale, even as some corporations have already adopted some of them.

The debate on family leave, however, offers a sobering example of a tendency in our public policy debate to seize on universal solutions. While a paid family leave after the birth or adoption of a child should be a right, experts who try to justify such a policy overstate the risk for babies when mothers work. Rather than say, as they might, that much infant care in this country is of poor quality and that good infant care is so expensive it might make more sense to allow parents time off, they declare that parents who do not stay home are putting their babies at risk.

In calling for a year's family leave, for example, the communitarian policy paper on working and child rearing stated flatly: "The best place for infants is at home, where they can bond with their parents."[31] Etzioni, in his book *The Spirit of Community,* goes even further: "No one can form the minimal bonding a newborn child requires in twelve weeks, a woefully brief period of time."

That undercurrent of coercion, as well as the blatant misstatement of the social science research, has no place in the debate. Even when policies are framed neutrally and do not single out mothers, a policy premised on the belief that infants should be at home may shame women into staying at home with them. Mothers will then pay the resulting price—lower pay in their jobs, possible lifetime second-class status in their professions, and a loss of the power that comes with advancement.

In several international studies, the United States has ranked among the bottom of industrialized nations in how well our children fare. A shameful 10 percent of this country's children live in extreme poverty, in families whose incomes are half the official poverty line. Jeremiads about working mothers and welfare mothers, about nature and biology, divert us from the real question: How can parents and society better care for children?

PART FOUR

MOTHERHOOD IN
THE TWENTY-FIRST CENTURY

Fathers and "Other Mothers"

I have a recurring image of the early weeks of my daughter's life. I am sitting in our living room, clutching a bathrobe around me, gazing at my husband and baby out of dark-ringed, puffy eyes. My husband holds our daughter in the crook of his arm; her head rests in his palm and her feet just graze his elbow. He stares down at her, his face glowing with the radiance that is supposed to be the exclusive province of new mothers. She starts to cry. Unruffled, he shifts her so her tiny head peeks up above his shoulder and walks her up and down. Her face is an uncanny replica of his.

I remember feeling torn between joy and envy. My husband seemed to have all the confidence I lacked. I spent many of those first weeks wondering what I was doing wrong and sure the answer was everything, but he claimed her as if she had always been with us. He seemed born to be a father.

My husband, I am told and I believe, is a rarity, that new man who is not supposed to exist. He is just as likely—often, more likely—to notice we are running out of diapers or that the children need new shoes. At night, he, just as much as I, will steal into their rooms to listen to them breathing, to close a window, or to cover them with an extra blanket.

Yet we are not interchangeable, and we are not parents to them in the same way. Often, I am the stereotypical mother, more patient, better at soothing and comforting. He is the stereotypical father, the one who rolls around with them on the floor and helps them build a spaceship. He is often the enforcer, the one who will slam his hand down on the table and say enough while I am still, futilely, trying reason.

Sometimes he is the stereotypical mother and I am the stereotypical father. It is harder on him if they cry when we leave; I am better able to assure him it will soon be all right. If someone hurts their feelings, he is quicker to swell with protective anger, while I tend to look for the other person's side of the story.

We slip nicely into some gender roles; we turn others inside out. We have different styles with our children, yet we divide responsibilities fairly equally. Neither one of us is the sole keeper of the list of what to do; we improvise together. My husband's willingness to be a partner has given me precious freedom professionally. By knowing that our children will be content with him, by knowing there is nothing he will overlook, I can work harder and longer. Although I may feel my children are thriving with him, that doesn't make me comfortable routinely coming home late. I want my time with them, too.

I don't think my marriage is the only template for happiness, even if it is the only way I can be happy. But we live in a prescriptive age. Just as polemicists from all sides are telling mothers what to do, so, too, we have rules for fathers. There is a chorus from the left: Good fathers are new fathers, but most fathers are bad fathers; they must split domestic chores equally, must nurture as well as provide, must learn how to relieve beleaguered women from their second shift. There is a chorus from the right: The old father is a good father; rather than harangue fathers to change diapers, we should honor those increasingly rare men who fulfill their responsibility as breadwinners and stop fighting the reality that men are biologically wired to compete, women to nurture.

Our public discussion of fathers, like that about mothers, is mired in confusion and all-but-terminal polarization. To pit androgyny against tradition is a false dichotomy; most mothers and fathers do not live that way. Most fathers are not new fathers, but neither are they old fathers. Most mothers still do far more at home than fathers do, but fathers do more than their fathers did. Although more involved fathers would spare mothers considerable pain, career sacrifice, and resentment, reflexive father bashing also muddies the debate.

THE TRADITIONALIST SALVO

A wave of political and cultural concern is sweeping the country about fathers—or more precisely, fatherlessness. There's no man in the house, the commentators proclaim, and children are out committing crimes, failing school, getting pregnant, doing drugs. Without a man, families are poorer, and more children are growing up in poverty. Irresponsible boys are getting girls pregnant and then failing to support them, swelling the welfare rolls.

There is a growing public policy consensus about the answer to these problems, endorsed by many psychologists, religious-right leaders, and some academics. Dust off the unfairly reviled old father and the traditional division of labor he represented. Bring back the good old days when men were men and women were women and each knew his or her place.

Just as in policy debates about mothers, public discussion about fathers is obsessed with natural differences between men and women and horror-stricken at androgyny. Although the champions of the old fatherhood do not speak with one voice, many share an unease about some elements of feminism and a call for men to reclaim their responsibilities as fathers. Promise Keepers, an evangelical phenomenon, draws tens of thousands of men to its football-stadium revival meetings to pray and weep and pledge to be better fathers, husbands, and Christians. It was founded in 1990 by Bill McCartney, the football coach at the University of Colorado who is famous for leading his team in prayer and condemning homosexuality. It has become the fastest-growing revival movement of this century. Its first rally in 1991 drew 4,200 people; the group says it had drawn 2.6 million men to rallies by 1997, culminating in an

October 1997 meeting attended by hundreds of thousands of men in Washington, D.C. Promise Keepers' explosive growth shows men's yearning for its message of faith and responsive masculinity, and, perhaps, the group's implicit embrace of more traditional family roles.

Promise Keepers has won notoriety because some of its literature and speakers seem to be calling for a return to the traditional family of the 1950s and a biblical ideal of wifely submission. Tony Evans, a pastor who often speaks at the meetings, is quoted in the group's publication, *Seven Promises of a Promise Keeper,* instructing husbands how to reclaim their manhood:

The first thing you do is sit down with your wife and say something like this: "Honey, I've made a terrible mistake. I've given you my role. I gave up leading this family, and I forced you to take my place. Now I must reclaim that role." Don't misunderstand what I'm saying here. I'm not suggesting that you ASK for your role back, I'm urging you to TAKE IT BACK. . . . Be sensitive. Listen. Treat the lady gently and lovingly. But LEAD![1]

Leaders of Promise Keepers say they are talking not about authoritarianism but an effort to lead by example in dedication and servanthood to Christ. Scholars and journalists who have studied Promise Keepers caution against caricaturing the group as unregenerate Neanderthals. They have reported a mix of male bonding, men's grief for their own or their fathers' failures as fathers, and an unusual emphasis on fighting racism. Many of the men in Promise Keepers have working wives, who generally tell journalists that their husbands have become more considerate and more engaged with their children. And yet many of the wives also say that their husbands are the final authority in their homes because that is the biblical way. One wife told *U.S. News & World Report* that she would not watch a television show if her husband forbade it (the husband beat her until he joined Promise Keepers); another called herself the chief operating officer to her husband's chief executive officer.[2]

The movement is still emerging, and it is not yet clear which face will win out: wifely submission or fatherly responsibility. *New Man* magazine, published by Promise Keepers, runs articles similar to those in Focus on the Family materials offering budget tips so that mothers can stay at home. Some writers offer different views in the same article; in one, the author refers to a wife as "your most valuable player," implying that she is not the coach, and as "your equal."[3]

A secular, less conservative variant of the Promise Keepers' themes has a far firmer hold on mainstream policy debate. Two recent books mounted a spirited attack on the "new father" ideal that has been the darling of feminist and academic circles: *Fatherless America*, by David Blankenhorn, and *Life Without Father,* by David Popenoe. The authors condemn a cultural message, conveyed to the public by experts, college textbooks, popular magazines, and parents' advice books, that the only truly good father is a father who equally shares child rearing.[4]

Blankenhorn described what he sees as a moral crusade among cultural elites to change American fathers—to make them more sensitive, less remote, and equally willing to get up in the middle of the night with a child. These are the fathers who win the accolades in the parenting magazines; they and the rare father who takes paternity leave are the ones featured on television for Father's Day.

Blankenhorn defends men who define the essence of fatherhood as providing for their families. "They say, 'I love my wife and children; therefore I bust my butt to make a lot of money and make it possible for my wife to specialize in the nurturing area'—and here the chorus of boos rises," he said. "I think that is good. I want to shake their hands and tell them they're being good fathers."

Men's failure to take their responsibilities as providers seriously is one reason why American society is in so much trouble today, Blankenhorn and Popenoe argue. Blankenhorn is trying to spur a grassroots commitment to fatherhood among both affluent and poor families through an organization called the National Fatherhood Initiative. Blankenhorn and celebrity members of the initiative, such as the former football player Don Eberly, traveled across the country asking fathers to sign a "fatherhood pledge" that they will provide for their children, teach them right from wrong, spend time with them, respect children's mothers, and put their families first.

Blankenhorn, Popenoe, and like-minded thinkers are not explicitly trying to restore traditional roles; their primary aim is to combat fatherlessness, discourage divorce and unwed motherhood, and reawaken fathers' sense of responsibility. Their argument has important implications as well for domestic life and how mothers and fathers share tasks at home. They believe the new father ideal has helped to spread fatherlessness because it blurs essential distinctions between men and women. Fathers are irreplaceable, they argue, because they are different from mothers. "A father is not an assistant mother," Blankenhorn said. "There is something specifically male about the father role."

Blankenhorn's and Popenoe's vision of the father's contribution relies on a laundry list of stock male and female stereotypes. Consider these excerpts from the literature of the National Fatherhood Initiative, which are nearly identical to the attributes Popenoe listed in his book:

"At times of crisis or stress, the traditionally male values—especially the ability to contain emotions and be decisive—are invaluable."

"Father encourages risk taking. Mother encourages caution."

"When a child has difficulty at school, a family car is wrecked, or a dispute with a creditor arises, it is often the father who confronts the issue."

Popenoe goes even further, noting that children of involved fathers often display superior intellectual skills that are probably related to "the unique mental and behavioral qualities of men; the male sense of play, reasoning, challenge and problem solving, and the traditional male association with achievement and occupational advancement."[5] If Popenoe had his way and most mothers stayed home with their young children, mothers would indeed lack an association with achievement and occupational advancement.

In welcome contrast to the religious right and to some of Popenoe's writings, Blankenhorn has stated repeatedly, and I think sincerely, that he is not trying to dictate that men should go out to work and women should stay at home. He and other new familists, along with many conservatives, believe that this is what most men and women want, and what they are naturally suited to do. They argue—and that argument has tremendous resonance for many men and women today—that women are naturally drawn toward children and men are naturally drawn toward the outside world of competition. They charge that feminism has ignored and insulted both these impulses, which are rooted in biological and cultural differences that have served most societies well for centuries. "As a general rule, as a very gross generalization, I think that men, if you look at the deep wiring, both social and to some degree biological, have certain propensities that lead them in the direction of male conflict and competition," Blankenhorn said.

It is tempting and all too easy to come up with examples that disprove every one of the stereotypes these writers claim is universal. The conclusion that men are innately drawn to competition, for example, is based, in part, on research conducted on elite, professional men; studies show that most men believe their family lives are more important than their jobs. In fact, a major new study, sponsored by the National Institute of Mental Health, showed that problems with children were more likely than trouble at work to take a toll on men's health.[6]

Blankenhorn and Popenoe are in the company of a large and growing group of experts who argue that not only do mothers and fathers experience being parents in profoundly different ways, but that children need them to do so. These experts point to studies showing that mothers and fathers typically relate differently to babies; mothers tend to be soothing and fathers tend to be robust and playful. In T. Berry Brazelton's studies, babies as young as six to eight weeks respond differently when a mother or father enters the room; a baby's heart rate, for example, shoots up when he sees his father because he already expects excitement.

These different styles, a number of eminent psychologists have argued, stem from the distinct psychological experiences of men and women and the distinct roles that fathers and mothers play for their children. Penelope Leach, who has a Ph.D. in psychology, suggests in her book *Children First* that children begin life in dependence on their mothers and learn from their fathers about autonomy. The mother represents the familiar and domestic; the father, the essential guide to the outside world. This holds true even if the mother works, Leach says, as long as the mother is the primary caregiver. Along with many psychoanalytic thinkers, Leach believes that mothers at birth become psychologically merged with their babies in a way that fathers do not. Fathers' role after birth is to protect mothers from the demands of the outside world and give them space and time to luxuriate in their new identities.[7]

Daniel Stern, the eminent psychiatrist, described this profound shift in a mother's psychological life as the "motherhood constellation." Once a woman becomes a mother, he said, her perspective shifts forever. She is now and always will be responsible for that child. She marks time by the child's milestones, not the regular calendar. She becomes more interested in women, particularly her own mother or other experienced mothers, and less in the world of men because men cannot help her learn how to be a mother. Fathers are on the psychological periphery.[8]

While Leach says that fathers' different roles by no means disqualify them from taking an equal share in babies' care, Stern and several academics challenge that premise. Fathers can be more involved than in the past, but except for the rare fathers who become primary caregivers for babies, mothers will be in charge and will feel primary responsibility. The new father is an unrealistic standard that has sown strife between men and women, they say. Mothers feel disappointed and betrayed by what seems to be the fathers' less intense experience of the babies, and fathers feel excluded, often bewildered, and resentful.

Stern, for one, has no idea—and no apparent interest in exploring any idea—of how to draw a father into this constellation. During an extended dialogue with Brazelton at a 1996 conference at Teachers College in New York City, Stern could hardly mask his impatience and contempt as Brazelton repeatedly asked him where fathers fit into his theories. "The father represents a problem here," Stern replied. "This business of sharing is partly fictive."

Brazelton, who has championed the ideal of a more involved father in his books, television shows, and research, politely pressed him again a few moments later. Stern said fathers can share more tasks, but most cannot do what mothers do—the more intimate kind of care that amounts to what he called "psychological holding," a notion derived from the psychoanalyst Donald Winnicott that means providing a child with a sense of safety and reliability that facilitates development.

"I'm saying we're putting too much on the father," Stern said. "A father can't do that kind of psychological holding. I'm not saying a father doesn't have a significant role as a support system. But we're asking something that's not realistic." In essence, as so often occurs in classic psychological theory, Stern's focus remains entirely on the mother. He offers a highly sophisticated, finely observed apology for the status quo. Blankenhorn makes a similar argument, in more down-to-earth terms: "It strikes me that what really makes a man feel like he's being a good man is going to lead him when the baby's born to get panic-stricken over the issue of insurance. Why do men do that? Why do women seem to become completely absorbed in caring for this new infant and wanting to remake the world in order to have the immediate needs met of this wonderful thing? You can say, that's terrible and men need to be rewired so they think the same way. Or maybe God wants it this way."

Blankenhorn and the psychological experts make some important points. It would be foolish to deny that most women and most men experience the arrival of babies differently, that they often play differently with children, and even that their styles as parents often fall into stereotypical divides.

Indeed, many mothers and fathers will recognize themselves in Stern's description. It is certainly true that most mothers—but not most fathers—are obsessed with their new babies and that almost everything else pales for them. For many women, motherhood and pregnancy are times of psychic reckoning, when they examine their childhoods and feel a new alliance with their mothers. And although I share the dream of a more just division of labor between mothers and fathers, I agree that much of the old discussion about it underestimated the power of women's pull toward motherhood—one that prompts many women to profound reassessments of their goals and others to establish a visceral territoriality that may keep the fathers playing a secondary role.

The debate goes awry when differences between men and women are confused with the ability to share tasks. Whatever biological or cultural differences exist do not rule out the possibility that men can experience children just as intimately, or feel just as responsible for them, or simply take on more of the grinding work of caring for them.

Countless anthropological and psychological studies have shattered the myth that men are incapable of nurturing; Kyle Pruett, of the Yale Child Study Center, is just one of several academics who have studied the rare men who became primary caregivers and found them well up to the task. In fact, Stern took pains to say that the men he had observed who did take primary responsibility for their babies were just as able as the women to display attunements to their babies of extraordinary finesse and subtlety. Nothing biological barred them from gaining that insight; it grew from their daily, hands-on experience. Indeed, Stern seemed to undercut his own argument when he answered a question about divorced fathers, who must take charge during the times their children live with them. In those cases, Stern said, fathers developed a "motherhood constellation," too.

Ron Taffel, a psychologist who conducts workshops with more than ten thousand parents a year, said that one reason women often experience a deeper intimacy with children is that they spend the time and perform the chores that lead to intimacy. This closeness is not innate, not biologically willed upon women or walled off from men; it arises from the daily tasks of child rearing.

"The myth continues that women are able to listen and talk to children more," Taffel told me. "The reality is that children talk in the midst of doing other things—when you're giving them a bath or wrapping presents. The one who does more of this is the one who finds more out. It's not inborn. It just happens that women happen to do more of that. That myth is truly a myth that keeps the status quo in place."

The Muddy Middle Ground

The public debate pits one extreme, tradition, against another, absolute equality. It bears little relation to the way people actually live. In fact, most families, and most fathers, are trudging along a muddy middle ground, one foot in the old and the other in the new.

At first glance, Peter Mubanda may seem like the dad of the 1950s. He works long hours as a Merrill Lynch financial consultant, riding the commuter train into New York City from New Rochelle; his wife, Valorie, stays at home with their young daughter and never knows when she'll see him at night. On weekends, though, he takes charge. He supervises diaper changes, naps, baths, and bedtime; he gets up when his daughter does. Valorie sleeps late, takes long walks or exercises, and vanishes for part of every Saturday to get some time for herself.

Peter found himself equally able to care for his daughter when he had to, even though his wife proudly proclaims child rearing to be her job. "It was a new experience," Peter said. "It was definitely scary. You know you're capable, but you never really know till you put it to the test. One of the first nights Valorie went out, our daughter woke up and I panicked. Then I thought, What would Valorie do? I went in, held her, talked to her a little bit, gave her some milk, and held her till she went to sleep. Basically, it's one of those jobs that you get better at the more time you spend at it."

Soon after Peter's weekend shift began, he noticed a transformation in his relationship with his daughter—and in his own confidence. "It made me so in tune," Peter said. "It made me understand baby talk. Now because of the time I spend with my daughter, whenever we go out as a family, she only wants to hold my hand when we walk down the street. She knows on the weekends to come to me, not to Valorie."

Mike King is another unlikely new father. He chases drug and alcohol offenders in his job at a state law-enforcement agency, then comes home to cook, clean, bathe, and tend his children. His wife, Donna, a hospital laboratory supervisor, has always worked, and the two of them have always shared child care and housework.

"Other guys are out hunting, and he's on the floor playing with the kids," Donna told me. "He gives them 110 percent of him. He does laundry. He likes to cook. He cleans. He does the dishes." In fact, when I sat with Donna in her immaculate living room, she told me that Mike had cleaned that morning before I arrived while she ran errands.

I asked Mike why he did so much more at home than many other men. He paused and gave me an answer that was true of many other fathers I talked to. He hadn't thought much about why; he just did what needed to be done, and he loved spending time with his children.

"I see it more as a responsibility," he said. "In my job, I see where a lot of kids don't have fathers. It kind of bothers me. If I'm in the mood, if I get home before her, I'll just go ahead and start cooking dinner. I won't say, 'How about giving the kids a bath?' I'll say, 'Let's go!' When I get up in the morning, I try to get up and get them fed. It's nothing I feel I've got to do. I just want to do it. "

Mike was also trained by his mother, who taught him to cook after his father died when he was fifteen years old. In a way, he practiced being a father to his younger sister, who was three years old when their father died. "Things came about when a father was supposed to be there, and I'd try to show up," he said. "She was in some Little Miss Beauty pageant, and I'd go there."

Mike knows he does more with the children and in the house than many of his friends and relatives do. "He even gets ragged on a little bit," Donna said. "The wives think he's wonderful. The men are like,'Yeah, yeah.'"

Praise makes Mike uncomfortable. "I've heard some people say, 'Look at all the things that Mike does,' and Donna says I shouldn't be saying stuff like this, but I really don't think I do that much," he said. "I think I should spend more time with them, more time with them to raise them right."

Mike may share chores like a new father, but he has plenty of old-father sensibility, too. He believes with Blankenhorn that the man of the house helps keep children in line. "There's got to be a father present somewhere," he said. "That's the missing factor I see.

You keep stepping over the bounds with the female, and the male comes in and sticks his foot in there so you can't cross over the bounds."

Yet Mike doesn't restrict himself to discipline; his traditional male qualities don't prevent him from performing many traditional female tasks or predispose him to be the mere helper while Donna takes charge. In fact, Mike said he would have been willing to stay at home with the children if he and Donna could have afforded it because although they were happy with the excellent day care center at Donna's work, he would have preferred his children to be at home in the early years.

WHO'S REALLY DOING THE WORK?

Peter and Mike are probably taking on more child care than most fathers, though the statistics on just how families divide household responsibilities are not only sketchy but hotly contested. While some studies suggest that nothing has changed, a research review by Joseph Pleck, one of the leading authorities on fathers, concludes that while women still do far more work at home than men, men do more than they used to. In the 1960s and 1970s, men spent about one-third as much time directly tending children than women did; now they spend about two-fifths as much time as women.

Pleck challenges the widely quoted figure in Arlie Hochschild's *The Second Shift* that fathers spend an average of twelve minutes a day taking care of children; that is a twenty-five-year-old statistic drawn only from weekdays, he notes. By his tally, a more accurate count is 1.9 hours on weekdays, and 6 on Sundays.[9]

In a major study of couples who both worked full time, Rosalind Barnett and Caryl Rivers found husbands and wives shared more tasks than many of the overall statistics might indicate, partly because many studies have counted up hours spent on tasks without adjusting for the number of hours men and women work; typically, women work fewer hours.[10] Even in households where both parents work, fathers who become primary parents are rare. The percentage of fathers who care for preschool children while mothers work has stayed virtually the same—between 15 and 16 percent—since 1977. And researchers have not found one child care task that most fathers say is their primary responsibility.[11]

Although the new father is more a myth than a reality, many fathers today like Peter Mubanda are consciously, often proudly doing more than their own fathers did. And although some studies have noted that men with egalitarian ideals divide tasks at home more fairly, there is evidence to suggest that while many upper-income professional fathers talk the egalitarian talk, it is often blue-collar men like Mike King, frequently caricatured as macho sexists, who actually spend more time directly tending their children. Blue-collar fathers do so partly because many nonprofessional families either work split shifts or want to save money on child care. Except in the poorest families, which are more often headed by single mothers, the lower a family's income, the more likely it is that the father will care for children during the hours mother works. Often it is possible for the fathers to do so because the mothers and fathers work different shifts, and several studies have found that split-shift families are the most likely to rely on fathers for child care and housework in the hours when mothers are at work. Shift work is more common in factory jobs or in the rapidly growing service industries that require night and weekend work, such as restaurants, convenience stores, and sales.[12]

In contrast, the findings of some recent studies of the corporate world have suggested that more traditional divisions of labor remain. A survey by Work/Family Directions of major corporations found that women spent nearly twice the hours per week on child care and household tasks than their husbands, even if both parents were working.[13]

In the upper echelons of corporate America, most men with young children still have wives who stay at home; more than two-thirds of the male professionals and executives surveyed by Work/Family Directions had wives who did not work. Although many upper-income professional men may be committed to egalitarianism in theory, the demands of their jobs—or their decision to climb the corporate ladder—often keep them away from home during the hours that their children are awake. Lawyers, doctors, journalists, investment bankers, and business executives must often work late into the night; many other fathers, from factory workers to civil service employees, have jobs that end at fixed hours and allow them more time at home.

In many cases, pragmatism may trump ideology. Studies have indicated that fathers who watch children, cook, do laundry, and wash dishes learned how to do so because they had to, not because they were philosophically committed to feminism. Parents may have wanted to save money on child care or have been uneasy at the idea of placing children in day care. Or fathers may have been arbitrarily assigned to a different shift and had to learn how to manage a household when their wives were not around. In many cases, one study of such families found, both parents continued to maintain that the mother was in charge and the father just helped out, even when the father was sharing much of the child care.[14]

WHAT'S FAIR? WHAT WORKS?

Families are struggling to figure out what a fair division of responsibilities should be now that the old ways are tarnished but the new ways remain largely a fantasy. Most are conducting negotiations fraught with guilt, rage, resignation, resentment, and even surprising accommodations.

Liz Forest, the economist who gave up her job when her second child was born, and her husband, Kyle Ward, are trying to figure out what is fair now that their lives have changed. Liz thinks of the children as her job. But it is a job that never ends, day or night, weekday or weekend. And she agonizes over how much she can ask her husband to share when he puts in a full workday, too.

With Liz emotionally spent from the task of caring for a six-month-old and a two-year-old on her own, with no money in the budget to hire a baby-sitter to spell her, virtually any negotiation can easily become a battleground. Kyle willingly does laundry and washes dishes; Liz really would like him to take over the children so she can clean the house and get a break. Kyle likes to work in the garden; Liz seethes because that chore, conveniently, is away from the children.

"He wanted to go out and plant the tomatoes," she said when we spoke in the winter of 1996. "I want him to be able to do that, I want the herbs and the tomatoes. But I said, 'I'm not going to be stuck in the house again while you're doing something that needs to be done but that you really enjoy while I take care of the kids.' He went out for a little while, but by the time he came in, I was feeling very upset. I said, 'I have been here three hours.' He said, 'That's all you need to say. You don't need to be angry and accusatory.'"

As Liz talked, she veered between gratitude and resentment, between praising her husband for his willingness to tackle anything she asks and her anger at having to ask in the first place.

"I don't think he's doing as much, but I don't necessarily fault him for that," Liz said. "It's me trying to do my 'job' during the week. I think, He's been working, doesn't he get to have time off? But I've been working, too, perhaps even harder. He says, 'If you need me to do this, just tell me.' But why do I have to tell him? Why doesn't he just say, 'Shall I give them a bath this morning?' He's going to do what he's 'told,' and I'm going to have to be the cruise director. I think up all the meals. I decide what the schedule is going to be. I invite the guests. Please, can you take over some of this?"

Just as soon as Liz vented her frustration, she felt she had been unfair. "He is really good. I don't give him enough credit. He is a fabulous spouse. The truth of the matter is, the husband will never ever be able to give 50 percent. It doesn't make sense for two people to know about the vaccination schedule."

Kyle has a different perspective. "I think in our house we do really share things pretty evenly," he said. Before Kyle's job at the United Nations moved to Switzerland, he told his supervisors that he wanted to leave at 6 P.M., a little earlier than normal, whenever emergencies did not intervene, so that he could spend an hour with his daughters before they go to bed. Once a week, he took the children so Liz could have a night out on her own. He cooked and changed diapers.

In fact, at times Kyle has felt as if he has no time to himself, either. "I have a half an hour on the train in the morning and a half an hour in the evening—that's not necessarily quality time by myself," he said. "From time to time I begin to feel like you get a night out and I don't." He says that's more of a visceral feeling than a real complaint; he has refused Liz's offer of a night out on his own because he does not want to give up the time with his daughters.

Yet Kyle readily acknowledges that Liz is the primary parent and says that was the case even when she was working. As for the cruise director complaint, "It absolutely rings true," he said. "She's watching the shoe sizes. I don't pay attention as to whether they had a bath this day or the day before."

The question for Kyle is whether Liz sees more and does more because of her personality, her gender, or some mixture of the two. He tends to be spontaneous; she needs to make lists. "She feels the need to have things planned, and I don't, so she often plans things," he said.

Just as Stern observed, Kyle has noticed that Liz and most women he knows seem caught up with their children in a way that eludes most men. Maybe, he mused, it's because of pregnancy and breast-feeding. He noted that he could go away for a weekend when his daughter was tiny, and Liz could not. "We can go to a football game and completely forget about it, and women never can and never will," he said. "They need to be completely—I don't want to use the word—obsessed."

Aside from whatever contributions biology makes to that obsession, Kyle also understands the impact of social expectations. He feels little guilt because he is doing more than fathers used to do. "I think there's a socialization aspect to this equation," he said. "The sensitive liberal nineties male still remembers—there's still this *Leave It to Beaver, Father Knows Best* sitcom lying in the back recesses of your mind, even though you have no intention or expectation of having a household like that. When men do pick up the slack—wash, cook, and clean—they basically expect credit for it at some level. I know, gee, I am not your average beer-swilling sit-on-the-couch-and-not-lift-a-finger kind of guy, and therefore I deserve some sort of notice for it. That's always lurking in the background."

These negotiations, conducted in virtually every household with children, can cut particularly deeply and bitterly when both parents work because the results affect not only personal happiness but often professional success. Many couples agree, at least in principle, that sharing child care and housework is only fair if both are working full time. I did not set out to find egalitarian poster families; in fact, I deliberately included families from a range of economic classes and ethnic backgrounds. I was struck by how many families, particularly nonprofessional couples, were committed to the ideal of sharing tasks at home.

When I asked Bill Rumsey why he was so willing to divide the work with Toni, he made a passionate case for fairness with no prompting from me. He couldn't understand the men around him who did less, he said. He looked at friends who would never think of throwing in a load of laundry; he looked at relatives where both husbands and wives worked, but where wives did virtually everything. "If the kids are sick, it's her responsibility," he said, talking of one couple he knew. "I have a hard time understanding that. It makes it a lot easier if both are willing to contribute some time and effort towards the kid. If it falls all on one person, if one person's not doing anything, what are they there for?"

Bill believes he is setting an example for his daughter and his son. "Hopefully, Lisa is not going to be expected to make meals and do all the laundry. Hopefully, Mike will realize it's a two-way street. The days of one person doing all that are gone."

THE PRICE OF UNFAIRNESS

For all the brave words, most mothers are still shouldering far more at home than most fathers, at a cost of considerable resentment, even rage. The Virginia Slims Opinion Poll, for example, asked working mothers their major sources of resentment. Fifty-six percent mentioned how little their husbands helped around the house, 50 percent replied how little men shared child care duties, 52 percent answered how much time they spent keeping the family organized, and 40 percent mentioned the time thinking about family responsibilities.

Indeed, Ron Taffel argued that the model that Blankenhorn believes is characteristic of most marriages, and probably the most natural state of affairs at that, does not satisfy many mothers and fathers. "The mom's-in-charge, we-help-out paradigm doesn't work," he said. "It makes her resentful. And it makes him feel resentful and locked out." The Barnett and Rivers study supports that assertion: It found that men were slightly more dissatisfied than women with how child care was shared, suggesting that many wanted more time with children. For their part, women reported stress because they felt responsible for making the child care arrangements.[15]

Women in all kinds of jobs, at all levels of responsibility, have felt the strains of working while remaining in charge at home. I spoke with a highly successful executive. She loved her work and tackled problems with a bracing optimism, but her husband traveled constantly for his job, often around the world. He was usually gone for most of the workweek, and she managed their two children and the household tasks by herself. She admitted to complete exhaustion.

"My husband travels all the time," she said. "I am like a single parent. There are times I feel, If I can go sit ten minutes, I'll be OK. After a very challenging day, you walk in and you're faced with the challenges of home life: homework, getting the bath, getting them to bed on time."

Even when her husband is home, he is up at 5 A.M. and soon out the door. It's not just a matter of sharing the daily chores. It's that she feels alone in making the judgment calls or assessing problems that arise with the children. "He misses all the chaos," she said. "I find that hard, more so now than before. Just to have another person's perspective—'This came home from school, what are your thoughts?'"

The unfair division of labor remains one important reason—pain at leaving children is certainly another—why working makes life miserable for many mothers and why some who are able to afford to do so pull back from the workplace. A study of women who graduated from Harvard Medical, Law, and Business schools between 1971 and 1981 found that 70 percent had reduced their hours of paid work because of their children and almost 40 percent had slowed their careers. Most said a supportive husband would have made their lives far easier.[16]

When fathers leave all the work at home to mothers, it not only compounds their fatigue, stress, and guilt, but can exact costs on the job, too. A father's help can make the difference between excelling, stalling, or dropping out altogether.

That is the lesson I draw from the saga of Jill Natwick Johnston, a corporate lawyer, though she had a different moral in mind. She wrote in the *Wall Street Journal* about her decision to turn down the job of a lifetime. Motherhood and wifehood, she said, got in the way.

"I turned my back on the temptingly tangible and esteem-enhancing benefits of a great job so that I could be there to cook dinner for my husband and help my kids learn their multiplication tables," she wrote. She concluded, "I realize I am my career's worst enemy." She left out someone else, though: her husband.[17]

Her husband had recently bought a new business 250 miles away from their home. He wanted her to move to the small town where his business was headquartered, where there would be little opportunity for her to practice her specialty. His new business made it far harder for her to accept what she once would have viewed as a dream job. She turned down a career opportunity because it would compromise her family responsibilities; he pursued a career opportunity that took him away from his children and ultimately led her to relocate and compromise her career.

Contrast that with the admittedly rare example of a two-career couple in which both the husband and the wife succeed, but the husband's easier schedule has allowed the wife to soar to unusual prominence. Alice Young is a partner and chair of the Asia Pacific practice in the New York law firm of Kaye, Scholer, Fierman, Hays & Handler. She conducts a dizzying array of negotiations for American clients in Asian countries and Asian clients in the United States and Europe. Her work requires her to make frequent trips to Asia and to field calls at all hours. Her job alone dictates a grueling pace, but like many prominent lawyers and business executives,

Alice also plays an active role in several organizations to stay informed, to remain visible, and to expand her network of acquaintances. She serves as a trustee of the Aspen Institute and secretary of the Japan Society; is on the President's Council of the Asia Society; and is a member of the Council on Foreign Relations, the U.S.–China Business Council, and the Committee of 100.

I have known Alice for more than fifteen years through my professional interest in Asia. Every time I met her—at a Council on Foreign Relations seminar, on a flying trip to Japan—I would marvel at her assurance, her unassuming warmth, and her personal flair. I watched as she married, had two children, and yet continued to move from career triumph to triumph.

I knew she spent time with her children in the morning and reserved her weekends for them; she usually left her home in suburban New Jersey at about 8 A.M., after giving the children breakfast and seeing them off to school. Although Alice leads one of the busiest lives I know, whenever we talked, I could sense her vigilance about the children's academic, moral, and emotional lives. The mother of one of Alice's daughter's best friends had died when we spoke one day, and Alice knew exactly how her daughter felt about it. She had drawn up a list of everyone she knew who had died.

I also knew that Alice could seldom get home before 8:30 P.M. and had to travel to Asia two to six times a year, often for three weeks at a stretch. After a while, I realized, as Alice freely admitted, that a large part of her secret was her husband, Thomas Shortall. Tom is an institutional bond trader with Citicorp. It is a demanding job that keeps him virtually tied to his chair between 7 A.M. and 6 P.M. Tom leaves before his children are awake, and Alice supervises the morning routine. Once the market closes, Tom can leave, and he is almost always home by 7 P.M. Thus, Tom can be there virtually every night to play with their two children and supervise their homework. Tom can stay home during the weekends that Alice travels. Although Alice and Tom have a live-in nanny, she is usually off duty on nights and weekends, and during those times, Tom is, as he puts it, "solo dad."

Tom is a confident man, secure in his own career and unperturbed about how others may view his domestic arrangements. "I'm not the house mom," he said when I asked him if he ever felt self-conscious. "I have been given an opportunity where I spend a lot of time around the kids. I don't really get involved in an ego thing with Alice. It's hard to compete on one level."

The point is not competition; Tom is choosing to do what he wants to do. "It happens to complement the idea that I enjoy being a father," he said. "I would prefer doing this than really shooting for the stars if it meant being on a business trip constantly. The advantage of this is the opportunity to really have quality—and at times not-so-quality—time with my children."

Tom's own childhood both drove him to be an involved father and accustomed him to working mothers. His parents divorced when he was three; he shuttled back and forth between them, and he was brought up primarily by a strong mother who always worked. "I'm very proud of my wife," Tom said. "She has, by her own accomplishments, a grueling schedule. I support that. My mother was a fairly successful working woman. I had some very very positive ideas about women and careers and I always have. There was no 'Gee, this is unheard of.' There was no educational experience I had to go through. It's a life choice that fits a lot of my own personal opinions."

Tom is no saint, and he doesn't mince words about his occasional frustration or fatigue, either. "I'm not overwhelmed. But do I feel put upon? Yes, sure, at some points." The worst times, Tom said, were when the children were infants and he was on duty while Alice traveled. "It was a terrible hardship being a new parent with her going to Japan," he said. "I can remember Alice going to Japan on our first anniversary, when Amanda was three months old and colicky. It was hell."

Now that the children are almost teenagers, it is far easier to tend them when Alice is away. There are still rough moments, when Tom worries about how Alice can sustain the pace without damaging her health or when he balks at her coming home and venting about her day. "I have enough need for downtime in my own life without having to carry her baggage, too," he said firmly.

As he is the first to admit, their full lives contain a full measure of stress. He's not always happy. Alice is not always happy. Their kids are not always happy. Most of the time, though, they thrive.

As Rhona Mahony argued, if there were more households like this, the gap between men's and women's earning power—and political power—would narrow or disappear. In the negotiations of couples like Liz Forest and Kyle Ward over household tasks, Mahony detects an imbalance of power fueled both by economics and psychology. Women, who bear babies, usually start out with more emotional attachment to them than do men. Because mothers feed and hold babies more, they often grow more adept at caring for them. And they often criticize fathers because they do not handle babies with the same sensitivity, thus preventing fathers from getting the practice they need to develop that skill.

Since mothers usually feel more connected, they balk at leaving the babies with someone else. They are more likely to quit their jobs or return part time after their babies' birth. Either of these steps usually reduces their future earning power and means their work will always be less important economically to the household than their husbands'. Mothers' lower earning power may erode their ability to ask for more help at home, particularly if doing so would compromise their husbands' jobs. It also makes them vulnerable at every stage of their lives. Every time there is a family crisis—not only child care, but the needs of a sick parent, for example—they, not the higher-earning and career-track fathers, curtail their work hours to cope.

Mahony's solution is to promote ways, both through negotiations by individual families and broader social policies, to induce fathers to take an equal share of the load or even to decide to stay home while mothers work. Her many provocative ideas include employers' affirmative action policies for men who took time off to rear children and encouraging new mothers to leave fathers in charge of infants for hours at a stretch so fathers can catch up on mothers' head start in attachment and skill.

Mahony's vision of a more just society, in which having children does not automatically mean curtailment of women's job opportunities, holds enormous appeal for me. If more working mothers had more help at home, who knows what they might be able to achieve?

Other Choices, Other Visions

Dividing child rearing equally is not the only model, and it is not even the preferable one for some families, either. I recognize that for many women, the abstract ideal of justice pales beside their passionate desire to spend more time with their children. Many mothers simply want to be at home more, to be more deeply immersed in their children's lives, even at the possible cost of advancement at work or bargaining power at home. And many mothers believe the rewards of a life with children bring with them their own sort of power and lasting influence, apart from the conventional—and certainly limited—measures of success.

Valorie and Peter Mubanda are thriving under a traditional arrangement, one that Valorie has felt free to improve. When their daughter was born three months premature and had to spend weeks in the hospital, Valorie decided to stay home. At first, Peter believed they had become the family he grew up in. "I committed 150 percent to my job," he said. "I just assumed that's what it was about: She would stay home and run the home, and I would go to work and run work."

After about a year, Valorie decided the time had come to make changes. "I was going out of my mind," she said. "Even though I created breaks for myself during the day, you still need more. When she was in the hospital, he did everything. He fed her, he would be the one to change her diaper. He was the first one to give her a bath. But as he got back into work and his schedule, he became a little more distant from her. I don't think he felt as confident of what to do. You withdraw. The other person knows better. Well, that wasn't going to happen in my house." So Valorie told Peter she wanted him to take over on the weekends, and he did. Valorie and Peter are not sharing tasks equally, but their arrangement strikes them both as fair.

Even when mothers work full time, some have been able to manage their households without much active help from their husbands and without cost to their careers. Diane Crispell, the executive editor of *American Demographics* magazine, had a four-year-old and a one-year-old when we spoke in 1996. Her husband is a construction worker, and before her children were born she thought he might be able to care for them during the seasonal layoffs. In the end, Diane said, her husband found that "he had a big problem with being home with the kids and feeling like it's a constructive use of his day."

Diane is the primary breadwinner, and when she gets home at night, she is the primary parent, too. She picks up the children from their family day care home, shops, cleans, fixes dinner, and bathes them. Her husband does the outside chores in their rural upstate New York home: chopping wood, caring for the small livestock they keep, tending the grounds, and remodeling their home.

"It's not like my husband comes home from work and sits on the couch while I'm running around," Diane said. "He is busy doing other things, too. Occasionally, when I grumble about how I have to do the dishes again, he'll say, 'Do you want to go out and chop wood?' It's not that I'm doing more work; it's that we divide up the work in stereotypical ways."

Occasionally, the pressure tells, and Diane and her husband have what she calls "silly little arguments, where we both say, 'I work harder than you do.' OK, we both work hard, we're tired, we're crabby, that's it; there's nothing we can do about it." Or Diane finds she does need help but discovers her husband cannot pitch in because he does not know where anything is or what to do.

Most of the time, Diane seems unruffled and unresentful, even though she has no hired help with housework. That is partly because her office is flexible, allowing her to leave early or bring work home when necessary, and partly because of her upbeat, organized, matter-of-fact nature. Although he is decidedly not a new father, Diane thinks her husband is a good father. He is playful and attentive with the children, and she says the children seem equally attached to both of them.

While some mothers carry their double loads uncomplainingly, others do not want to cede control of children. They not only want to spend more time with them than do fathers, but believe they know better how to care for them. Without even being fully conscious of it, some mothers may discourage fathers from taking on more by criticizing when they do help. Such "gatekeeping" is extremely common, as psychologists at Boston University found when they tracked one hundred new parents for five years.[18]

Kyle Ward noted of his wife, "She is of the impression that I couldn't survive a minute if I don't do things exactly the way she would. Men are far more casual about things they're doing with kids than mothers are. I tell her it won't be exactly the same way she would do it, but we'll make it."

Sometimes it is not a matter of control, but of longing. One of my friends, whose husband has taken on considerable responsibility for their children after she decided to take a demanding job, nonetheless balked at Mahony's idea of giving fathers a chance to catch up on mothers' attachment. For every hour she handed a baby over to her husband, she said, she felt she would be missing a chance to deepen and strengthen her attachment to the baby.

OTHER MOTHERS, OTHER HELP

When fathers are unable or unwilling to help, mothers can and should be able to turn to "other mothers"—relatives; friends; neighbors; members of their churches, synagogues, or mosques; paid helpers; the wider community; and, on occasion, the state.

I suspect, for example, and Liz Forest does, too, that her life in those early years would have brightened immeasurably if she could have afforded a baby-sitter for just a few hours a week. It wasn't necessary that Kyle spell her, only that someone did.

Women have always relied on relatives to help them bear the burdens of child rearing, and if families live nearby, as in the case of Toni Rumsey or Ahling Deng, they still do. Many mothers today have no relatives living close by and sometimes no neighbors around during the day either. These mothers can end up, as Liz did, and as I did during my maternity leaves, spending days virtually alone and overwhelmed.

To their credit, some members of the Christian right understand that isolation breeds despair, even if at times their literature presents an unrealistically rosy picture of at-home motherhood. While they campaign for mothers to stay at home, organizations like Focus on the Family offer practical advice on combating the occupational hazards of staying at home. An article in the February 1996 magazine, for example, details how a "lone ranger Mom" sought out other mothers and formed a co-op to swap baby-sitting, chores, and health and fitness tips. After her loneliness and exhaustion gave way to depression, the author, Donna Partow, found solace, practical help, and considerable savings in her co-op. She and the mothers exercise together, attend mothers' nights out, organize book exchanges, and take turns hosting a weekly play group.

In a typical week, one mother took Partow's daughter for the day so she could earn some money from home and another baby-sat so she and her husband could celebrate their wedding anniversary at home, saving money for dinner out and baby-sitting. Partow then took in a neighbor's daughter so the neighbor could have an uninterrupted talk with a visiting relative; in return, the neighbor took all the children to the local swim club, whose membership is too expensive for Partow.

In my own apartment building, in supposedly anonymous, unfriendly New York City, there is a large community of other mothers and fathers, who keep an eye on each other's children. Nearly ten children were born the year before my daughter and six or seven the year my son was born. One adult can often be found watching a brood of children playing, riding bicycles, or blowing bubbles on the wide sidewalk outside the building. Our children are often in each other's apartments.

Networks of friends can help, too. When the deadline loomed for this book and I realized, with extreme reluctance, that I would have to work six days a week for a while, friends generously rallied. They kept my husband company when he was alone with our two children and offered to let him drop off the children so he could take a desperately needed break.

Many working mothers today struggle without help from fathers, family, or neighbors. That is where the community and the state can help. Leach outlined an appealing vision of government-supported community "child places," where parents could drop off children if they needed a breather, attend workshops on child development, or consult books on children and parenting. These places could offer children a relaxed haven after school or play groups during the day for children of different ages.

One version of such a child place exists in Illinois. Called Family Focus, it is the brainchild of Bernice Weissbourd, whose credo is that all families need support. Family services should not be offered just to families in desperate trouble; all parents have questions about how best to handle their children and all families endure a normal range of stress. Family Focus has four centers near or around Chicago, in poor neighborhoods, middle-class suburbs, and semirural areas.

I visited two of the centers, one in an inner-city Chicago neighborhood and the other in Evanston, a suburb with a range of incomes but which is primarily middle-class. Mothers (and some fathers) drifted in and out, attending discussion groups on how to handle the terrible twos or consulting the staff about individual problems. The centers offered child care during their programs and held occasional activities on Saturdays as well for the entire family. In Chicago, parents could study for their high school equivalency degrees and meet with counselors who referred them for services like welfare or housing. The programs vary, depending on parents' needs, but include toy-lending libraries and workshops on how to help children get ready for school. Family Focus has several sources of funds: state or federal money, because some of the families it serves qualify as high-risk; private donations from corporations and foundations; and money it earns from training other communities to reproduce its model.

If fathers do not help, mothers who can afford to can buy help, from modest to substantial. I know that such expenses are out of reach for many mothers, and that is where social supports provided by the state can ease working parents' loads—and, to some extent, pick up the slack left by fathers.

As the author Sylvia Ann Hewlett pointed out in her writings, feminism in Europe has focused more on supports for families such as child allowances, extended family leaves, and subsidized child care, and less on revising traditional sex roles. This emphasis has eased the toll on children both of mothers working and of deadbeat dads.

Our debate about fathers has grown stale and acrimonious. Society blames fathers, but fails to recognize that fathers are facing terrible pressures, too—from social expectations, an inflexible workplace, and the looming threat of downsizing. While we condone mothers' desire to pull back from work as natural, we regard with suspicion a man who does the same. Mothers still are accorded the luxury of choosing to be at home if the family can afford it; in some cases, fathers will pay the price of working longer hours and possibly seeing their children less to make up for the mothers' lost income. Some fathers who might have wanted more daily, intimate involvement with child care are discouraged by well-meaning gate-keeping mothers. The rare father who tries to assert his legal right to take family leave often faces thinly masked scorn from peers and risks being dismissed as a less committed employee. The tyranny of the workplace and our failure to imagine ways to rethink work to be more accommodating to family life take their toll on fathers as well as mothers.

These strains—a sense of disorientation about their roles as men and fathers, economic anxieties, and grief at the loss of their own fathers, whether real or psychological—appear to be fueling movements like the Promise Keepers, the Million Man March, and Robert Bly's retreats just as much as or perhaps more than overt antifeminism. David Hackett, an associate professor of religion at the University of Florida who has studied these movements, noted that Promise Keepers' surveys show that more than half its members report the absence of their own fathers while growing up, either through death, divorce, or emotional distance. Many of the

African American men on the Million Man March brought their sons, to stand as bulwarks against the fatherlessness that has afflicted their community. The climactic moment at Bly's retreats often came when men realized the depth of their sadness about their distance from their fathers.

None of this excuses those fathers who evade responsibility, particularly those whose selfishness and fixation on their careers blights their wives'. We must not use real differences between men and women as a rationale for a forced march back to fixed gender roles. And we still need a vision of a father whose distinct male traits do not prevent him from experiencing the intimacy and toil of child rearing. Fairness does not always mean splitting tasks down the middle, as long as mothers are not coerced into staying home out of misplaced guilt or forced to cut back on jobs they love because fathers will not do their part. The real issue is that most mothers, working outside the home or inside it, need more help. They must either get it from fathers or somewhere else.

Reimagining Motherhood

Mothers today, as they have for centuries, live under the unforgiving glare of public judgment. Mothers have for too long made society's harsh verdict their own. The pundits' pronouncements become the nasty inner voice that scolds, How can you be a mother when you don't act like the mother I have always imagined?

Mothers who work outside the home have to give up the intense, prolonged immersion in the daily lives of their children—the immersion we have been told, and many of us still believe, is the only way to be real mothers. It is true that for eight to ten hours a day, someone else is wiping our children's noses, changing their diapers, playing peekaboo and other games with them, rocking them to sleep, and hearing confidences.

Yet working mothers are still raising their children. They are still deeply connected to them. They are still shaping their values. They are still beloved by them. When I feel vulnerable to the criticism that I don't want to do the messy, grinding work of everyday child care, that I just want the fun times, I think about my life for the past seven years. It is filled with countless staggerings out of bed at 3 A.M. to soothe a teething baby, run an oatmeal bath for a screaming chicken pox sufferer, and cuddle a child sobbing from a bad dream. I have washed and boiled and poured more bottles than I could ever count. I have changed enough diapers to fill a landfill. I resent the charge that working mothers are shunning the real work of mothering. There's a lot of that work to go around.

I have learned, even as I continue to battle doubts, that my bond with my children endures although I am not the good mother of song and story. Countless other mothers have learned that, too. So why can't we refute with more passion and conviction the distortions of the Jeremiahs around us? Because they speak to that deep, dark place where the ideal of the good mother lives inside all of us.

For many women—even at times for me—the good mother is someone we cannot be if we work outside the home. She remains lurking in our brains and hearts as a kind of June Cleaver vampire: No matter how many times you kill her, she never dies.

That mother is a pernicious fantasy—equally out of reach for the mother who works outside the home and the one who works within it. Yet many mothers at work and at home are in the grip of that ideal. They cannot live their lives that way, but they cannot imagine motherhood any other way.

WHY WE CLING TO THE OLD IDEAL

The good mother may be a false god, but she is an alluring one, with a tenacious hold on our hearts and imaginations. Why has the ideal of the good mother survived so many assaults and so much pain? The answers are moral, economic, and psychological.

The good mother seems particularly resonant now because we are living through a profound cultural and moral crisis that opens the door to absolutism. No matter how often revisionist family historians expose the dysfunctions of the 1950s or other eras glorified in our collective imaginations, adults in the 1990s cannot afford to be complacent. While the right glosses over the heartbreak and repression that lurked beneath the fixed smiles of the family grouped around the Christmas tree, it would be folly to deny the signs of depression and despair that cloud so many children's lives today. Concern over moral decay and the pervasiveness of sex and violence in our culture extends far beyond the Christian right; it is shared by most parents in most communities.

The voices from the right and, increasingly, in the center are offering a clear, ringing answer that has the comfort of familiarity and simplicity in a time of uncertainty and dislocation: Keep mothers at home. Mothers, as they were in Victorian times and have been for centuries, are seen as bulwarks against evil—or held responsible for inculcating evil in the next generation.

Even though economic forces have pushed many women into the workforce, economics also helps to keep many wedded to the traditional ideal of the good mother. Those who urge women to heed the call of nature and stay home are also restoring them to their traditional position of economic powerlessness. Staying at home offers many joys, but it can also mean giving up bargaining power in making decisions and sharing household tasks. If a husband makes more or all the money for a family, he is less likely, and may be less able, to cut into his valuable breadwinning hours to share the work at home.

Most of us also have a deep emotional attachment to the ideal of the perfect mother. As the psychoanalysts and scholars Jessica Benjamin, Nancy Chodorow, and Susan Contratto suggest, many people cling even as adults to the image of the mother they formed as infants. To a baby, a mother is the source of all comfort and reassurance; that romanticized memory is one reason mothers continue to be sentimentalized in public policy and public debate.[1]

Those memories of the perfect mother, of course, are a distortion. Accepting a mother or a father as flawed, as only human, is one of the hardest tasks of adulthood. The fantasy of the perfect mother often lives on when girls become mothers in two ways: They try to re-create for their own children the parts of their mothers they revered, and they try to avoid the mistakes they feel their mothers made.

Even if a mother has accepted her own mother as imperfect, she often clings to the hope that she can somehow be a perfect mother to her own child. I remember my mother telling me that as a child she had written down all the things her mother had done wrong in a little black book that she meant to use as a guide when she became a mother. Surely one of a mother's deepest satisfactions is the opportunity to try to heal her childhood wounds by treating her own child differently. And surely one of the most piercing sorrows of motherhood is when a mother, inevitably, fails in that quest for perfection and hurts her child in some way she never anticipated.

THE DANGER OF THE PERFECT, SACRIFICIAL MOTHER

What, then, is wrong with an ideal that has proved so sacred to so many for so long? In one sense, all mothers, all parents, are sacrificial, and should be. The desire to give is one of the most elemental and most honorable impulses of love. To make the decision to marry or to have a child should mean a willingness to sacrifice, to curb your own urges to accommodate another's. Adults are better able and morally obligated to defer their needs when their children's are overriding.

Yet there is a line between reasonable self-deprivation and martyrdom. To give a child what he or she needs, a mother must have a healthy sense of her own self. In fact, the sacrificial model hurts children as well as mothers. Just as we spoil children by giving them too many things, we can spoil them in more profound emotional ways by allowing them to grow up feeling entitled to place their own needs before anyone else's.

To cite just one example, the writer bell hooks believes the ideal of the sacrificial mother, an icon of African American culture, has helped produce a crop of selfish African American men. "The notion of mothering that is placed onto black women by traditional black culture is that you should never say no, you should never have a boundary," she told me in 1994. "There is an expression that black mothers love their sons and raise their daughters. Those of us who get these sons that have had the mother who was ever-giving get men who are completely unadult in their expectations."

It is a parent's responsibility to curb children's natural fantasy that they are the center of the universe. A mother who never says,

"No, I can't because this is my time now," is a mother who convinces children she lives only for them. She is doing her children a grave injustice. Children cannot understand that they, too, have rights to claim time for themselves and to set limits on others' demands of them unless they have seen their mothers claim those rights for themselves.

A mother who lives an entirely sacrificial life, with the psychological costs such a life entails, is also likely to fail her children in other important ways. She may be so distracted by her anger or sadness that she will find it harder to be attuned to her child. Mothers and fathers who deny their own frustrations or dreams will have more trouble hearing and responding to their children.

The champions of the sacrificial mother argue that children learn to be grateful and honor their mothers for this sacrifice. That is a poor substitute for having the emotional experience of making way for someone else's needs. Indeed, that gratitude can easily become a tyranny of its own, one that carries a heavy burden for a child. Sacrifice is often served up with a large dollop of guilt. A mother who lives only for her child can be a suffocating mother; her very weakness can become a form of control.

A sacrificial mother also cannot help her child with what most Western psychologists believe is a crucial task for children: learning to see themselves as separate beings from their parents. Children have to feel free to separate, but they cannot get that sense from sacrificial mothers who live only for them and have nothing if they pull away.

Some attachment theorists preach that a mother who leaves will have children who feel abandoned. To the contrary, a mother who never leaves her children never allows them to gain the confidence that she will also return. If a mother never leaves her child, then the child will feel that the mother is afraid to do so. And the child will then come to feel that he can never leave the mother without feeling afraid either. The child grows unable to distinguish his feelings from his mother's feelings—and so cannot really separate from her psychologically.[2]

I am not suggesting that a mother must work outside the home to allow her child to separate from her. A mother at home can encourage separation, too, but it is hard to let a child go if a mother's world is wholly built around that child. That void could be filled by many things that have nothing to do with paid employment: charity, community service, volunteering at school. The crucial task is to be able to give permission for children to enter the wider world without their believing that by doing so their mothers will feel abandoned and alone.

There are also social costs in the ideal of the sacrificial mother. If a child's first relationship is with a mother who sacrifices for him, he may grow up believing that in every relationship, someone wins at someone else's expense. And that belief, in turn, means it is harder to imagine any relationships of equality, at home or in the world at large.[3]

If mothers continue to be the ones doing most of the child rearing, these patterns will be repeated down the generations, Chodorow argued. Girls will grow up thinking that they are the ones in charge of nurturing, and boys will believe that their turf is the outside world, where relationships take a distant second place to autonomy. That is because girls tend to identify with their mothers, who have traditionally represented self-sacrifice, while boys have had to make a psychological break with their mothers to assert their identity as men.

These arguments are familiar in academic circles, but they have been caricatured to the public at large as meaning that unless all mothers work, they are setting back the cause of equality; or unless all fathers share child care fifty–fifty, they are derelict; or unless we eradicate all differences between men and women, women will remain oppressed. I believe that the point is to allow the broadest possible range of responsible choices, not to dictate another set of rules just as confining as the old ones.

Even now, the sacrificial model is being used, quite deliberately in some quarters, to shame women back into a life of self-denial— and to offer them the sop of reverence as compensation. Maligned as it is, feminism is really about the freedom for women to imagine themselves and their lives as *they* wish. They can broaden their sphere to the workplace or stay at home if they can afford to. They can press the men in their lives to ease their load or accept a traditional division of labor if they find that tolerable. Feminism remains threatening because it does not accept the traditional path as the only way, as inevitable or even just.

All you have to do is read the vitriol about working mothers in the *Wall Street Journal* or *Commentary* to see how explosive is the simple premise that women have a right to dreams that may extend beyond—though they usually include—home and children.

A New Vision of Motherhood

As hard as it is, we must try to banish the good mother from our dreams and nightmares. Instead, we can substitute a motherhood that is more generous, more forgiving, less isolated, and better for children, mothers, and society than the one we worship now. Doing so means letting go of the old images and accepting that working mothers' lives will not look or even feel the same as traditional mothers'. It means believing that new rituals can be just as meaningful as the old.

Reimagining motherhood requires understanding that working does not destroy the joyous sense of connection to a child or diminish the all-important influence of the family on a child's life. It means enduring children's resentment of work while explaining that work has value. And it means embracing a new psychological ideal of motherhood, one that abandons the pursuit of perfection and the reverence for sacrifice.

It is hard for many working mothers, particularly if their mothers did not work, to accept that they may not be able to re-create for their children all the memories and experiences they cherish from their own childhoods. Our society is so obsessed with the rituals we have lost that we can't figure out how to create new ones. Is it really the end of the world if a mother is not at home when a child returns from school? How about doing what one of my friends does: programming the phone so that her young son can push a button; get her office; tell her he's home; chat a little about his day; and then, reassured, play with his friends?

Although I treasure the memories of my childhood, I am not going to re-create all of them for my children. When my daughter turned one, I sought advice from my aunt, whose elaborate birthday cakes for her son were a highlight of my childhood. They must have taken her hours and were astonishing: circuses featuring animals artfully composed from bits of candy and train tracks, toy trains, bridges, and stoplights concocted from icing and gumdrops and pipe cleaners.

I spent a nasty hour struggling with jelly beans before calling my husband in despair, allowing him to spell out my daughter's name, and retiring from the cake-decorating game. I wish that I had that skill, and I still feel a pang when I see the imaginative homemade birthday cakes created by friends of ours—who spend hours on them even though they both work.

Yet when special occasions loom, with visions of perfect meals dancing in my head, I think of a new ritual my children enjoy as much as I do. Around Christmas, which we do not celebrate, we visit a friend who holds down a challenging job and seldom ventures into the kitchen. She nonetheless labors once a year to produce gingerbread slabs for gingerbread houses. Every year we try to assemble the houses with the icing that is supposed to harden into cement. We carefully prop up the sides, slather on icing, and hold them fast. Finally, breath held, we put on the roofs. The houses invariably collapse, and so do we, in giggles. Then we jerry-rig the houses with rubber bands, hide the rubber bands with gobs of icing, and hand them over to the children to decorate.

Rather than torment themselves about what they cannot do, working mothers can take solace in the different gifts they may be able to offer their children. For me, my work is part of my delight in the world of ideas. I believe that this is a heritage I can offer my children that is just as precious and enduring, just as much a token of love, as the traditional mother's baked goods or spotless house. I once heard a story about a young man studying in a yeshiva in Europe before the war. His grandmother appeared one day near the gates of the school hiding something under her coat. She quickly thrust it at him, and he took it, thinking it was some home-baked treat. When he opened it, he found a volume of Schopenhauer. His grandmother wanted to make sure that amid his Talmudic studies, he kept a mind open to the great philosophers.

Much as I hope that my children can see my love of work as a legacy that they may one day share in whatever path they choose, I also must accept that there are times when they see my work as a burden and a competitor. Any mother has to contend at times with her children's anger, resentment, and pain, but working mothers, in particular, tend to blame their jobs, and themselves, for inflicting that pain. By the very nature of work, a mother and a father may have to disappoint a child. They can't go on every field trip, even if they can get free for some; they may not be at home waiting after school; they must go out the door in the morning, even when their children desperately want them to stay.

"My nine-year-old would like nothing more than to have me at home every day," said Paulette Xamplas, who is majoring in biology and English at Kalamazoo Valley Community College. "She's really acting out. Every two minutes she asks, are you done studying yet?"

If children do chafe at times because of jobs, they must understand why mothers work. Many mothers, like Ahling Deng, can say that without work, there is no food on the table. There is another equally valid explanation—that work is important to the mother, that helping support her family makes her proud, that the work itself makes her happy, maybe even that it contributes something to other people or the world at large. Work has an intrinsic value, one that mothers can convey to their children.

The new vision of motherhood also requires relinquishing the fantasy that a good mother is always perfect. It is natural for most mothers to strive for an ideal of excellence, and children deserve and should command our best efforts. Yet mothers are not omniscient. They cannot always see into their children's souls and spirits well enough.

How many times does a mother let some complaint pass by, only later to find that a seemingly offhand remark was a clue of something more seriously awry? How many times does a mother make the wrong call about when to clamp down and when to ease off?

Both mothers at work and mothers at home lambaste themselves for these lapses. Benjamin suggested, however, that what may leave a more lasting imprint on children is how a mother handles her inevitable mistakes. "If you're stressed and you lose your temper, are you going to apologize?" Benjamin asked. "There may be a deep recess in the child that will always retain that memory, that mother let me have it unfairly. But another part will go on to say mother knows when she is being unfair. I can rely on her. But if the mother's not self-forgiving, she's not going to apologize because she can't bear to admit her imperfection."

If a mother believes she must be perfect, she may hold her child to similarly punishing standards. Benjamin believes that children who grow up nursing resentment at their mothers' shortcomings may simply be turning the critical eye on their mothers that had always been cast on them.

We endure our children's anger when we refuse to let them watch that third television show, but we lash ourselves if they complain we're not at home after school like so-and-so's mother. We have no trouble banning candy because it would hurt children's teeth, but it's much harder to convince ourselves that learning that a mother has a right to some time or purpose of her own is good for children in the same basic way—that it forces children to confront the fact that their mothers are separate persons with equally legitimate needs, not extensions of themselves who are there only to wait on them.

At heart, we must imagine a motherhood that is not defined by servitude. I dream of a motherhood that is not synonymous with self-immolation, one that accommodates the needs of the mother and child without sacrificing either. My good-enough mother would teach her children to revel in their own individualism, but to respect hers as well. She would understand that pursuing her dreams, whatever they are, can enrich her children. She would know that she cannot do her job alone, and she would expect help from fathers, neighbors, friends, and the society.

This vision includes mothers at home as well as mothers at work. We are linked by a mutual passion for children. Working mothers should honor the traditional mother and recognize her pull on many Americans' hearts. We should respect that mother's joy in her child rearing and its emotional and intellectual appeal. Mothers like Valorie Mubanda are not sacrificial mothers; they are not interested in martyrdom.

The motherhood I imagine holds the promise of more happiness for mothers and children. It is not a second-best motherhood, but a better one, for mothers at work or at home. Mothers are freed from the tyranny of perfection and their own ceaseless recrimination. Children are freed to be separate without guilt and to acknowledge the needs of others around them. They can grow up to be adults who, because they do not see their mothers as both perfect and threatening, may be able to free society from the constant seesawing between sentimentalizing and demonizing mothers.

AN HONEST ACCOUNTING

The new vision of motherhood offers more freedom, but it demands responsibility as well. Nothing in this book should be read as permission for mothers or fathers to neglect their obligations to children. I agree with many of those whose opinions I otherwise attack that moral relativism has become a societal sickness. Not everything is all right. Having children and pretending that you can lead your life exactly as before is not all right. Ignoring children's pain is not all right.

For me, the hardest questions to answer, in this book and in my life, are what my dream of new motherhood means in practical terms. How do we know which disappointments are bearable for children and which are not? How are parents to lead their lives, to make decisions that honestly weigh the consequences of their actions for children?

When I began this book, I hoped to give mothers some reassurance and sustenance to brace them against the attacks they endure. I pressed experts I interviewed for answers: How do you know you've worked too long and too hard? How could women work at grueling or even rewarding jobs and still give children what they need? What, indeed, do children need from parents? Is there a checklist that parents could consult of general indicators when children are thriving and when they are sinking? I should have known that answers would not be that simple; too much depends on individual factors like a child's temperament, a mother's dreams, a father's involvement, and a family's past.

There are no set rules or formulas for bringing up children. We cannot say that three hours at home with a mother at night is enough, or two hours woefully inadequate. We cannot pronounce that four months is the minimum time a new mother must stay home with her baby, and any less risks an insecure attachment.

It is easy to see why experts want to make rules and mothers so eagerly seek them. Rules are reassuring, and there is a fear that without them, parents will blind themselves to children's suffering and ignore real problems. Instead of rigid rules, we need to enunciate principles and judge ourselves honestly about how well we meet them. Here are mine.

I believe mothers should command respect not for totems of devotion like handmade Halloween costumes or birthday extravaganzas, but for the real hallmarks of mother love: an unwavering commitment to children, a sense of responsibility that often includes breadwinning, and psychological sensitivity.

I admire a mother who can, more of the time than not, differentiate between a bored tug on the skin and a cry for help, who asks for help, and who can acknowledge imperfection to children while still sheltering them from too much adult uncertainty. The mother I honor allows children emotional privacy while offering reassurance and stability. She cherishes her own independence and her children's. She is available to her children when she is there, whether for most of the day or just part of it.

Mothers should make the effort to study and observe their children. Are they robust or frail? Do they forge straight ahead in new situations or hold back? Do they find structure comforting or confining?

This is the real work of motherhood—and fatherhood. It is a daunting task, and mothers must understand they will sometimes fail. It takes effort and time to make these observations, and the working parent may well have to scramble harder to do so, but dedicated parents will try.

Parents must ultimately judge themselves not by what they did, but whether they met their children's needs. Although such needs vary with age and individual personalities, most experts agree that children must be able to forge a sense of trust and affection with at least one adult. They need a moral compass and limits on their behavior. Children must believe that they will be heard, that they can rely on a parent time and again.

"Children need a sense of safety," said Dr. Leon Hoffman, director of the New York Psychoanalytic Society's Parent–Child Center and a Freudian psychoanalyst. "They need to know this is the person who knows me and can sense the problem. A child senses something from within the mother. A very strong message can be given that you are the mother and you know what to do."

From the perspective of a psychiatrist who is skeptical of Freudian theory and of a mother of four who worked long before most others did, Stella Chess offers a similar definition. "Children don't have to have every moment of a mother's time if they are assured of her," she told me. "If when Mom gets home from work and gets on the telephone and says I'm busy, that's different." Chess had a rule at work that her children would always be put through to her, and she recounted how she would settle fights over the telephone about who got to practice the piano first.

Once parents understand a child's basic needs, they can then ask if they are the ones who must meet all those needs or whether someone else can help. A baby-sitter or day care worker can help foster a baby's sense of trust, can cuddle and talk to her, can soothe and hold her. A housekeeper or an after-school program can help supervise an older child or occupy him so there is less risk of getting into trouble. Only parents, though, can fulfill some tasks. Only they can explain their personal moral standards, and only they can live that example for their children.

Although staying at home does not guarantee success in the essential tasks of sustaining emotional connection and supervising children, it's only fair to admit that working outside the home often makes those tasks more challenging. Being a responsible working mother and father means accepting the need for constant vigilance. Although there is no simple checklist, psychologists say that classic signs that children are not thriving include trouble sleeping, poor appetite, problems at school, outbursts of anger, or periods of withdrawal.

Kathy Klema, the investment banker, drew a line by insisting on returning home in time to give her children baths and put them to bed despite her demanding profession. "It's pretty clear to me that where kids really are the parents' first priorities, kids know," Kathy said. "When David and I talked about having children, we knew we would have less time for the two of us. We weren't going to institute one night out. All of our time spent not working is with our kids."

Once home, Kathy said, she and her husband also resolved that they would act as parents, not delegate chores to their live-in nanny. "We change the diapers. The nanny is in her room. We believe that once we're home, we're on."

To get home on time, Kathy takes work home with her and works until 3 A.M. crunching numbers if necessary, after the children are asleep. She can invite clients home to dinner to meet her children instead of taking them out; she says many of them tell her that her openness about being a mother makes her human and appealing to them.

In the end, I asked, has her decision to leave earlier than many others in her office caused trouble at work? Kathy did not hesitate. "If I made the decision, whatever the ramifications may be, I don't give a hoot."

REFRAMING THE DEBATE

Once we redefine motherhood, we can also change the shallow, misleading debate about working mothers to cut through the distortions that blind us. If we can ask the right questions, we can focus on the real problems, not the false villains. First, we must stop assuming that good mothers stay at home and bad mothers go out to work, that children of mothers at home thrive and children of mothers at work suffer. It is time to acknowledge that working is not the gauge of parental success or failure. A better guide might be what David Blankenhorn, citing the Bible, called "right spirit," or what could be called personal responsibility.

There are working mothers who did not or could not convey that spirit; Brenda Coffey remembers a perennially tired mother who worked two jobs; Toni Rumsey remembers a "cranky mom." Working can deaden and coarsen the soul, as can poverty or marital strife or depression or, for some women, staying at home. Of course, some working mothers are negligent, beaten down, or worse.

In some cases, the problem lies with the person's character, not occupation. Every time the accusatory finger points to work as the reason a mother neglected her child, we should also ask whether that mother would do any better if she were at home. Would a news anchor who leaves her children with a nanny during the week and visits them only on weekends be more committed to them if she did not work? Might she not leave them with the nanny while she spent her days playing tennis, working out with a personal trainer, and planning the local charity ball?

Just as we must not brand a working mother as automatically negligent, we must not label a mother at home as inevitably oppressed and exploited. To stay at home with a child these days is a luxury, a coveted one for many women. Many have found great joy in doing so. And many take on virtual second careers in volunteer and charity work, unpaid tasks that keep them almost as busy—or in some cases, just as busy—as their paid jobs once did.

Second, we must realize that we can't help children by talking only about their needs, as if somehow we can magically separate what happens to their parents from what happens to them. Psychologists, pundits, and politicians prate on about "putting children first." Of course we must, but we cannot do so if we consider children in a vacuum. Psychologists believe and studies have found that the emotional health of mothers (and fathers, although they are less studied) shapes their ability to be sensitive and responsive to their children. Children's well-being depends on the material, moral, and emotional well-being of their parents.

For these reasons, it is wrong to describe the mother-child relationship as a zero-sum game, although that is the metaphor that dominates our discussions. In ways large and small, parents must always make excruciating decisions about whose interests prevail. Should parents divorce because they are miserable together, or should they endure unhappiness because divorce would make their children miserable? Should a family move so that one parent can advance in a career or stay put because moving is too disruptive to children?

It is never as simple as one side winning or losing. The reality is that if one loses, both lose. A conscientious mother will suffer if her child suffers because her happiness and her sense of effectiveness are bound up with how her child fares. She will not relish her victory if the result is a child in pain. Nor does a child win if the mother is frustrated, despairing, angry, or distracted.

While we have to understand how mothers' and children's needs are intertwined, our public and private discussions of motherhood often confound them entirely. Mothers may talk of children's needs when they are really describing their own. I have heard countless mothers say they are staying at home because their children need them to. That may be true in some cases; perhaps a child has a severe disability or a temperament that does not adapt well to separation. But heretical as it is to say so, I believe that in many cases the truth is that it is the mother who needs to be home—and there is nothing wrong with that.

One of my earliest forays into thinking through the ideas in this book came in the form of an essay for the *New York Times Book Review*. My suggestion that not all children need their mothers to stay at home and that much guilt is unnecessary drew an irate phone call from an acquaintance. She told me that I had, in effect, betrayed her and other mothers by undermining their attempts to win permission to work part time. How could she tell her boss that her children needed her when I was arguing that mothers who work full time can still meet their children's needs?

My answer is that if a mother feels she needs to be at home more, then she probably does. It is telling that, as a society, we think that the only acceptable and convincing way to make the case for job flexibility is to talk about children suffering. As usual, mothers' feelings are discounted. It's a perfectly legitimate argument to say that some mothers need more time with their children to feel properly attuned to them.

I think many women at home today need to convince themselves that their children will turn out better than those whose mothers work partly because they have given up a great deal to stay home and must believe that whatever sacrifices they have made will pay off. I say, yes, their children are likely to turn out better because they are following their hearts—and my children are likely to turn out better because I am following mine.

Third, we must stop judging motherhood by arbitrary, external measures. We tend to rate mothering by what economists would call inputs: how many hours mothers are at home or how often a mother joins children for a family dinner. The better measure is outcomes, even though we must remember that we cannot always know precisely how much to attribute to parents, to genes, or to the broader culture.

Most people know what they believe a good mother and a good father help to produce: a person with sound moral values and an ability to engage in productive work (of whatever kind) and loving relationships. The shifting fashions of child rearing ought to have taught us by now that there are many different ways to reach these goals and no simple symbolic cure-all.

The best test of what is good for children is not what actions mothers and fathers perform, but how their children experience them. Take the family dinner, most commentators' favorite test of parental devotion. For some children, that meal can be a warm occasion to exchange confidences; for others, it can be an excruciating hour of quizzing and reprimands. One therapist I know treated a patient with a devoted stay-at-home mother who ate a formal dinner with the children every night. During dinner, the mother and father grilled the children about their days, required them to discuss political topics, and quizzed them on schoolwork. The child grew up alternating between bouts of obesity and anorexia, and one reason was her association of eating with fear and approval.

I am not saying that a family dinner is a bad idea. It is clearly important for parents and children to have regular, predictable time together and clearly a good thing to have family rituals. It's just that the mere presence of such rituals does not guarantee closeness or empathy between parents and children, and the presence or absence of such rituals does not constitute a good measure of the mothers' or fathers' devotion.

Fourth, we must shift our society's exclusive focus away from mothers and widen it to all those who are responsible for the welfare of children: fathers, extended family members, "other mothers," communities, and the government. We must finally rid ourselves of the cruel pretense that mothers can do their job alone. Throughout history, they have not; in most cultures, they do not. That is equally true for mothers at home and mothers at work.

Mothers bear responsibility, but they must not be condemned to bear it entirely by themselves. We must look beyond mothers' failings to the failings of the communities that once encircled and buoyed them. Many mothers today try to rear children in menacing neighborhoods amid a culture blaring messages of sex, violence, materialism, cynicism, and apathy. They live in a society that denigrates both mothers at home and mothers at work. Yet mothers continue to blame themselves for failings that are exacerbated, if not caused, by the larger forces around them.

Finally, we must acknowledge the folly of blanket prescriptions. It is worse than absurd, it is actively harmful, to pronounce that mothers should stay at home because doing so would be best for their children. For some families, that would indeed be the best choice. For others, it would mean condemning the mother and child to all but certain unhappiness—and near penury. No one solution will work for all families; an elixir that cures one could well poison others.

THE REAL VILLAINS

Once we reframe the debate, the real issues emerge. All too often, the champions of working mothers, trying to repel attacks, counter by denying that any problems exist or charging that the problems are exaggerated, viewed through the prism of nostalgia. We must avoid replacing the half-truths of working mothers' critics with half-truths of our own.

There are clear signs that many children are in trouble today, from the shameful rates of poverty to the soaring instances of violence. The campaigners for "family values" have been right to raise the specter of children suffering and parents' irresponsibility, even if they often wrongly accuse working mothers.

Some of these problems are so painful that parents avert their eyes and hearts. Patricia Nachman, a psychoanalyst who found that children of working mothers were more advanced developmentally in several ways than children of mothers at home, nonetheless talked about her concern that many working mothers were ignoring their children's genuine sadness at their departure each morning because they could not bear it. Without acknowledging their children's pain, they had no hope of comforting them.

Many teachers and child care workers I spoke with complained bitterly about parents who seemed to be growing more selfish by the year. On the whole, I have found teachers and day care workers among the severest critics of parents (with the lucky exception of the ones who cared for my children). They are so trained to focus on children that they sometimes forget that to help children, they must help mothers.

Nonetheless, I feel honor bound to report teachers' tales of parents who refused to adjust their work schedules even when teachers judged their children needed more time with them, who would not change baby-sitters even after teachers noticed problems, who balked at taking time off from work even to help phase their children into a new school or day care center, and who screamed at staff members who would not allow them to drop off their feverish or infectious children.

In my years as an educational reporter, I heard countless teachers vent their disgust with parents, rich and poor, who did not bother to show up for conferences, who dismissed teachers' concerns about their children, who refused to have children tested, or who seemed profoundly out of touch with their children's worlds. They told of students who ranged from poorly dressed, hungry, and sleepy to forlorn, lost, and unloved.

There are plenty of horror stories to go around, but they apply both to mothers at work and mothers at home. Both can display this kind of indifference, this ability to ignore children's pain and comfort themselves with inane rationalizations like, Whatever makes me happy makes them happy.

One of the most chilling stories I have heard of a loveless childhood came from a friend who grew up in a wealthy home. Her mother was, as she put it, a "clubwoman," who never held a job but was simply resentful of and uninterested in her children. She told her children she was too busy to attend school events. She left their care to servants they still cherish. One of my friend's recurring memories is of waking up with a nightmare and being comforted by a nanny. Her mother lived in another wing of the sprawling house, too far away to hear her.

The evidence from teachers, day care centers, and society at large suggests that there are working parents who are not taking their responsibilities to children seriously enough. The question is whether these parents are neglecting their children because they are working. I believe these parents would neglect their children whether they were working or not, because something is missing inside them and they had children without understanding what a solemn and profound commitment that entails.

Some of these tales of neglect are cautionary tales of the failure of individual responsibility. Some, however, are pitiable reflections of the harshness and economic precariousness of many parents' lives, parents who will be fired if they take off time from work to go to school conferences or tend sick children. As such, these cases expose a broader failure, one of our society as a whole—to honor our obligation to our children.

WHAT IS TO BE DONE?

We know what we could do as a society and as individuals to help mothers both at work and at home, and we have refused to do it. This is not a book about policy because I am convinced that no changes will come unless we cut through the disinformation and reshape the way we talk and think about work and child rearing.

The French provide an instructive example. The United States spends millions of dollars a year on research examining the effect of child care on intelligence, emotional stability, behavior, and bonds to parents, all in the service of asking the question, Does a mother's work harm her children? The French ask a different question: How do we make sure that child care is the best it can be?

Bettye Caldwell, one of the pioneers of child care research and still a leading expert, traveled to France a few years ago to observe the child care offered to all families there: day care for children under three years old with fees on a sliding scale adjusted to parents' incomes and publicly funded nursery school for all children three to six years old.

When she described her research to her French counterparts, she said, they asked her why Americans did not spend more money instead on practical measures like teacher training to ensure high-quality child care. France requires five years of training for the teachers who will work with infants and toddlers; in most American states, teachers need only about ten hours of training. More than 72 percent of Frenchwomen with children under age three work, compared to 62 percent in the United States.[4] There isn't much discussion in France about generations of lost children, and you don't find the abysmal day care centers we have in the United States.

Americans would probably never feel comfortable with a centralized system of child care that fits the French emphasis on national control of education. Rather, because we are stuck on the first question of whether working harms children, we do not move on to the more important question of how we can make sure it doesn't.

Our political and public policy debates ask the wrong questions, too. The great feminist causes célèbres—sexual harassment, date rape, women's studies, gender issues, and abortion—are not the issues that consume most women's lives. How to afford to spend as much time as possible with their families, how to find good child care if they must or want to work, how to shelter children from a corrosive popular culture—these are the issues that grip women and, increasingly, men.

The religious right and the Republican Party have been shrewd to focus on family issues not only because voters care about them the most, but also because these issues tap the widespread sense that something is rotten in our society and that new leaders may help. The Democrats belatedly recognized that fact by co-opting many of the same ideas in the 1996 campaign. Yet neither party offered much beyond token gestures. The tax credits both parties endorse are too small either to enable a mother to stay at home or to pay the costs of child care. School uniforms and curfews are cheap ways to appease fears about the lack of discipline and children out of control.

These issues are also routinely slighted by the press. The proposals of the Christian right on family tax breaks or, indeed, of the left or the center on how to attain a better balance between work and family are relegated to the "soft news" ghetto in many newspapers and magazines or confined to the women's talk shows on television.

With a handful of exceptions, virtually no one in our society has grappled with the real costs of putting children first. How many of those who preach that children are better off with their mothers at home have considered what that would really mean? A family would have to forgo a mother's salary, and since many mothers cannot afford to stay home, someone would have to help replace it. How much are employers, the government, and individual families willing to pay to achieve that goal? How long should we help mothers stay at home? The first year? Longer? Should the benefits extend to all mothers—wealthy, middle class, working class, and poor?

The answers offered by advocates on the right and the left are often woefully inadequate. Many pretend that mothers don't really have to work and ritually denounce materialism. James Dobson of the Christian right, David Gelertner in *Commentary,* communitarians like Amitai Etzioni and the New Age gurus of movements like Voluntary Simplicity gamely press for better budgeting and the virtues of doing without, but many families need the mothers' paychecks for necessities like mortgage payments and college savings—or, in poor families, food.

Christian-right groups and conservative Republicans alike call for radical tax cuts and a radical rethinking of the role of government, reasoning that mothers could stay home if taxes returned to the levels of forty years ago. Would most families be willing to accept drastically reduced services in return? Could they give up the many governmental subsidies that have aided the middle class—the tax breaks on mortgages and government-subsidized low-interest loans that allowed generations of Americans to afford their own homes or federal subsidies for highways that linked cities to the suburbs, to name only two? Nor would lower taxes help poor mothers stay at home with children who need most the benefits of healthy parental bonds, intellectual stimulation, and structure to help them survive the neighborhoods and family stress that threaten them.

The left is often similarly unrealistic. It champions a European model of generous social welfare payments that offer women the option either of staying at home and keeping their jobs for several years or working with the aid of first-rate child care and flexible hours. It is a model that deeply appeals to me, but it involves taxation and governmental spending on a scale that is unacceptable to many Americans and that violates the American political ethos of individualism. It may well be that we need to forge our own American version of these European ideas, one that mixes market incentives with governmental largesse.

I'd be willing to pay more taxes if they went to helping poor and working-poor families and their children, but many people would not. The resentments of many working-class families about such benefits helped power their exodus from the Democratic Party. I think that many on the left have not grappled honestly enough with the question the right raises: Is it fair to impose taxes that force all families to pay for services like child care that some would rather not use because they prefer mothers to stay at home?

However we pay for it, deciding that society should encourage mothers to stay at home effectively means condemning many women to a life of economic dependence. Women will need jobs not only to put food on the table now, but also for their own and their families' long-term economic security, particularly in an age of downsizing and high divorce rates. Mothers at home may not only be stranded if their husbands leave, but may be stuck in bad marriages because they have no ties to the world of work or no skills to enable them to earn decent salaries.

If we decide that women who want to work deserve social support, how do we ensure that their children are safe? Good child care, especially during the first year of life, is extremely expensive. There must be enough people around to make sure that babies are responded to, hugged, rocked, and talked to. New discoveries about the way the structure of the brain is formed during the early years make clear the terrible price we pay for neglect or bad child care.

A recent report by the Center for the Future of Children estimated that the United States now spends about $40 billion a year on child care—with half the burden borne by parents; about 45 percent by federal, state, and local governments; and 5 percent by business or foundations.[5]

Even that sum, which sounds huge, is by no means enough. Much of the governmental money is spent on child care for very poor parents, but working-poor parents do not get help with child care that might enable them to keep their jobs. Several studies have found that the children of working-poor and working-class parents often receive the lowest-quality care.

The state of most American child care is a national disgrace. One of the most recent studies of child care, the Cost, Quality, and Child Outcomes in Child Care Centers Study, offers a stark picture of why it is dangerous to leave child care entirely up to the market. The fierce competition among centers created pressure to drive costs down; parents were not willing or able to pay more for higher quality.

That study, like many others, found the best child care in centers that were subsidized in some way, by governments, businesses, or universities. A Harvard study of child care found that tax credits or parental vouchers had no impact on the quality of child care and that tax credits disproportionately benefited upper-income families. In international comparisons, countries with government-funded, well-regulated care rank highest in child-care quality, while countries like the United States, which depend largely on the market, provide the worst care on average.[6]

As Heidi Hartmann, of the Institute for Women's Policy Research, and Barbara Bergmann, of American University, argued, we could decide that child care should be a national priority, like public schooling. If every working mother could place her child in affordable, high-quality care, we could protect children and reduce poverty.

Ideally, that system would be funded by the government, available on a sliding scale to any parent who needed it. Child care workers would be paid decent wages. They would have to meet some basic standards and undergo some framing, as public school teachers now do. Child care standards should be national to ensure that good-quality care is widely available.

Opponents of regulation say it would drive many small child care providers out of business and create an administrative nightmare. But there are several ways to lighten the regulatory load, according to William Gormley, of Georgetown University. Family day care workers, for example, could be exempted from all local regulations, such as zoning, except for fire safety; they could be subject only to broad state or federal standards. Child care providers might be given incentives to obtain training; for example, family day care workers could be allowed to care for a larger number of children if they received better training. If a first inspection turned up no problems, good providers could be inspected less often.

There may be many mothers who would rather stay at home with their children and who would view a government-funded system as an unfair subsidy of working mothers at the expense of mothers at home. One alternative, then, might be a substantial, refundable child-rearing tax credit, which mothers could use either to rear their children at home or help pay for child care. Our current tax deductions are too small either to help mothers afford to stay home or to pay the real costs of good day care. And they are not refundable, so they do not help poor or working-poor mothers.

Phil Robins, of the University of Florida, estimated that making the current tax deduction refundable would increase governmental expenditure from about $8.8 billion a year to $9.2 billion. Making the credit large enough to enable mothers to stay home or afford good day care would cost about $23.7 billion a year. If we opt for a tax credit, though, we still need federal standards, as well as some federal money to improve quality, since the market tends to drive quality down, not up.

We need some consumer protection, including inspections, and information on resources and referrals for parents to help them choose good care, as Barbara Reisman, of the Child Care Action Campaign, urged. Parents, for example, should be able to review state inspection reports of child care providers; lists of repeated violators should be circulated.

Even if child care is top flight, all parents should be able to take a year's leave, at some lower percentage of their salaries, after the birth or adoption of a child, in whatever combination of mother and father they choose. There are several ways to pay for these leaves, but all will be expensive and will require sacrifice. Gormley suggested that in essence the government and the employer should split 80 percent of the cost of a mother's or father's salary and that parents would forgo 20 percent of their pay.[7]

Virtually everyone agrees in principle about the benefits of flextime, telecommuting, and sequencing. The problem is to convince most employers that offering these options is a worthwhile investment—and in persuading most parents that their jobs will be safe if they take advantage of these benefits. Several studies have shown that only a tiny fraction of employees use these benefits even when they are available because of their fear that they will be marked as less dedicated and more vulnerable to being fired.

The findings of other studies, though, have suggested that these policies can be a powerful lure: Mothers in companies with such benefits return to work sooner. Even the *Economist*, the Bible of classic laissez-faire economics, warned that relentless layoffs could destroy morale and suggested that companies offer employees a new bargain: flexibility and benefits, including sabbaticals, job sharing, child care, and subsidized education instead of job security.[8]

We could go even further and explore how to reimagine work, perhaps forgoing wage increases for several years in return for moving toward a four-day week for most workers. Shorter workweeks would give more people jobs and more workers time. Perhaps we could offer more European-style flexibility to parents, so that mothers or fathers could work part time for several years, as they can in Sweden.

I do not offer new answers here because the right ones are obvious and numbingly familiar. For more than twenty years, women have been asking for higher-quality, more affordable child care, more participation from fathers, and more generous family leaves. For years, working mothers have anguished over how to meet their responsibilities to their children and their jobs.

Parents need more time with their children. Those who work need high-quality, affordable child care. Those who want to stay home should be able to do so. Those who are poor need enough social supports to keep them in the workforce. Help must come from individuals, from communities, from business, and from the government. Fathers could decide that having children requires a conscious reassessment of their priorities. Groups of concerned people could band together to protect children by establishing programs, such as

Mad Dads, in which fathers patrol the neighborhoods, or Safe Zones, where adults take responsibility for the children around them.

These ideas are just a few of many alternatives that deserve a hearing and vigorous public discussion. We must change policies and reshape work, for the sake of men as well as women and children. Yet for the most part, we have refused to act. We resist solutions partly because of the American belief that every family should be able to manage on its own. That belief persists even though historians like Stephanie Coontz have shown that from colonial times on, families were aided by the state and joined together to help each other. That belief has intensified in this time of disillusionment with big-government solutions.

In addition to the political resistance to change policies, there is a personal one. What hobbles mothers from asking for help, reaching out to their communities, or rallying politically to demand better policies? The misguided but widespread belief that they should be able to make it on their own, a pervasive sense of shame in admitting failure, and a gnawing feeling that they are not good mothers because they work.

We have to fight this fight on two fronts: the world outside us and the one within us. Americans are curiously reluctant to consider our children a public good worth protecting. While we wait and work toward that day, we can do something about our own internal visions of who mothers are and what they are supposed to do.

A Truce and a dream

It is time to stop the chorus of condemnation about working mothers. Toni Rumsey, Ahling Deng, and Sue Henderson are good mothers, dedicated and responsible, but women like them are pilloried in the public hand-wringing about working mothers.

This is not only insulting, but worse, it instills in many mothers a corrosive but groundless fear that they are harming their children. The evidence I marshal in this book proves that it is absurd to argue that a mother who works condemns her child to an emotional, intellectual, or moral wasteland. Instead, we should recognize that mothers at work or at home who claim their own dreams without neglecting their responsibilities can help their children learn to do the same.

We should be worried about the state of children, far more worried than we are, but not because so many mothers work. We should be worried because we continue to balk at finding ways to help parents at work take care of children. Society's branding of working mothers as bad mothers is even crueler for those mothers who work because they must. Such mothers often have regimented, joyless jobs, and they labor at them with the painful knowledge they have left their children in second-rate child care or worse, because they could not afford anything better. We offer them only criticism, no help in affording better child care, no assurance that the people who look after their children are screened or well-trained.

The debate about work and child-rearing is poisoned by defensiveness on both sides. Mothers at home tend to attack mothers who work outside the home because they, in turn, feel demeaned, written off as uninteresting drudges. The pull toward home that many mothers feel is a perfectly defensible one; it does not need to be rationalized by insisting that to do otherwise is bad for children.

Many mothers may read the research results on child care, the theories of Jessica Benjamin, or any of the other offerings of this book and still not feel comfortable with working at all. Even making British-trained nannies available to all families in the country for free would still not make many mothers want to work. I'm not writing this book to urge that all women take power in the world by ignoring their own legitimate desires to stay home with their children.

In turn, mothers do not need to apologize if they long for the stimulation, adult company, money, and independence that work provides. We need to cast off the taboo that prevents many women—and not just highly educated or professional women—from admitting that staying at home all day with children can be stressful, frantic, and boring. Working mothers should not have to resort to what magazines like *U.S. News & World Report* label "lies," the excuse that they only work because otherwise starvation lurks. Though many mothers indeed must work, others offer that excuse in public because any other reason is still judged selfish and unmotherly.

The public debate about working and children also ignores one of the most obvious lessons of adulthood, that each choice carries with it some degree of loss. Just as mothers at work mourn the time they give up with their children, many mothers who left the workforce also have bouts of longing for their old identities and the relative calm of the workplace. Some of the public breast-beating by mothers about the pain of working seems to be a futile longing for the impossible. No one can escape trade-offs.

Ultimately, the right balance of work and mothering can only be decided after struggles with our own hearts. In the end, individual decisions will and should vary. Is giving up a job so painful that doing so will sour time with children and make mothers feel their lives are failures? Is giving up time with children so painful that doing so will poison the hours at work and torture mothers with the belief they've failed their children?

Mothers must be given the freedom to make choices without being blinded and hounded by the false debate, the confining ideal of the perfect mother, and the taunts of the self-righteous. Only then, unencumbered, can mothers make the decision that works best for them and their children. I only ask that no mother should curb her dreams—whether to be at home or at work—out of baseless fear or guilt.

Epilogue

I wrote this book out of hope and fear, to confront my own demons and share my exhilaration. I used to quail inside whenever I met a mother who had chosen a different path from mine; in my heart, I felt challenged and questioned my own choice. When I started my research, I worried that if I met even one working mother who was negligent or who had found her work unbearable, my book would turn out to be a fraud.

Writing the book exorcised many of these fears. I came to see that swayed by the distorted debate about motherhood, I had been searching for absolutes that did not exist. My arguments that mothers can work and responsibly raise children were not undermined by evidence that working mothers can be irresponsible, that many are riven by fears, and that some do not want to work at all.

I have come to accept that breaking with the old images of the good mother means living with a certain measure of uncertainty and self-doubt—just as many mothers at home feel they are at odds with a new ideal that trumpets working as the norm. Writing this book helped me to see that the task is not to find some elusive peace, but to learn how to ask the right questions to make decisions that are fair to myself and my family. I will have to constantly test the right balance between work and family, and my sense of what feels right will change over time, as my needs and my children's do.

I continue to struggle with how to weigh one desire—to work, to contribute, to strive, to dream—against the longing to have time with my children, to enjoy them, teach them, and love them before they leave. Before my children were born, I was a foreign correspondent in Japan and Korea; it was a golden time, filled with an intoxicating sense of adventure and an awed sense that I was present at great moments in a country's history. I watched Japan grow ever richer and ordinary Japanese struggle to understand what that meant for their own lives. I scrambled onto rooftops and gagged on tear gas and watched as ordinary Koreans defied their government and ultimately helped topple a dictator. When phone calls came at 3 A.M., I was out on the next flight, and I never knew when I would get back.

I worried that such a life would be too much for me as a mother and hard on children. Eventually, a chance came to return to New York, and I grabbed it. After my daughter was born, I was astonished and grateful to find that I could indeed be a responsible working mother. Yet I could not go on as if my child did not exist. I traveled less and planned shorter trips. I worked fewer hours and saw the number of articles I wrote fall. I turned down tempting assignments because I felt they required too much travel or too many late nights and weekends. As happy as I was being a mother, at times I felt stunted professionally. I wondered constantly if I was shortchanging myself; I knew I could not shortchange my children.

As my children grow, I find my responsibilities more challenging than when they were babies. Very young children usually gladly accept the love of a surrogate, as long as that person is sensitive. They bask in trust and the knowledge that their needs will be attended to. When my daughter entered elementary school, I felt a new urgency about getting home to her. While she was content doing her homework with her baby-sitter or my husband, I wanted to be able to work with her, too. I wanted to be involved in school discussions about curriculum. That meant making sure I could take time from work to perform these tasks.

As I wrote the last chapters of this book, over me loomed my return to a job that I loved, but one that would inevitably keep me away longer hours than my book-writing schedule. Being able to arrive home a little earlier, having the flexibility to interrupt my workday, were precious freedoms. As the time to go back drew closer, I could feel a band tightening around my heart.

I work for a newspaper, and a newspaper's rhythms are hard on families. The very hours when most people are leaving the office, when children are ready for dinner and bed, are the hours when the deadlines loom and the heart of a newspaper begins to pound. As I thought about what to do at the paper, I was swept by a wave of defeatism.

In the few years before my book leave, I had battled a sense of being on the margins at work. I longed to change that situation, but the positions of responsibility at the paper seemed to keep my colleagues chained to their desks well into the night. I could not imagine how to take on more demanding jobs while remaining the kind of mother I wanted to be.

As if to test my newfound resolution, a few months after I returned to work, a job opened up that offered me the chance to return to that earlier calling of foreign news. The job would mean more responsibility and being on call in a way I had resisted since my children were born. I agonized for weeks, and at several points decided I would not apply.

In the end, I decided to apply the principles I had been writing about. I talked to my husband about what he was willing to do and what would be too much for him. We realized my first months back at work had put too much strain on him and that we needed to hire some extra help to spell him at night when I did have to work late.

I asked myself what my children needed and what I needed to feel close to them. The answer was enough time every night before bed—to play, to talk over the day, to establish that elusive but essential sense of connection. My months back at work had taught me that I could tolerate some late nights, but I could not bear regularly arriving home after my children were asleep, or even getting home just in time to kiss them good night.

I was honest about my need to go to school meetings and the pediatrician's office. And I knew that the foreign job, because articles arrived in waves from different time zones, offered the best chance of leaving in time to see my children alert and awake. When I tried the job for a few weeks, I was surprised to feel the same joy that had swept over me when I first returned to work after my daughter was born. The excitement of being challenged infused me with energy when I arrived home. I decided to take the job, and I have not regretted it.

There is a price for my work; my life is often more harried, my burdens greater, because I am trying to honor my obligations to my family and my job. There are moments when I feel depleted, guilty, distracted, and deprived of time with my children.

I remember a day I spent at lunch in my daughter's nursery school, time I had because I was on maternity leave after the birth of my son. She chatted away to her classmates and occasionally turned to me and grinned. I could hear the siren call of freedom, freedom to drop in at lunchtime any day I wanted. At that moment and many others, I could understand the longing to stay at home or work part time so I could have an extra day with my children.

In the end, though, I have made another choice, and I am happy with it. My daughter is older now, and there are times when she complains about my work in a way she did not when she was younger and more disposed to accept as normal whatever happened in our house. Not long ago, my husband brought her by my office; unexpectedly, she asked to stay with me on a night when I was the editor on duty and would be very busy. She busied herself with the computer and brushed off my attempts to explain what I was doing when I conferred with reporters, edited an article, or fielded requests from the top editors.

When we finally got home that night, my husband asked her how she liked it. I thought she might have been bored. "It was great," she told him. "Mommy was in charge." I don't know what that meant to her, exactly; it is tempting but probably facile to draw a simple feminist lesson such as it's good for her to see a woman exercising authority. I think that's true, but I also believe that her satisfaction sprung as well from seeing her mother in a different place, in a different set of relationships, acting in a different way but also remaining the same mother she knew. It was a way of being together while watching me in a different guise, but also a proof that my other identity as a working woman did not wipe out my identity as her mother.

Working and raising children is hard, but so is any job worth doing. Staying at home with children all day is hard and draining work, too. I found that holding myself back at work was debilitating and depressing. It infected my time at home with my children and my husband. I have learned that whatever the price of working, if I give up the struggle, I will pay a greater price—one of defeatism and despair.

A friend of mine once told me about someone she knew who was trying to decide whether or how much to work after the birth of a third child. In the end, she decided, "I'm just a working girl." It was a sentence that struck me with the force of revelation. Becoming a mother did not change that commitment or dislodge that identity; it grafted a new self and a new mission onto the old one.

What I resent most about the discussion of working motherhood is the premise that working means valuing work more than children. I am not placing one above the other; I am choosing both. The exhilaration I feel because I am not dividing my soul and my mind helps buoy me in times of struggle.

When this book was on the verge of publication, I found my convictions tested by the illness of one of my children. My child's life was in danger, and the crisis lasted many, many months. I discovered that work can be a lifeline not only in normal times but in dire times as well.

I was lucky to work for a generous and compassionate employer, who allowed me to take as much time off as necessary to care for my child. There was no question in my employer's mind—or my own—about what came first. Going to work when I could, though, allowed me to visit a world far removed from the one of sickness and sadness that we inhabited. Working also signaled to my children that life could be normal and they could feel normal, too.

Without my work and the restorative sense of identity and community it provided, I could not have mustered the strength to do what was indeed my most important job: nursing and reassuring my child. I was told by the doctors that my child would take cues from me. I could not break down. I could not show fear. That would have been contagious. Along with the support of friends and family, working helped me compose myself. It helped distract me from terror, and it helped replenish me so I could give again.

While I cannot predict what lies ahead for me as mother or professional, I know that I refuse to listen to those who tell me I cannot honorably do both. I wrote this book because I wanted to say to the voices of doubt outside me and within me, Be silent. I want my daughter and my son to be able to choose a life rich with both work and family without the same hobbling sense of dread that afflicts so many of us today. I am tired of hearing women told that they should not dare to want it all—or as much as anyone can reasonably hope to get. I am going to shut my ears to the drumbeat, and I am going to keep my eyes trained on my children.

ACKNOWLEDGMENTS

I thank all the mothers and fathers I interviewed for allowing me to enter their lives; I have tried to do justice to their complexity and their everyday heroism.

I am grateful to the many experts and scholars who patiently bore with my questions; in particular, for their time and generosity, I thank Drs. Jessica Benjamin, Stella Chess, Alexander Thomas, Bettye Caldwell, Barbara Nordhaus, and Dr. Donald Cohen of the Yale Child Study Center; and Jeff Atkinson, for his repeated searches for custody cases. I am particularly grateful to Dr. Michael E. Lamb, who guided me through the maze of child care studies and read early drafts of my chapters on attachment theory and child care research.

Joe Lelyveld understood how important this book was to me and generously allowed me to take a leave of absence from the *Times*. For their patience and support when I had to take vacation time to finish the revisions, I thank Bill Keller, Dean Baquet, Steve Engelberg, and my colleagues on the Foreign and National Desks.

My colleagues Fox Butterfield, Jason DeParle, Robert Pear, Robin Toner, Janet Elder, and Michael Kagay kindly shared their expertise on crime, welfare policy, the gender gap, and polling.

For helping to arrange interviews, I thank Jane Lii, who introduced me to Ahling Deng and translated for us; Alvin Aviles and Dr. Bart O'Connor of Project Chance; and Sofia Stefatos of Unite, who also kindly translated from Spanish to English. Jean Hardesty of Political Research Associates guided me to the publications of the religious right.

With unflagging goodwill and calm, Steve Ross and Andrew Lih rescued me from several computer disasters. Sarah Kidwell allowed me to rent a room of my own in which to write. Sam Freedman and Ari Goldman came to the rescue with loans of their offices and cups of hot tea during the last weeks of revision.

In the early months of working on the book, Kevin Heldman gave me tips on computer journalism and computer searches, and Janet Goldstein gave editorial advice. Samy-Leigh Webster-Woog provided invaluable research help in the last weeks of revisions.

Dr. Judith Isaac has not only shared her insights about working motherhood but has been a patient midwife to this book, which in many ways is a collaboration.

I am deeply grateful to the many friends who, despite their own busy lives, took on the task of reading a balky six-hundred-page draft. The finished work has been vastly improved by Kami Kim, David Remnick, Lisa Gubernick, Tanya Luhrmann, and Jan Hoffman, who read the entire manuscript and offered trenchant, enormously useful criticisms. David was kind enough to read several subsequent revisions. Ada Yonenaka's expert eye, as an editor and a working mother, was invaluable in reshaping my second draft. Lisa Gubernick came up with the perfect title.

Diane Reverand of HarperCollins took this book on despite a prodigiously busy schedule and edited it with a deft hand. David Flora was ever patient and efficient.

Barney Karpfinger is not only a wonderful agent but a dear friend. He believed in this book when I despaired of ever writing it, encouraged me at every turn, sustained me through the upheavals of the publishing process, and added insightful editing to his many other contributions to this book.

My friends have been extraordinarily generous. They sent me

clippings, taped radio shows, introduced me to interview subjects, housed me when I traveled, propped me up when I felt like giving up, and hashed over the issues in their own lives. As well as the friends acknowledged elsewhere, I thank Miles and Diane Corwin, Rebecca and Jim Fowler, Martha Greenough and David Pitt, Catherine Manegold, Amy McIntosh and Jeff Toobin, Susanna Rodell, Elisabeth Rubinfien and Dan Sneider, and Ann Wizer.

This book would never have been finished without the moral and practical support of my own network of "other mothers," my extended family: Kami Kim and Tom McDonald, for pushing me to take more time to work in the last frantic months and keeping my husband and children company while I did; Carol Phethean and Peter Yawitz, staunch allies in the struggle to make it all work and inveterate clippers of articles in the *Wall Street Journal;* Lisa Gubernick and Paul Fishleder, the kind of neighbors whom people think exist only over a white picket fence; Esther Fein and David Remnick, whose hearts are as open as their intelligence is keen; and Shirley Matthews, my oldest friend and surrogate sister. I can leave for work each day only because of Paula Heeralall, who has lovingly tended my children and imparted her values of dignity, decency, ambition, and responsibility.

In a time when the family is supposed to be in shards, I am lucky to rely on mine. I thank my in-laws, Lorraine and Herbert Shapiro, for their unfailing support and understanding of a working mother's life and for raising a feminist son, and my sisters, Diane and Nancy Chira, for their encouragement and interest. My parents, Joe and Estelle Chira, are models of all that is generous and loving; they brought me up to value both the mind and the heart and have always cheered me in whatever I took on. I thank my father, who was a "new father" long before it became fashionable, and my mother, who taught me my first, lasting lessons in mother love.

For their compassion, dedication, and consummate medical skill, I thank the doctors, nurses, and staff of Babies Hospital, Mount Sinai Hospital, and Advanced Care; in particular, Terry Coffey, Dr. Jean Emond, Laura Flanigan, Naomi Hawkins, Dr.

Ken Gorfinkle, Ria Hawks, Genevieve Lowry, Cathy Mazzella, Marni Rubin, Jackie Simpson, Karen Suchoff, Dr. Jakca Tancabelic, Laura Tralongo, and Dr. Michael Weiner. I will always marvel at the surgical wizardry and commitment of Drs. Charles Miller and Myron Schwartz. No words can ever fully express my gratitude to Dr. Leonard Wexler, who lifted this mother's heart time and again and who understands that to treat a child, he must treat a family.

I have written this book for my own children, Eliza and Jake, who are my dearest reminders of the stakes and the joys of a new kind of motherhood.

My greatest debt is to my husband, Michael Shapiro, who endured much, and gave more, during the long struggle that was this book. As a husband and father, he gives me the freedom not only to dream my dreams, but to live them.

NOTES

CHAPTER I

1. *Newsweek,* May 12, 1997; *Wall Street Journal*, May 9, 1995; *Time*, May 20, 1991; *Barron's*, March 21, 1994.
2. *Commentary,* February 1996.
3. Arlie Russell Hochschild, *The Time Bind* (New York: Henry Holt and Company, 1997); "The Myth of Quality Time: How We're Cheating Our Kids, What You Can Do," *Newsweek*, May 12, 1997; and "The Lies Parents Tell About Work, Kids, Money, Day Care, and Ambition," *U.S. News & World Report*, May 12, 1997.
4. "Child Care and Working Parents," *Nightline* transcript, ABC News, October 21, 1997.
5. Hochschild, *Time Bind,* p. 83.
6. Ibid., pp. 75, 192, 219.
7. Interview with Sandra Scarr.
8. Natalie Angier, "Fighting and Studying Battle of the Sexes with Men and Mice," *New York Times*, June 11, 1996.
9. Betty Friedan, *The Feminine Mystique,* rev. ed. (New York: Dell, 1983), pp. 191–92.
10. Kathryn Keller, *Mothers and Work in Popular American Magazines,* Contributions in Women's Studies series, no. 139 (Westport, Conn.: Greenwood Press, 1994), p. 19.

11. Gay Sheldon Goldman and Kate Kelly, "Choices of Modern Mothers," *Parents,* October 1988, as quoted in Keller, pp. 116–17.

12. Julie Fudge Smith, "Welcome Home," *The Family in America,* December 1993.

CHAPTER 2

1. Shari L. Thurer, *The Myths of Motherhood: How Culture Reinvents the Good Mother* (Boston: Houghton Mifflin Company, 1994), pp. 8–16.

2. Ibid., p. 49.

3. Ibid., pp. 79–80.

4. Ibid., pp. 56, 176.

5. Laslett, cited in Ann Dally, *Inventing Motherhood: The Consequences of an Ideal* (New York: Schocken Books, 1982), p. 107.

6. Claudia Goldin, *Understanding the Gender Gap: An Economic History of American Women* (New York: Oxford University Press, 1990), pp. 46, 47.

7. Sharon Hays, *The Cultural Contradictions of Motherhood* (New Haven: Yale University Press, 1996), p. 30.

8. Ibid., citing *Journal of Pediatrics* study.

9. Interview with Goldin.

10. Goldin, *Understanding the Gender Gap,* p. 43.

11. Hays, *Cultural Contradicions,* p. 33.

12. Barbara Ehrenreich and Deirdre English, *For Her Own Good: 150 Years of the Experts' Advice to Women* (New York: Doubleday, 1978), p. 190.

13. Jeanine Basinger, *A Woman's View: How Hollywood Spoke to Women, 1930–1960* (New York: Alfred A. Knopf, 1995), pp. 48, 458.

14. Wendy Martin, "Women's Work," review of *Daughters of the Great Depression,* by Laura Hapke, *New York Times Book Review,* February 4, 1996.

15. Goldin, *Understanding the Gender Gap,* p. 32.

16. Ibid.

17. Diane Eyer, *Motherguilt: How Our Culture Blames Mothers for What's Wrong with Society* (New York: Random House, Times Books, 1996), pp. 53–54.

18. Ibid.

19. As quoted in Ehrenreich and English, *For Her Own Good,* p. 246.

20. Interview with Robert Thompson, director of the Center for the Study of Popular Television at Syracuse University.

21. Ibid.

22. Goldin, *Understanding the Gender Gap,* p. 158.

23. Ibid., p. 120.

24. Eyer, *Motherguilt,* p. 60.

25. Goldin, p. 18.

26. Donatella Lorch, "Is America Any Place for a Nice Hispanic Girl?" *New York Times*, April 11, 1996.

27. Ellen Hock, Debra DeMeis, and Susan McBride, "Maternal Separation Anxiety," in A. E. Gottfried and A. W. Gottfried, eds., *Maternal Employment and Children's Develpment: Longitudinal Research* (New York: Plenum Press, 1988), p. 198.

CHAPTER 3

1. Penelope Leach, *Children First: What Our Society Must Do—And Is Not Doing—For Our Children Today* (New York: Alfred A. Knopf, 1994), p. 50.

2. Penelope Leach, *Your Baby and Child: From Birth to Age Five* (New York: Alfred A. Knopf, 1989), p. 190.

3. Penelope Leach, *Babyhood,* 2d ed. (New York: Alfred A. Knopf, 1983), p. 219.

4. Ibid., p. 218.

5. Leach, *Your Baby and Child,* p. 192.

6. Ibid., p. 87.

7. Ibid., p. 78.

8. Jan Weyl, "I Can't Afford to Work," *Ladies' Home Journal,* October 1953, as quoted in Keller, *Mothers and Work in Popular American Magazines,* p. 17.

9. Leach, *Children First,* p. 94.

10. Ibid., p. 77.

11. Ibid., p. 95.

12. Leach, *Babyhood,* p. 218.

13. Gwen Kinkead, "Spock, Brazelton . . . and Now Penelope Leach," *New York Times*, April 10, 1994.

14. Leach, *Your Baby and Child,* pp. 28, 30.

15. *The Right Start Catalogue,* 1995.

16. T. Berry Brazelton, *Infants and Mothers: Differences in Development* (New York: Dell, 1983), p. xxviii.

17. Ibid., p. 173.

18. T. Berry Brazelton, *Working and Caring* (New York: Addison-Wesley, 1985), p. xvi.

19. Ibid.

20. Ibid., p. 78.

21. Ibid., p. 111.

22. Sheila Kitzinger, *Ourselves as Mothers: The Universal Experience of Motherhood* (New York: Addison-Wesley), 1995, p. 10.

23. *Time,* August 28, 1995.

24. Kitzinger, *Ourselves as Mothers,* p. 116.

25. *The Year After Childbirth: Surviving and Enjoying the First Year of Motherhood* (New York: Charles Scribner's Sons, 1994), p. 282.

26. Kitzinger, *Ourselves as Mothers,* p. 11.

CHAPTER 4

1. *Atlantic Monthly,* February 1991; Robert Karen, *Becoming Attached: Unfolding the Mystery of the Infant-Mother Bond and Its Impact on Later Life* (New York: Warner Books, 1994).

2. Dr. Ken Magid and Carole A. McKelvey, *High Risk: Children Without a Conscience* (New York: Bantam, 1987), pp. x, 3, 4.

3. David Blankenhorn, Steven Bayme, and Jean Bethke Elshtain, ed. *Rebuilding the Nest: A New Commitment to the American Family* (Milwaukee: Family Service of America, 1990), p. 127.

4. A point made in the writings of Diane Eyer, Barbara Ehrenreich, Lois Hoffman, and Michael Lamb.

5. Interview with Kagan.

6. Karen, *Becoming Attached,* pp. 30, 448 nn. 17, 18, 19, 20.

7. This synopsis of Bowlby's development of attachment theory is drawn from *Becoming Attached.* I have given short shrift in the narrative to the influence on Bowlby of ethnologists like Robert Hinde and Harry Harlow, who found that monkeys left in a cage with an iron mother with bottles sickened, while those with a wire monkey covered in cloth nuzzled and thrived. Bowlby wanted to replace Freud's idea that drives motivate behavior with a biological and emotional impetus: the need for attachment, which the new animal studies were showing to be present in many animals. In his observations of deprived and institutionalized children, Bowlby also relied heavily on the work of Rene Spitz.

8. The Unabomber, Theodore Kaczynski, was hospitalized for a week when he was nine months old in 1942, but was allowed to see his parents only once or twice for an hour during that week.

9. Samuel Pinneau was one of the first critics to make this point; Michael Rutter, an eminent British child psychiatrist, gave a fuller rebuttal in his important book, *Maternal Deprivation Reassessed* (Hammondsworth, England: Penguin Books, 1973).

10. Ehrenreich and English, *For Her Own Good,* p. 230.

11. Karen, *Becoming Attached,* p. 325.

12. Ibid., pp. 342–43.

13. Thurer, *Myths of Motherhood,* pp. 241–43, 246.

14. Steven A. Frankel, M.D., "The Exclusivity of the Mother-Child Bond," *The Psychoanalytic Study of the Child* 49 (1994): 86–106.

15. Thurer, *Myths of Motherhood,* p. 281; Ehrenreich and English, *For Her Own Good,* p. 221.

16. Ribble, "The Rights of Infants," as quoted in Thurer, *Myths of Motherhood,* p. 273.

17. Spitz, as quoted in Ehrenreich and English, *For Her Own Good,* p. 227.

18. See also Diane Eyer, *Mother-Infant Bonding: A Scientific Fiction* (New Haven: Yale University Press, 1992).

19. Janna Malamud Smith, "Mothers: Tired of Taking the Rap," *New York Times,* June 10, 1990.

20. Katharine Davis Fishman, *Behind the One-Way Mirror: Psychotherapy and Children* (New York: Bantam, 1995), p. 364.

21. Karen, *Becoming Attached,* pp. 131–177. But also note Michael Lamb's research, which found that these effects were only true when nothing else changed in a child's life.

22. See description of the NICHD study in chapter 5.

23. Rutter, *Maternal Deprivation Reassessed.*

24. Sandra Blakeslee, "Beyond the Veil of Thought," *New York Times*, August 29, 1995; Sharon Begley, "Your Child's Brain," *Newsweek,* February 19, 1996. For example, the *Times* article noted that the same brain chemistry may be available to adults in the hippocampus, so that brain circuits caused by early experiences may be changed through therapy or other means. The *Newsweek* article cited one experiment that found that drilling learned disabled children with computer-generated sounds for three hours a day seemed to cure their inability to distinguish between certain sounds, a skill that many scientists believe becomes wired to the brain; thus the therapy may actually change brain circuits.

25. See Stella Chess and Alexander Thomas, "Infant Bonding: Mystique and Reality," *American Journal of Orthopsychiatry* 52, no. 2 (April 1982): 214; see also the writings of Michael Lamb, Jerome Kagan, and Edward Zigler.

26. They and Dr. Herbert Birch followed 136 mostly white middle-class children and 95 children of working-class Puerto Rican families from childhood through adulthood.

27. His longitudinal study following such children began in 1978, and he believes these traits have a genetic component. He has found distinct physiological markers in shy children, such as faster heart rates and elevated levels of cortisol, a stress hormone.

28. Winifred Gallagher, "How We Become What We Are," *Atlantic Monthly,* September 1994; Lawrence Wright, "Double Mystery," *New Yorker,* August 7, 1995.

29. Daniel Goleman, "Child Development Theory Stresses Small Moments"; *New York Times*, October 21, 1986; Karen, *Becoming Attached;* Daniel N. Stern, *The Motherhood Constellation: A Unified View of Parent-Infant Psychotherapy* (New York: Basic Books, 1995).

30. Jessica Benjamin, *The Bonds of Love: Psychoanalysis, Feminism, and the Problem of Domination* (New York: Pantheon, 1988); and *Like Subjects, Love Objects: Essays on Recognition and Sexual Difference* (New Haven: Yale University Press, 1995).

31. Benjamin describes this experiment, performed by Elsa First, in *Like Subjects, Love Objects,* pp. 41–42.

CHAPTER 5

To research this chapter, I interviewed several of the leading authorities on child care research as well as several participants in the NICHD study: Jay Belsky, Cathryn L. Booth, Jeanne Brooks-Gunn, Bettye Caldwell, Alison Clarke-Stewart, Tiffany Field, Sarah Friedman, Lois Hoffman, Carolee Howes, Michael E. Lamb, Sandra Scarr, and Deborah Lowe Vandell.

To sort truth from fiction about the effects of child care on children, I turned to reviews conducted by scholars summarizing the available studies on child care and its effects on attachment, aggression, and intelligence. These included Lois Hoffman's 1989 review of effects of maternal employment, Sandra Scarr and Marlene Eisenberg's assessment in the 1993 *Annual Review of Psychology,* Alison Clarke-Stewart's book *Daycare*, and several published and unpublished papers by Jay Belsky. I relied most heavily on a comprehensive assessment by Michael E. Lamb, with a fifty-page bibliography of existing studies. I also read more than a dozen individual studies. I provide the full citations below for all studies I refer to, in case the reader wants to look them up.

1. *Time*, June 22, 1987; *Wall Street Journal*, March 3, 1987; *Washington Post,* April 23, 1988.

2. Jay Belsky, "Infant Day Care: A Cause for Concern?" *Zero to Three* 6, no. 5 (September 1986); interview with Jay Belsky; and K. Alison Clarke-Stewart, "Infant Day Care: Maligned or Malignant?" *American Psychologist*, February 1989.

3. Michael E. Lamb, Kathleen J. Sternberg, and Margarit Prodromidis, "Nonmaternal Care and the Security of Infant-Mother Attachment: A Reanalysis of the Data," *Behavior and Development* 15 (1992): 71–83.

4. Peter Barglow, Brian E. Vaughn, and Nancy Molitor, "Effects of Maternal Absence Due to Employment on the Quality of Infant-Mother Attachment in a Low-Risk Sample," *Child Development* (1985): 949.

5. Ibid., p. 951.

6. Karen, *Becoming Attached,* pp. 147–63.

7. Ibid., pp. 181–94, 215–26.

8. As the book went to press, the attachment results for age three had not been tallied.

9. S. Stith and A. Davis, "Employed Mothers at Family Day Care Substitute Caregivers," *Child Development* 55 (1984): 1340–48; and M. J. Zaslow, "Maternal Employment and Parent-Infant Interaction at One Year," *Early Childhood Research Quarterly* 4 (1989): 459–78. Both cited in Michael E. Lamb, "Non-Parental Child Care: Context, Quality, Correlates, and Consequences," manuscript copy of chapter to appear in I. E. Sigel and K. Ann Renninger, eds., *Child Psychology in Practice*, W. Damon, gen. ed., *Handbook of Child Psychology*, 4th ed. (New York: Wiley, in press).

10. Preschool study: B. Rabinovitch, M. Zaslow, P. Berman, and R. Hyman, April 23, 1987, "Employed and Homemaker Mothers' Perceptions of Their Toddlers Compliance Behavior in the Home," a poster presented at Meetings of the Society for Research in Child Development, Baltimore, Maryland; S. Crockenberg and C. Litman, "Effects of Maternal Employment on Maternal and Two-Year-Old Child Behavior," *Child Development* 62 (1991): 930–53; Nazli Baydar and Jeanne Brooks-Gunn, "Effects of Maternal Employment and Child-Care Arrangements on Preschoolers' Cognitive and Behavior Outcomes: Evidence from the Children of the National Longitudinal Study of Youth," *Development Psychology* 27, no. 6 (1991): 932–45; B. Volling and L. Feagans, "Infant Day Care and Children's Social Competence," *Infant Behavior and Development* 18 (1994): 177–88.

    Elementary school: R. Haskins, "Public School Aggression Among Children with Varying Day-Care Experience," *Child Development* 56 (1985): 689–703; B. Egeland and M. Hiester, "The Long-Term Consequences of Infant Day Care and Mother-Infant Attachment," *Child Development* 55 (1995): 474–85.

    Missouri: K. R. Thornburg, P. Pearl, D. Cropton, and J. M. Ispa, "Development of Kindergarten Children Based on Child Care Arrangements," *Early Childhood Research Quarterly* 5 (1990): 27–42.

    Dallas: D. L. Vandell and M. A. Corasiniti, "Variations in Early Child Care: Do They Predict Subsequent Social, Emotional, and Cognitive Differences?" *Early Childhood Research Quarterly* 5 (1990): 555–72.

    Indiana and Tennessee: J. Bates et al., "Child-Care History and Kindergarten Adjustment," *Developmental Psychology* 30 (1994): 690–700.

    Above studies all cited either in an unpublished review by Jay Belsky of aggression research or, Lamb "Non-parental Child Care."

    Aggression in normal range: S. Scarr and M. Eisenberg, "Child Care Research: Issues, Perspectives, and Results," *Annual Review of Psychology* 44 (1993): 613–44.

11. C. Howes, "The Peer Interactions of Young Children." *Monographs of the Society for Research in Child Development* 53, 1988, Serial No. 217; T. Greenstein, "Maternal Employment and Child Behavioral Outcomes: A

Household Economics Analysis," *Journal of Family Issues* 14 (1993): 323–54; Crockenberg and Litman, "Effects of Maternal Employment," as cited in Lamb, "Non-parental Child Care," and Belsky.

12. C. Howes, "Peer Interactions"; C. Howes, "Can the Age of Entry into Child Care and the Quality of Child Care Predict Adjustment in Kindergarten?" *Developmental Psychology* 26 (1990): 292–303; C. Howes, C. E. Hamilton, and C. C. Matheson, "Children's Relationships with Peers: Differential Associations with Aspects of the Teacher-Child Relationship," *Child Development* 65 (1994): 253–63; Deborah Vandell with C. Powers, "Day Care Quality and Children's Free Play Activities," *American Journal of Orthopsychiatry* 53 (1983): 493–500; Deborah Vandell et al., "A Longitudinal Study of Children with Day Care Experiences of Varying Quality," *Child Development* 59 (1988): 1286–92, as cited in Lamb, "Non-parental Child Care."

13. Tiffany Field, "Quality Infant Day Care and Grade School Behavior and Performance," *Child Development* 62 (1991): 863–70; Tiffany Field, Wendy Masi, Sheri Goldstein, Susan Perry, and Silke Parl, "Infant Day Care Facilitates Preschool Social Behavior," *Early Childhood Research Quarterly* 3 (1988): 341–59; Bengt-Erik Andersson, "Effects of Day Care on Cognitive and Socioemotional Competence of Thirteen-Year-Old Swedish Schoolchildren," *Child Development* 63 (1992): 20–36.

14. Alison Clarke-Stewart, *Daycare* (Cambridge: Harvard University Press, 1993), p. 74.

15. Dennis R. Ryerson, "Strong Parents, Strong Children," *Des Moines Register,* September 27, 1997.

16. Richard Neely, "Social Breakdown, Coming to Your 'Hood," *Wall Street Journal*, March 24, 1995.

17. Patrick F. Fagan, "The Real Root Causes of Violent Crime: The Breakdown of Marriage, Family, and Community," *Heritage Foundation Reports*, March 17, 1995.

18. Robert L. Maginnis, "Unprecedented Surge in Future Youth Crime Predicted," *Family Research Council Insight Paper*, February 6, 1996.

19. Robert J. Sampson and John H. Laub, *Crime in the Making* (Cambridge, Mass.: Harvard University Press, 1993).

20. Lamb, "Non-parental Child Care," p. 135.

21. Interview with Deborah Lowe Vandell; Lamb, "Non-parental Child Care," p. 135, citing Vandell and J. Ramanan, "Children of the National Longitudinal Survey of Youth: Choices in After-School Care and Child Development," *Developmental Psychology* 27 (1991): 637–43; V. S. Cain and S. K. Hofferth, "Parental Choice of Self-Care for School-Age Children," *Journal of Marriage and the Family* 51 (1989): 65–77.

22. Lamb, "Non-parental Child Care," pp. 127, 129, citing N. L. Galambos and

J. Garbarino, "Identifying the Missing Links in the Study of Latchkey Children," *Children Today,* July/August 1993, pp. 2–4, 40–41; H. Rodman, D. Pratto, and R. Nelson, "Child Care Arrangements and Children's Functioning: A Comparison of Self-Care and Adult-Care Children," *Developmental Psychology* 21 (1985): 413–18; Vandell and Ramanan, "Children of the Longitudinal Survey."

23. Vandell and Steinberg described these studies to me in interviews.

24. Sandra Blakeslee, "Studies Show Talking with Infants Shapes Basis of Ability to Think," *New York Times*, April 17, 1997. The issue of brain development has gotten widespread publicity. *Time* and *Newsweek* had extensive articles on the topic—"How a Child's Brain Develops," *Time* Special Report, February 3, 1997; *Newsweek,* February 19, 1996.

25. Blakeslee, "Studies," quoting Betty Hart and Todd Ridley.

26. Lamb, "Non-parental Child Care," p. 90, citing S. Ackerman-Ross and P. Khanna, "Study of Middle-Class Three-Year-Olds: The Relationship of High Quality Day Care to Middle-Class Three-Year-Olds' Language Performance," *Early Childhood Research Quarterly* 4 (1989): 97–116; Burchinal et. al., "Study of Middle-Class Black and White Six- to Twelve-Year-Olds: Early Child Care Experiences and Their Association with Family and Child Characteristics During Middle Childhood," *Early Childhood Research Quarterly* 10 (1995): 33–61.

Kindergartners: Thornburg et al., "Development of Kindergarten Children."

Higher scores for day care: Field, "Quality Infant Day Care."

27. See overview in Lamb, "Non-parental Child Care," pp. 86–95, 112–16; and see S. Desai, P. L. Chase-Lansdale, and R. T. Michael, "Mother or Market? Effects of Maternal Employment on the Intellectual Ability of Four-Year-Old Children," *Demography* 26 (1989): 545–61; M. Caughy, J. A. Di Pietro, and D. M. Strobino, "Day Care Participation as a Protective Factor in the Cognitive Development of Low-Income Children," *Child Development* 65 (1994): 457–71.

28. Karen Bogenschneider and Laurence Steinberg, "Maternal Employment and Adolescents' Academic Achievement: A Developmental Analysis," *Society of Education* 67 (1994): 60–77.

29. See Lamb, "Non-parental Child Care," citing several studies by Ramey and colleagues, the New York City Infant Day Care Study; and Bogenschneider and Steinberg, "Maternal Employment."

30. Major reviews include the National Academy of Sciences, 1982; Lois Wladis Hoffman, "Maternal Employment and the Young Child," in M. Perlmutter, ed., *Parent-Child Interaction and Parent-Child Relationship in Child Development*, (Hillsdale, N.J.: Erlbaum, 1984); and "Effects of Maternal Employment in the Two-Parent Family," *American Psychologist,* February 1989.

31. Frank R. Furstenberg and Gretchen A. Condran, "Family Change and Adolescent Well-Being: A Re-Examination of U.S. Trends," in Andrew J. Cherlin, ed., *The Changing American Family and Public Policy* (Washington, D.C.: Urban Institute Press, 1988), pp. 117–33.

32. Adele Eskeles Gottfried and W. Allen Gottfried, eds., *Redefining Families: Implications for Children's Development* (New York and London: Plenum Press, 1994), pp. 55–93; Gottfried and Gottfried, eds., *Maternal Employment and Children's Development,* pp. 12–55, 270–84. The percentage of mothers who worked while their children were under seven years old ranged from 36 percent to 64 percent; by the time the children were twelve, 80 percent of the mothers were working.

33. See Clarke-Stewart, *Daycare*.

34. Patricia A. Nachman, "The Maternal Representation: A Comparison of Caregiver- and Mother-Reared Toddlers," *Psychoanalytic Study of the Child* 46 (1991): 69–90.

35. Sylvia Ann Hewlett linked worsening child indicators to maternal employment in *When the Bough Breaks: The Cost of Neglecting Our Children* (New York: Basic Books, 1991).

36. Nicholas Zill and Carolyn C. Rogers, "Recent Trends in the Well-Being of Children in the United States and Their Implications for Public Policy," in Cherlin, ed., *The Changing American Family and Public Policy;* Nicholas Zill, "The Status of Children and Families in the United States: Conditions and Needs," a paper presented at the Early Childhood Leadership Development Program Seminar, September 9–11, 1994; U.S. Department of Health and Human Services, *Report to Congress on Out-of-Wedlock Childbearing,* DHHS Pub. No. 95-1257, pp. 138–39; Furstenberg and Condran, "Family Change."

37. Nicholas Zill and Carolyn C. Rogers, *U.S. News & World Report,* May 5, 1997. Note that there are some questions about whether the teen suicide rate is rising because reported increases are based in differences in classification.

38. Jeanne Brooks-Gunn, "Early Experience and Human Development," in Franz E. Weinert, ed., *International Encyclopedia of Education,* 2d ed. (Oxford: Pergamon Press, 1996).

39. See Lamb, "Non-parental Child Care."

40. Clarke-Stewart, *Daycare,* pp. 114, 134.

41. Ibid., pp. 123–24.

42. See Brooks-Gunn, "Early Experience."

CHAPTER 6

1. James Dobson and Gary L. Bauer, *Children At Risk: What You Need to Know to Protect Your Family* (Dallas: Word Publishing, 1990), p. 143.

2. *Focus on the Family* magazine, April 1994.

3. Amitai Etzioni, excerpts from *The Spirit of Community: Rights, Responsibilities and the Communitarian Agenda*, in *Utne Reader*, May/June 1993; Leach, *Your Baby and Child,* p. 274.

4. Edward Zigler and Nancy W. Hall, "Day Care and Its Effect on Children: An Overview from the Pediatric Health Project," *Developmental and Behavioral Pediatrics* 9, no. 1 (1988): 38–46; Sandra Scarr and Marlene Eisenberg, as cited in Lamb, "Non-parental Child Care": D. C. Farran and C. T. Ramey, "Infant Day Care and Attachment Behaviors Toward Mothers and Teachers," *Child Development* 48 (1977): 1112–16; R. C. Ainslie and C. W. Anderson, "Day Care Children's Relationships to Their Mothers and Caregivers: An Inquiry into the Conditions for the Development of Attachment," in R. C. Ainslie, ed., *The Child and the Day Care Setting: Qualitative Variations and Development* (New York: Praeger Special Studies, 1984), pp. 98–132.

5. Rita K. Benn, "Factors Promoting Secure Attachment Relationships Between Employed Mothers and Their Sons," *Child Development* 57 (1986): 1224–31.

6. Dally, *Inventing Motherhood*, p. 89.

7. M. Weinraub, E. Jaeger, and L. Hoffman, "Predicting Infant Outcome in Families of Employed and Unemployed Mothers," *Early Childhood Research Quarterly* 3 (1988): 361–78; Hock, DeMeis, and McBride, *Maternal Separation Anxiety*.

8. Benn, "Factors Promoting Secure Attachment"; D. L. Vandell and J. Ramanan, "Effects of Recent Maternal Employment on Children from Low-Income Families," *Child Development* 63 (1992): 938–49; A. M. Farel, "Effects of Preferred Maternal Roles, Maternal Employment and Sociodemographic Status on School Adjustment and Competence," *Child Development* 51 (1980): 1179–96; M. T. Owen and M. J. Cox, "Maternal Employment and Transition to Parenthood," in Gottfried and Gottfried, eds., *Maternal Employment,* pp. 87–115.

9. Faye J. Crosby, *Juggling: The Unexpected Advantages of Balancing Career and Home for Women and Their Families* (New York: Free Press, 1991), pp. 78–79, citing Nancy Pistrang, "Women's Work Involvement and the Experience of New Motherhood," *Journal of Marriage and the Family* 46 (1984): 433–47; Farel, cited in Clarke-Stewart, *Daycare,* p. 107; E. L. Dienstag, "The Transition to Parenthood in Working and Non-Working Pariparous Mothers," paper presented at the August 1986 meeting of the American Psychological Association, Washington, D.C., as cited in Hoffman, "Effects of Maternal Employment."

10. Farel, in Clarke-Stewart, *Daycare,* p. 107.

11. E. Hock and D. DeMeis, "Depression in Mothers of Infants: The Role of Maternal Employment," *Developmental Psychology*, as cited in Hoffman, "Effects of Maternal Employment."

12. Tiffany Field, "Infants of Depressed Mothers," *Development and Psychopathology* 4 (1992): 49–66; Field et al., "Effects of Maternal Unavailability on Mother-Infant Interactions," *Infant Behavior and Development* 9 (1986): 473–78; Jane Brody, Personal Health column, *New York Times*, November 2, 1994.

13. *Pediatrics*, September 1994, pp. 363–68.

    Note: I cite several studies suggesting that working may help combat depression. It is important to remember, though, that just as in the child care studies, the results may be open to different interpretations, and correlations do not prove cause and effect. So these studies do not prove a definitive link between working and protection against depression.

14. Rosalind C. Barnett and Caryl Rivers, *She Works/He Works: How Two-Income Families Are Happier, Healthier, and Better Off* (New York: HarperCollins, 1996), pp. 26, 28–30.

15. See Hoffman, "Effects of Maternal Employment"; Crosby, *Juggling,* pp. 61–74; Grace Baruch and Rosalind Barnett, unpublished study of 238 middle-class women in a Boston suburb.

16. Crosby, *Juggling,* p. 79, cites a study of tellers and clerical workers by Rena Repetti; study of waitresses, factory workers, and domestic workers: D. V. Hiller and J. Dyehouse, "A Case for Banishing 'Dual-Career Marriages' from the Research Literature," *Journal of Marriage and the Family* 49 (1987): 787–95, cited in Sandra Scarr, Deborah Phillips, and Kathleen McCartney, "Working Mothers and Their Families," *American Psychologist* 44 (1989): 1402–9.

17. Crosby, *Juggling,* p. 103, citing studies by Crosby, Repetti, and Mavis Heatherington.

18. Barnett and Rivers, *She Works/He Works,* pp. 99, 110, 125–26, 139.

19. Sue Shellenbarger, "It's the Type of Job You Have That Affects the Kids, Studies Say," *Wall Street Journal*, July 31, 1996.

20. *New York Times*, March 25, 1995.

21. David Blankenhorn, *Fatherless America: Confronting Our Most Urgent Social Problem* (New York: Basic Books, 1995), p. 108.

CHAPTER 7

1. *Newsday*, September 25, 1997.

2. Transcript of *Today* show, September 26, 1997.

3. Dobson's letter appeared in his August 1994 mailing; *Arizona Republic*, July 19, 1994; Gannett, June 26, 1994; Newhouse, June 5, 1994; *Christianity Today*, September 12, 1994; *Advertising Age*, September 19, 1994.

4. Howard V. Hayghe, interview and articles in the July 1995 and September 1997 *Monthly Labor Review*.

5. Gary Bauer, *Our Journey Home: What Parents Are Doing to Preserve Family Values* (Dallas: Word Publishing, 1992), p. 72.

6. A Louis Harris & Associates survey of 1,502 women conducted as part of a larger study by the Families and Work Institute for the Whirlpool Foundation. Louis Harris & Associates 1981 study of family values found that 39 percent of women polled preferred to stay home. In 1994, 31 percent wanted to stay at home.

7. 1994 Harris poll for Whirlpool Foundation: 56 percent of women polled said they would not give up their responsibilities; *Redbook* magazine October 1992 poll conducted by EDK Associates; the 1995 Virginia Slims Opinion Poll, conducted by Roper Starch Worldwide Inc.; "Working Women Count," survey conducted by the Women's Bureau of the U.S. Department of Labor, in *Daily Labor Report*, April 11, 1995; CBS News poll, as reported in Sarah Boxer, "One Casualty of the Women's Movement: Feminism," Week in Review, *New York Times,* December 14, 1997, p. 3.

8. Rhona Mahony, *Kidding Ourselves: Breadwinning, Babies, and Bargaining Power* (New York: Basic Books, 1995).

9. "Back From the Mommy Track," *New York Times*, October 9, 1994, citing a study by Joy Schneer and Frieda Reitman.

10. Interview with Polachek; Leslie S. Stratton, "The Effect Interruptions in Work Experience Have on Wages," *Southern Economic Journal* 61, no. 4 (April 1995): 955–70.

11. Barnett and Rivers, *She Works/He Works* p. 32; Patricia Boyle and Sylvia W. Sirignano, "Balancing Work and Family During the First Year of Parenthood," unpublished paper.

12. James Cosgrove and Mark Mongomery, "Are Part-Time Women Paid Less?" *Economic Inquiry* 33, no. 1 (January 1995): 119–33.

13. Harriet B. Presser, "Can We Make Time for Children? The Economy, Work Schedules, and Child Care," *Demography* 26, no. 4 (November 1989): 530.

14. William R. Mattox, Jr., "The Parent Trap: So Many Bills, So Little Time," *Policy Review*, Winter 1991; Carnegie Corporation of New York, "Starting Points: Meeting the Needs of Our Youngest Children," 1994.

15. Elizabeth Fox-Genovese, *Feminism Is Not the Story of My Life: How Today's Feminist Elite Has Lost Touch with the Real Concerns of Women* (New York: Doubleday, 1996); Gelertner article, February 1996.

16. Mattox, letter to the editor, *Policy Review,* September/October 1996.

17. David Whitman, "The Myth of AWOL Parents," *U.S. News & World Report,* July 1, 1996.

18. Interview with Geoffrey C. Godbey, who noted that women's hours of housework dropped from twenty-seven hours a week in 1965 to nine in

1985; interview with Suzanne Bianchi; Zill and Rogers, "Recent Trends in the Well-Being of Children"; Whitman, "Myth of AWOL Parents."

19. Steven L. Nock and Paul W. Kingston, "Time with Children: The Impact of Couples' Work-Time Commitments," *Social Forces* 67, no. 1 (September 1988): 59–85; Paul W. Kingston and Steven L. Nock, "Time Together Among Dual-Earner Couples," *American Sociological Review* 52, no. 3 (June 1987).

CHAPTER 8

1. "Child Care and Working Parents," *Nightline*, ABC News, October 21, 1997.
2. "Ex on Clark: Bad Mom, Good Prosecutor," *Newsday,* April 3, 1995.
3. "Parents Share Blame in Baby's Death: Poll," *New York Post*, November 2, 1997.
4. "Gender Bias Study on the Court System in Massachusetts," Supreme Judicial Court, 1989; "Gender, Justice and the Courts," report of the Connecticut Task Force, 1991; "Gender and Justice: Report of the Vermont Task Force on Gender Bias in the Legal System," a joint project of the Vermont Supreme Court and the Vermont Bar Association, January 1991.
5. "Gender Bias in the Court," Maryland Special Joint Committee, May 1989; New York report as printed in the *Fordham Urban Law Journal* 15 (1986–87); Minnesota Supreme Court Task Force for Gender Fairness in the Courts, 1989; "Justice for Women: Nevada Supreme Court Gender Bias Task Force," 1989; "Louisiana Task Force on Women in the Court, Final Report," 1992; the 1990 "Report of the Illinois Task Force on Gender Bias in the Courts"; "Gender and Justice in the Court: A Report to the Supreme Court of Georgia by the Commission on Gender Bias in the Judicial System," August 1991; Washington, D.C., Task Force on Racial and Ethnic Bias and Task Force on Gender Bias in the Courts, May 1992.
6. Nancy Polikoff interview in July 1994, citing the North Carolina study of trial courts, 1983–1987, published in 1991.
7. Massachusetts gender study.
8. Jeff Atkinson, *Modern Child Custody Practice, 1994 Cumulative Supplement* (Charlottesville, Va.: The Michie Company Law Publishers), p. 50.
9. See gender studies above and "Gender and Justice in the Colorado Courts," Colorado Supreme Court Task Force on Gender Bias in the Courts, 1990; "Wisconsin Equal Justice Task Force Final Report," January 1991; "Reports of the Florida Supreme Court Gender Bias Study Commission," 1990; "Gender and Justice in the Courts," Washington State Task Force on Gender and Justice in the Courts.
10. Jeff Atkinson, *Modern Child Custody Practice, 1986* (New York: Kluwer Law Book Publishers), p. 224.
11. Ibid., p. 235.
12. Ibid., p. 238.

13. Atkinson, *Modern Child Custody, 1994,* p. 55, citing Cummings *v.* Cummings.

14. The appeals court did, however, fault Judge Taylor for failing to consider Prost's charges, which were corroborated by several witnesses, that Greene had pushed her, choked her, stamped on her foot, and threatened her, sometimes in front of the children. Greene denied the charges, though several of Prost's friends backed her up. The court suggested that the charges, if found to be true, could affect the custody decision and returned the case to the judge on that basis only. The judge dismissed the charges and issued a decision in February 1995, writing that Greene was a pacifist and doubting the testimony of the medical expert.

15. When I reported on this case for the *New York Times,* Greene declined, through his lawyer, to be interviewed. In an interview with the English newspaper the *Guardian* ("Mother of All Custody Battles," October 20, 1994), however, he said that he had wanted a friendly arrangement in which he and Prost would "co-parent" the children, but that she had resisted and consistently tried to cut back his time with the children, so he went to court.

16. Marc Fisher, "Trials of a Female Lawyer: Should Marcia Clark Be in Court or in the Kitchen?" *Washington Post*, April 3, 1995.

CHAPTER 9

1. Rockford Institute, August 1995 issue.

2. Bauer, "Our Hopes, Our Dreams," in *Focus on the Family* magazine, March 1996; Dobson, August 1994 letter.

3. *Focus on the Family,* April 1994.

4. Ibid.

5. Bauer, *Our Journey Home,* p. 134.

6. Ibid., p. 215.

7. "What Moderate Feminists?" *Commentary*, June 1995.

8. Danielle Crittenden, "Yes, Motherhood Lowers Pay," *New York Times,* August 22, 1995.

9. U.S. Bureau of the Census, March 1997 supplement. This figure overstates the income a single worker would make because it counts only those people who work year round and full time, and because it includes both men and women. Many workers hold jobs only part of the year, and their salaries tend to be lower. For example, according to the Bureau of Labor Statistics' 1997 figures, the median weekly earnings of full-time workers was $503, but for part-time workers it was $149.

10. "The Lies Parents Tell About Work, Kids, Money, Day Care and Ambition," *U.S. News & World Report*, May 12, 1997.

11. David Popenoe, "Modern Marriage: Revising the Cultural Script," a Council on Families in America working paper for the Marriage in America Symposium, August 1992.

12. Barbara Dafoe Whitehead, "The New Family Values," *Family Affairs*, summer 1992, excerpted in *Utne Reader,* May/June 1993.

13. The following discussion draws on writings by Carol Tavris, *The Mismeasure of Woman* (New York: Simon & Schuster, 1992); Katha Pollitt, "Are Women Morally Superior to Men?" *The Nation*, December 28, 1992; Benjamin R. Barber, "Beyond the Feminine Mystique: Feminist Ideology Is Moving in a New Direction," *New Republic*, July 11, 1983.

14. Tavris, *Mismeasure,* pp. 51–52, 63–64, 288, 294.

15. Ibid., pp. 290–301.

16. Gail Collins, "Wooing the Women," *New York Times,* July 28, 1996.

17. *Austin American Statesman*, July 7, 1996.

18. *Des Moines Register*, August 9, 1996.

19. *The Hill*, July 17, 1996.

20. Neil MacFarquhar, "Don't Forget Soccer Dads; What's A Soccer Mom Anyway?" Week in Review, *New York Times,* October 21, 1996.

21. *Washington Post*, October 21, 1996.

22. Camille Paglia, "A Drag Queen of Gender Roles," *New Republic,* March 4, 1996, p. 24.

23. "Word for Word," Week in Review, *New York Times,* March 26, 1995.

24. *New York Post,* December 14, 1996.

25. Robert Pear, "House Backs Bill Undoing Decades of Welfare Policy," *New York Times*, March 25, 1995.

26. Alison Mitchell, "Gingrich's Views on Slayings Draw Fire," *New York Times,* November 23, 1995.

27. Tamar Lewin, "Study of Welfare Families Warns of Problems for Schoolchildren," *New York Times,* February 29, 1996.

28. "Lies Parents Tell . . . " *U.S. News & World Report*, May 12, 1997.

29. Dobson and Bauer, *Children At Risk,* pp. 84–85, 174–75; LaHaye testimony before Congress, January 17, 1995.

30. Gary Bauer, "Leaving Families Out," *National Review*, March 29, 1993.

31. "A Communitarian Position Paper on the Family," prepared by Jean Elshtain et al., p. 4.

CHAPTER 10

1. As quoted in Jeff Wagenheim, "Among the Promise Keepers," *New Age Journal*, March/April 1995, reprinted in *Utne Reader*, January–February 1996.

2. Marci McDonald, "My Wife Told Me to Go," *U.S. News & World Report*, October 6, 1997.

3. Interviews with David Hackett and Mary Stewart Van Leeuwen, religion scholars who have studied the Promise Keepers movement.

4. David Popenoe, *Life Without Father* (New York: Martin Kessler Books/The Free Press, 1996).

5. David Popenoe, "A World Without Fathers," *Wilson Quarterly*, spring 1996, p. 21.

6. Barnett and Rivers, *She Works/He Works,* p. 59.

7. Leach, *Children First,* pp. 31–48.

8. Stern, *Motherhood Constellation.*

9. Joseph H. Pleck, "Paternal Involvement: Levels, Sources and Consequences," draft; "Families and Work: Small Changes and Big Implications," *Qualitative Sociology* 5, no. 4 (1992).

10. Barnett and Rivers, *She Works/He Works,* pp. 178, 226.

11. Lynne M. Casper, "Who's Minding Our Preschoolers?" *Current Population Reports,* U.S. Census Bureau, March 1996; Martin O'Connell, "Where's Papa? Fathers' Role in Child Care," *Population Trends and Public Policy,* September 1993; interview with Joseph Pleck, University of Illinois.

12. Interview with O'Connell, director of the fertility and family statistics branch of the Census Bureau; 1996 Census Report; Presser, "Can We Make Time"; Harriet Presser interview.

13. Work/Family Directions survey of 60,000 employees at fifteen major corporations between 1986 and 1991.

14. Presser, "Can We Make Time"; Barnett and Rivers, *She Works/He Works,* p. 230.

15. Barnett and Rivers, *She Works/He Works,* p. 228.

16. Mahony, *Kidding Ourselves,* p. 138, citing a 1993 study by Swiss and Walker.

17. Jill Natwick Johnston, "Of Glass Ceilings and Sticky Floors," *Wall Street Journal,* May 10, 1996.

18. Mahony, *Kidding Ourselves,* p. 109, citing R. William Betcher and William S. Pollack in *A Time of Fallen Heroes: The Recreation of Masculinity* (New York: Atheneum, 1993).

CHAPTER 11

1. Benjamin, *Like Subjects,* p. 107.

2. Ibid., p. 91.

3. Ibid., Dorothy Dinnerstein, *The Mermaid and the Minotaur: Sexuality and Human Malaise* (New York: HarperPerennial, 1976); Nancy Chodorow, *The Reproduction of Mothering: Psychoanalysis and the Sociology of Gender,* Berkeley: University of California Press, 1978; Nancy Chodorow and Susan Contratto, "The Fantasy of the Perfect Mother," in *Feminism and Psychoanalytic Theory* (New Haven: Yale University Press, 1989).

4. Mahony, *Kidding Ourselves,* p. 206; Bureau of Labor Statistics, 1996.

5. *The Future of Children* 6, no. 6 (summer/fall 1996).

6. Bruce Fuller, Susan Holloway, Stephen Raudenbush, and Li-Ming Wei, "Can Government Raise Child Care Quality? The Influence of Family Demand, Poverty and Policy"; Harvard University Graduate School of Education researchers examined 1,800 child care centers located in thirty-six states; Cost, Quality, and Child Outcomes in Child Care Centers study had researchers at University of Colorado at Denver, University of California at Los Angeles, the University of North Carolina, and Yale University examine 400 day care centers in four states and tested 826 children to examine the impact of their child care experience on their intellectual and emotional development; Lamb, "Non-parental Child Care," p. 22.

7. Under this plan, the government would offer matching funds to businesses that pay 40 percent of a worker's salary during a year of family leave; see also in *The Future of Children* James R. Walker's suggestion of a combination of an employee-paid payroll tax and low-interest government loans with a child allowance for poor and working-poor families.

8. Interview with Sandra L. Hofferth, May 1996; "Effects of Public and Private Policies on Working After Childbirth," Institute for Social Research, University of Michigan, May 1996, p. 25; *The Economist*, July 17, 1993, pp. 13–14.

INDEX

Aber, Lawrence, 81, 118–19, 125
Abney, Gail, 214
Abraham, 204
Adoption, 76–77
Adventures of Ozzie and Harriet, The
    (television program), 29
Advertisements, 5–6
African Americans
  treatment of sons versus daughters, 256
  working mothers among, 31–32
Aggression, day care and, 98–100, 118, 119
Ainsworth, Mary, 68, 78–79, 92–94
Alter, Eleanor B., 188
Anderson, Bonnie, 204
Andrews, Delynn, 32
Androgyny, 196, 224–25
At-home mothers
  cost of, 274–76
  cult of domesticity and, 17–18, 26, 28–29,
    53–54, 193
  direct interaction with children by,
    162–63
  homemaker IRA and, 218
  opinion polls concerning, 152–53
  "other mothers" and, 249–50
  religious right and, 195, 198, 274
  television portrayals of, 14–17, 29–30,
    32–34, 239
  unhappiness of, 127–28
  working mothers versus, 196, 258–59, 281
Atkinson, Jeff, 180
Attachment theory, 58–64, 67–73, 202
  day care and, 90–94, 95–101, 118
  gender and, 205
  insecure attachment and, 90–94, 95–100,
    118, 126–28
  maternal deprivation and, 91–94
  mother-infant bonding and, 68, 76–77,
    84–87
  mystery of bonding and, 125–26, 140–42
  separation in, 72–75, 79–81, 257–58

Strange Situation and, 92–94, 95, 110
  surrogate care and, 122–23
Attunement, 84–85

Baby-boom generation, 53, 202
Baby cult, 47–56
Bank, Rita, 188
Barglow, Peter, 91
Barnes, Brenda, 12, 100, 146
Barnett, Rosalind C., 129, 235–36, 241
Barrett, Nina, 52
Bateson, Mary Catherine, 159
Bauer, Gary, 33, 121, 149, 194–98, 218, 219
Becoming Attached (Karen), 71
Beecher, Mrs., 26–27
Belsky, Jay, 90–92, 97, 98, 100, 118, 124
Benjamin, Jessica, 85–87, 255, 262, 281
Benn, Rita K., 125, 126
Bergmann, Barbara, 277
Bettelheim, Bruno, 75
Blacks. *See* African Americans.
Blankenhorn, David, 141, 201, 227–29,
    231, 234, 241, 267
Bly, Robert, 251–52
Booth, Cathryn L., 81
Bowlby, John, 68, 70, 71–74, 78–82, 91, 101,
    124
Boyle, Pat, 156
Brain research, 107–10
Brazelton, T. Berry, 45, 56–60, 69, 77, 128,
    219, 229, 230–31
Brock, David, 208
Brown, Ronald, 186
Bruch, Carol, 179
Bureau of Labor Statistics (BLS), 147–49
Bureau of the Census, U.S., 104
Burkett, Larry, 196, 197

Caldwell, Bettye, 273
Carlson, Allan, 194–95
Carmona, Dorothy, 212–14